GLOBAL NEWS ACCESS

GLOBAL NEWS ACCESS

The Impact of New
Communications Technologies

Carla Brooks Johnston

Westport, Connecticut
London

Library of Congress Cataloging-in-Publication Data

Johnston, Carla B.
    Global News Access : the impact of new communications
technologies / Carla Brooks Johnston.
        p.   cm.
    Includes bibliographical references (p.   ) and index.
    ISBN 0–275–95774–8 (alk. paper)
    1. Mass media policy.   2. Mass media—Technological innovations.
3. Mass media—Influence.   4. Democracy.   I. Title.
P95.8.J64   1998
303.48'33–dc21   97–50036

British Library Cataloguing in Publication Data is available.

Library of Congress Catalog Card Number: 97–50036
ISBN: 0–275–95774–8

First published in 1998

Praeger Publishers, 88 Post Road West, Westport, CT 06881
An imprint of Greenwood Publishing Group, Inc.

Printed in the United States of America

The paper used in this book complies with the
Permanent Paper Standard issued by the National
Information Standards Organization (Z39.48–1984).

10 9 8 7 6 5 4 3 2 1

To those who care about the children's future.

May you move beyond fascination with the new hardware
to create uses for it. Enable the exchange of news and information
appropriate to building a democratic, egalitarian, and peaceful
global village for us all.

Contents

Photo essay follows page 153.

Preface

The pace of change caused by the new communications technologies is like that of a cyclone. It will be many decades before the full impact of this change on society is fully understood. It is clear, however, that, as with all new structures, the time for determining the use of these technologies is short.

The time is now to step back from fascination with the technology and its power; it's time to establish the patterns for its use. Otherwise, civilization will have no role in determining whether its impact will be favorable or unfavorable.

My special thanks to the scores of persons who have contributed interviews to this book. Their words, valuable in their own right, lend a global authenticity to the discussion. A thank-you to the numerous individuals at Greenwood Publishing Group, especially Nina Pearlstein, Terry Park, and Elisabetta Linton. Their ongoing support and assistance have been critical to the book's publication. A special thank-you to Bob Hilliard, who continues to believe that manuscripts do get finished and that books do make a difference in whether or not the larger society chooses to influence the policies that affect its life. Elise and John, Eric and Debbi, you have provided inspiration and ideas in countless ways.

Political Map of the World

Scale 1:75,000,000

Robinson Projection
standard parallels 38″ N and 38′ S

Source: CIA, <u>The World Factbook</u>, U.S. Government, 1995.

1

Tomorrow's News and Information

PREFACE

A thirty-six-year-old divorced princess, alienated from Britain's royal family, brought a larger crowd to the streets of London in September 1997 than any event since the celebration of the end of World War II. By all reports, the eerie sound of silence from the millions watching Princess Diana's funeral procession was unforgettable.[1] Public pressure over the royal neglect of her funeral caused the Queen of England to appear live on television for the first time since 1959. The European Broadcasting Union estimated that 600 million people in 190 countries watched the funeral on live television. In the United States, an estimated fifty million watched.[2] What accounted for this outpouring of public interest and respect? Did Diana's life and tragic accident make her funeral so monumental? Or did the media merge news and entertainment to create a larger-than-life spectacle? In the long run, does it matter whether the media create events? Can an event happen of its own accord, apart from the media, in today's world?

An eleven-year-old whose family is part of a sophisticated academic community thought the Gulf War was a sitcom. Does it matter whether an intelligent adolescent knows the difference between fact and fiction?

One man who survived the Nazi concentration camps has spent a lifetime trying to explain how events can affect innocent people. He said it once in a picture at the beginning of his biography, in a 1929 photo of a couple and their three children sitting on the grass in a nicely kept yard in Lodz, Poland. Fifteen years later everyone in the picture except the five-year-old, the author, had been killed by the Nazis in Auschwitz and other camps. Should the story matter to anyone outside the ghettoized Jewish community?

Now young adults from Europe and the United States visit Viet Nam as tourists. Thirty years ago, in the late 1960s, their parents' friends were killed in Viet Nam or arrested trying to stop the war. Today, that's just the plot for an evening's movie. Does it matter whether people understand the forces at work in these transitions? Can history repeat itself?

A young Chinese woman who dared to marry an American and come to the United States had been warned repeatedly by her compatriots not to leave China. "America is plastic and dangerous." "Not so," she concluded after coming here. "People in the United States care about so much." Why did she conclude that? Is it perception? Is it true? Who communicates the reality? How are these myths that influence the behavior of nations created?

Is there a point at which people's emotional or physical comfort might be threatened by their ignorance of news and information? For example, if a government doesn't warn the public about a potential environmental hazard, can people be prepared when it happens? If government then covers up its failure to safeguard the public, who is hurt?

In decades past, there seemed to be a time for everything—a time to work, a time to be entertained, a time to benefit, and a time to be responsible. It was all easier to grasp because the environment was comprehensible—with visible borders—a home, a business, a town, a country. Today, we live in a totally different world. Rapid changes in communications technologies have eliminated borders and compressed time. These changes affect everyone. Industrial society is moving beyond television to the Internet and technology convergence. Developing countries are marveling at what appears in their living rooms on that little box—the TV set. The poorest villages in rural areas have cell phones, or wind-up radios, or homemade satellite dishes.

As Albert Einstein once said, "Everything has changed except the way we think."

Do the viewers, the consumers of news, the ones who believe the reality shown on the screen, become victims or victors in society? How can we effect our futures? But, first—can we even talk about the options? Where is the table for discussion? We need the media to provide that table and to turn on the microphones.

This book introduces the reader to two parallel "media worlds": a "have" world that is grand, global, and gratuitous and a "have-not" world that is silent, segmented, and secluded. These worlds exist in a larger environment generally united on the idea that global society can benefit from democratization. Beyond that idea, few people think through what it means to provide *access* to media as the forum for everyone, and *access* to participation in economic and political decision-making.

LET THE PEOPLE KNOW

No More "Business As Usual" News

Technology is responsible for the changes that leave us somewhat confused, suffering from information overload but substance underload. The media professionals have a tiger by the tail; industry changes are leaping ahead at such a pace that evaluating the situation to plan for maximum benefits is next to impossible. Many new TV channels are available for new programming. Reception of "live" news is possible in wholly new regions of the globe. Concurrently, in some parts of the world, individuals are turning away from broadcast TV to get their news "online" and on demand through the Internet. Newspapers are appearing online and on paper—and in regionally tailored editions. Radio is reaching new audiences in rural areas, and shortwave radio is being replaced by the Internet. The new technology hardware is, by and large, in place. We are at a crossroads. What do we *do* with the technology?

Ongoing modernization of the hardware is far less challenging than addressing the task before us now—figuring out what to communicate on the many lanes of this splendid new "information superhighway." To whom, and why? How can you measure return on investment? What kind of "software" or news programming maximizes the potential of the hardware?

When assessing these questions in regard to news and information, the ideal is to mesh viewer self-interest with industry self-interest. For example, the standard U.S. approach has been to match a presumably entertainment-starved third world and an entertainment-saturated first world with "infotainment" news programming. Presumably, if viewers get what they want, industry gets the investment return it wants—financial strength and political stability. However, just as the technology changes who gets these broadcasts, the public changes, too. People's horizons are different from those of a decade ago. Business requires them to engage with people half a globe away—people they never knew about before. New neighbors from other countries bring with them new customs. As people in developing countries see on TV things previously censored or unavailable, it may be less simple to mesh public self-interest with industry self-interest.

Who's News Is It?

Technology has expanded community borders. It sends news and information to millions, more than ever before, and millions are participating more than ever before in the information dialogue through global business, global travel, global education, and global media. It is no longer possible to avoid intermingling of the globe's two billion Christians, one billion Muslims, 750 million Hindus, 111 million Buddhists, sixteen million Sikhs, and 12.8 million Jews.[3] It is essential to transcend the language differences of over one billion Chinese speakers, approximately one-half billion English speakers and the speakers of the following principal language groups, in descending order of numbers: Hindustani, Russian, Spanish, Arabic, Bengali, German, Portuguese, Japanese, Malay, French, and Italian. This diversity doesn't even begin to account for the political and economic differences caused by historical alliances and hatreds. How can we share the planet together?

There is no longer a choice about living with diversity. Will global news and information transmission increase goodwill with understanding, or will it increase hatred with intolerance and fear of the unknown? In large part, it's because of the new communications technologies that we face these problems. Will the media, who brought us diversity, also lead the way in showing us how to celebrate its opportunities?

One thing is certain. The reality of diverse cultures competing in the world for economic and political stability will only expand. The world's ten most populous countries all have access to TV and Internet information about each other as a technical, if not a political, possibility. China, the most populous country, is making phenomenal strides economically and has now taken over the economic giant Hong Kong; 1.2 billion people live in China (one in five inhabitants of the globe.) In India, TV access and the media are changing with unprecedented speed; 870 million people live in India. In these two countries, the emerging middle class may be a small percentage of the population; nonetheless, they account for an enormous consumer-market expansion. The same growth in TV markets exists in most of the other eight most-populous countries. The former Soviet Union was third in population size; the shift by its governments to market economies will lead to large and important markets. The United States, fourth in population size with 293 million people, has well-developed media, but major changes in the market are occurring. Indonesia, Brazil, Japan, Nigeria, Pakistan, and Bangladesh all represent new markets affecting the future of global TV news. The well-developed markets also exist in the European Union, in emerging democracies such as South Africa, in many of the Middle Eastern nations, and in most of Latin America.

Access to News Making?

> "The community I know wasn't on the screen. If we're not on the screen, we're not in the future."
>
> —Latina news watcher

It's an issue of access, access to opportunity. The West has flourished by operating within a paradigm that assumes some level of democratization, that is, access, as a base for economic and social exchange. There are two principal reasons for upholding this paradigm. One reason is pragmatic: Democratization averts conflict over place, property, and personal security. It encourages stable transitions in political leadership and philosophy, thereby avoiding wars that destroy capital. The second reason is ethical: Is it not right for all people to have a voice in determining the policies that govern their communities?

Since the media set the news and information agenda by selecting what topics will be offered for public debate, media policy is crucial to fostering or neglecting and abandoning the paradigm of democratization. The presentation of all news and information implicitly, if not explicitly, includes messages about the acceptable paradigm for conducting society's business. For example, Graham Mytton, head of international broadcasting audience research for the BBC, makes the following observation:

> [For some people] the electronic media may be doing rather more than giving information. They are thought to enhance the power of the already powerful. They are criticized for lowering the cultural standards and blurring the distinctive richness of many world cultures. They are seen by critics as promoting false values. Electronic media are viewed by others as having mostly beneficial effects. They make democracy possible by widely disseminating the kinds of information people need when making democratic choices. They cut across social and economic barriers and provide equal access to education and other information by which people can improve their own personal circumstances.[4]

No longer is it possible to reach agreement quietly among a select elite of industry, media, and political leadership. It's not so easy to have everyone else just "go along." In part, the tenuousness that is felt in all sectors of society is caused by this change in the "game rules" for doing business. In this climate, what is the media's role in presenting news and information that foster democratization?

How Can News Foster Democratization—Access?

Just creating a headline isn't enough. It does get audience attention, which is crucial, but only a starting point. The difference between ordinary reporting of news and information and reporting in an environment that fosters democratization lies in what's done after the headline is printed.

The definition of "democracy" implies that people govern themselves, not that people watch others govern them. Access to the policy-making process—transparency—is the news. Does any entity other than the media amplify the policy-making process in such a way that an enduring democratic government is possible?

The journalism of inclusion and constructive "watchdog" journalism can advance democratization and minimize the anarchy that results from cynicism. Later chapters of this book will explain these concepts by offering case studies and models.

PUBLIC INFORMATION OR PAPARAZZI

With "live" news, the conquerors of mind and heart have a weapon more powerful than either the sword or the pen: the little picture box in everyone's living room and office.[5] Can these new technology tools be harnessed for constructive purposes? Live television is creating both victims and victors.

Max Frankel noted that without the paparazzi, "Diana would have been merely a royal highness."[6] He claims that she was the idol of the people precisely because her privacy was invaded and her image was exploited.

As a human incarnation of the royal family, Diana was victor. Her death was caused, in part, by an effort to outrun the pursuing paparazzi. Her brother, Earl Spencer, eulogized her as "the most hunted person of the modern age."[7] In this instance, Diana was both victim and, again, victor.

What about the 600 million viewers of her funeral? Were they victims or victors? Was this event "news" in the sense that it affected the quality of life for viewers? Or was it entertainment and, to that degree, irrelevant? Did it mix news and entertainment to make an important point about the lack of relevance of a remote royal family for today's common people?

Certainly, this is an age in which the media can conquer hearts and minds, but there's a fine line between news and entertainment. News has often become infotainment, and entertainment is often believed to be information. Can a civilized society set any standards for itself in determining what it needs as news? How would it do that?

Assessing News Needs

It's commonly understood by the industry and by sociologists like Saul Alinsky that people understand only what is within their experience. That's true. However, people have changed, and their experience has changed. Tomorrow's news and information will be more understandable if it does not replicate that which was relevant to the generation before the technology revolution. For example, young people everywhere are interested in emerging workplace opportunities and life in neighboring parts of the globe. This is as true for the village dweller in Samburu tribal lands in Africa or for the pueblo dweller in Chuquito, Peru, as it is for the high-tech junkies in California's Silicon Valley. Because of the technology, these opportunities differ greatly from those in their parents' generation. Because of TV, they all know about many things their parents never experienced. Across the globe, education levels and economic opportunities may differ, but levels of intelligence and curiosity do not. Issues that grew out of World War II and the Cold War lose their relevance to those not in the affected generation, not to mention those not in the affected parts of the world.

Customarily, the media industry extrapolates from the Nielsen ratings of current television programming to assess popular or unpopular programming. A fallacy lies in the belief that what worked yesterday will work tomorrow. Furthermore, one cannot assume that what works in one culture will work in another. It might be far more useful for the ratings experts to learn from financial experts to take a "zero-base" look at the options, that is, to wipe the slate clean and do a range of different assessments of what news and information will work: Look at news and information from the point of view of a psychologist knowledgeable in human motivation. Look from the point of view of a scientist examining the environmental health of the planet. Look from the point of view of individuals across the globe who seek opportunity for themselves and their families. Look from the point of view of advancing the democratization that will enhance human opportunity, promote market stability, and expand markets. Look from the point of view of a business entrepreneur who knows that it is not enough to be content with yesterday's market.

The construct presented by the psychologist Abraham Maslow is a useful starting point for a zero-based assessment of the needs of recipients of news and information.[8] Maslow presents his picture of human motivation in pyramid form. It begins with the need to deal with basic survival—food, drinking water, shelter, and clothing. Maslow contends that until individuals have satisfied that need, they cannot focus on the next level of concern—safety. After people are confident that they are free from danger, they can focus on social concerns—belonging in a community, friends, family. Those who have successfully met these areas of need are the few who, near the top of the pyramid, are able to deal first with esteem—achievement, recognition, respect—and finally with self-actualization, the sense of meaning and fulfillment associated with directing one's own life.

How could Maslow's hierarchy of needs be useful in assessing needs for news and information? To provide news and information that address the general level of needs of a community will obviously attract an audience. Similarly, it is useful to understand that those who make the decisions from their vantage point near the top of the pyramid may not appreciate the experience of those dealing with the more basic levels of need. Maslow's theory might be applied to news to examine the considerable allocation of news time to crime coverage, that is, to safety. Those deciding on this time allocation make an accurate judgment in thinking that everyone who has TV (everyone who has managed to rise above the basic survival skills) is interested in personal safety. However, they err in failing to realize that there's an interest in the next levels of the pyramid—being part of a viable community and realizing achievement. To keep the broadest audience, one shouldn't exclude the sizable number of people who have moved beyond the bottom of the pyramid. Whatever a person's current level of need, hope springs eternal for movement to a "better life." Programming that takes these psychological factors into account may provide new opportunities for both the industry and the consumer.

Take another example of zero-based assessment for news and information programming. A scientist examining the environmental health of the planet might highlight critical areas where the global public and global leaders need certain news and information critical to survival, never mind safety. The UN Earth Summit elicited the following facts on sustainable development:

- *Population*—The number of people added to the world's population each year peaked in 1990 at 87 million. By 1996, it had dropped to 80 million more people per year.
- *Poverty*—The number of people living on less than $1 per day continues to grow; by 1996 they represented more than 1.1 billion of the world's 5.8 billion people.
- *Fresh water*—One-third of the world's population presently lives in countries with moderate to severe problems of access to fresh water; by 2025, two-thirds of the world's population may live in countries with fresh-water shortages.
- *Global warming*—Each year the global carbon dioxide emissions increase. They were 5.9 billion tons in 1990 and 6.2 billion tons in 1996. Carbon dioxide contributes to global warming.
- *Forests*—Each year the earth has 35 million fewer acres of forest, lost to cutting or burning. Forests help to reduce the carbon dioxide levels.[9]

From this UN perspective, clearly news and information are needed about environmental protection. The knowledge needed differs greatly from a few decades ago, in that the planet's safety is jeopardized in ways quite different from those of the past.

Look at news and information in a zero-based assessment of priorities from the perspective of a global policymaker like the former U.S. secretary of state Warren Christopher.[10] Christopher's concern for global peace and security was to increase understanding of the need for diplomacy. He warned that isolationism results in the need to respond to crisis—a costly and dangerous practice. He further highlighted issues like the environment, terrorism, and drug trafficking as the likely catalysts for conflict.

If one accepts this assessment of global need, one would conclude that it was crucial for the U.S. public, as well as others across the world, to understand what diplomacy means in terms of government budget appropriations. In the United States, only 1% of the federal budget is so allocated, while well over 25% of the whole is spent on the military or responding to conflict. In a democratic system, those allocations are altered only when the elected decision makers are confident that they have support for such action from those whose votes (or money) keep them in office.

Against these more systematic "needs assessments" that determine news priorities, one also has the assessment made by networks and stations—partly ratings based and partly intuitive. An example cited by ABC's Richard Wald illustrates the process.

This country went through a very long period of very difficult civil rights arrangements and it was never on the front page of any newspaper or on the main news programs until Martin Luther King and that whole explosion of demand for civil rights in the 1960s. It wasn't news in a big time way until something happened that made it coalesce and made it news. The situation hadn't changed. It was merely that consciousness was concentrated. It took a personality. It took events. It takes all kinds of things. It takes a peculiarity of history. The same is true for almost every great movement in our lives. There has been a difficulty with paying for medicine in this country for a long time. Clinton may or may not have gotten elected on his pledge of a new system for the payment of health and medicine, but clearly he coalesced the interest in it. When you say what is the future of these things, I don't know the answer. There are great social questions at issue.[11]

The Impact of News and Information

If the news media were not the most powerful force in the world, why would they be the first institution to be taken over at times of political instability? For example, the 1991 attempted coup by the old guard in the Soviet Union failed because they failed to understand how to disconnect the high-tech media. The news got out. Yeltsin came to Gorbachev's rescue, and the transition to a market economy continued. In the 1997 political power struggle in Serbia, the president took control of the TV stations as a way to solidify her base.

A journalist's criterion for good news may be that which will win an award, is easy to present, or seems to meet the protocol needs for the station. An industry criterion may be that which will bring in the most advertising revenue, provide an advantage over the competition, or curry favor for future business transactions. Those criteria certainly represent personal and industry self-interest, but they represent only a short-term self-interest.

To satisfy media professional and industry long-term self-interest, one must appreciate the impact the mass media have across the globe. The news and information media operate on the assumption that they are reporting and interpreting events and opinions. The truth is that all forms of news—hard news, soft news features, and public affairs commentary—are also creating the opinions by which countless critical decisions are made.

It's not hard to create opinion, because people believe TV. The Times Mirror Center for the People and the Press found that TV is replacing the church as the authoritative source of information. Sixty percent of Americans regarded the church as believable, and 73% said TV was believable. In Mexico, the church still has a small lead, but the gap is closing: 79% believe the church and 75% the news media. In Canada, 47% believe the church and 81% believe TV news. In five European nations, the church ranks even farther behind TV news than it does in Canada.[12]

Adding to that understanding, research results show that whenever at least 25% of the individuals in a social system adopt an innovation, idea, practice, or object, "it is probably impossible to stop the further diffusion of a new idea, even if one wishes to do so."[13]

Fortunately, this means that the public are not lemmings at the mercy of whatever tyrant seizes the microphone. In some measure Richard Wald, senior vice-president of ABC News, has a point:

> We educate the public. We help them to understand what some of the problems are. They do understand. People are not dumb. People are very smart. Most people. There's a sort of funny non-news case in point. You think that people will accept what authority figures tell them. But they don't. They're not foolish children. They're not the Christian right or the non-Christian right, or whatever. They're just people. They have a reasonable expectation of life. They have a reasonable expectation of what you put on the air. You put on something lousy, and they understand it's lousy. You put on something pretty good, and they understand that it's pretty good. What's wrong with that?
>
> Why is it that there's a sort of gentle political fascism at work in the world all the time—and that is that other people are not as smart as you and me? People who are committed politically tend to think that they're aware of the issues, and therefore they are smarter than other folks. They're not smarter. They're just committed. Smart and educated are two different things. I'm not sure that they meet all that often.[14]

The bottom line is that the potential is enormous for both fulfilling media short- and long-term self-interests and simultaneously fulfilling some of our commonly held ideals for the quality of life we would like to see across the globe. Fulfilling that potential requires a fresh zero-based needs assessment of what news and information are relevant into the coming century.

STONEWALLING CHANGE

For countless reasons, the media industry could benefit from rethinking the news and information it presents to global audiences. These reasons apply to print media and to radio, but especially to television. The Internet is another matter, to be discussed in a subsequent chapter.

There are new channels to program and new audiences to reach. New production equipment and methodologies have arrived. New competitors have entered the communications field, and securing operating revenue and advertisement revenue is a constant challenge. Industry sales and mergers affect business practices. The list goes on.

In reality, it's all rather overwhelming for the industry, where it's difficult enough to do one's regular job from day to day, never mind rethinking one's approach.

The Swiss Watch Approach

The beauty of a Swiss watch is its ability to continue to run well day after day, year after year, without any attention. Anyone with management experience can tell stories about how remarkable it was that, in a specific circumstance, a given institution continued to carry out its routine job functions despite a total leadership vacuum.

In an environment where everything is in a state of flux, it is reassuring to dig in and say, "But, we've always done it this way." Unfortunately, this satisfaction is short-lived.

Business consultant Timothy Nolan and his colleagues tell a story about frogs:

> In a laboratory, frogs were placed in shallow pans of room-temperature water, They were free to jump out of the pans at any time. Under each pan was a Bunsen burner, which heated the water very gradually. As the temperature rose, degree by degree, the frogs adapted to the new temperature. Unfortunately, regardless of how hot the water became, the frogs never became uncomfortable enough to jump out of the pan. In fact, they stayed right there until the heat was so intense that the frogs died. Now, *that's* adaptability![15]

Dealing with "Others"

A common problem for people and institutions (and cultures) confronted with something new is the failure to leap eagerly into the unknown of dealing with "the different." It's risky. One who lives with victors might have to encounter a victim; and while learning to communicate in those circumstances, one risks becoming a victim. The longer people follow the same practices—"business as usual"—the harder it is to change. That which is different requires adjustment, maybe new learning, and certainly a conscious effort to chart a new course.

Such inertia is evident in the person comfortable with the typewriter who resists learning to use a personal computer or in the person who's used to a darkroom who must now deal with video and digital images. It's evident when people who've always spoken English find themselves surrounded by people who speak Spanish. It's evident for those who know that news broadcasts and newspapers were created to provide economic information to those who financed them—and now, even economic interests have new, broader definitions. It's clear that "we" are protecting the status quo when newcomers (new technicians, new leaders, new populations, new economic or racial groups) are not folded into the "we," but are referred to as "they," the victims. Second-class status is communicated, and perception becomes a reality affecting a wide range of business, professional, and personal decisions. The chance to expand the number of victors is lost. Opportunity is cut short.

Nolan explains the risk-taking required for successful change with the cartoon of a coach advising his team of trapeze artists just when the moment is right to leap into the grasp of the person swinging on an approaching trapeze. It's necessary to leave one trapeze in order to catch the oncoming one. He notes that the coach or leader's job is to provide "encouragement, timing, and a safety net for those who must let go of today's stability for tomorrow's opportunity." There is no final destination. Change is ongoing.

In the business of news and information transmission, the situation is the same. Tomorrow's opportunity will be missed if the industry clings too tightly to the security of the past. Thanks to technology, the trapeze is swinging faster than ever.

Needing to Be An Expert

A problem for the journalist and for just about every other professional in this era of transition is being expected to deal with new and strange topics. Why should one who understands journalism necessarily understand nuclear physics? It's not easy to get the story straight if the hazard requires knowing whether there's a blowup or a meltdown. Furthermore, it's not easy to translate complex and specialized material into something understandable by people who need to know what affects their safety and what their options are, but don't need (or want) to know the intricacies of physics.

The journalist is not alone with this problem. Edith Wiener, president of the New York firm Wiener, Edrich, and Brown, describes the new era we are entering. Skills are no longer relevant; technology can do surgery. Time is no longer compelling; everyone sets his or her own pace. "What's important is knowing what questions to ask and where to look for the answers."[16]

Fortunately, technology has also helped solve this problem. Computers make it possible through the Internet for anyone to derive any level of knowledge desired on most topics; and computers also make it possible for television, radio, and the print media to complement each other in offering varied aspects of a story.

Unfortunately, the journalist will need to leap from old trapezes to new ones in learning to master these technologies and incorporate this knowledge into story preparation. Industry management will need to engage in enough similar activity to understand the changes and how to use them for the benefit of the industry and—simultaneously—for the benefit of the citizenry in their consumer market.

This investment in news content may not occur if, as Negrine and Papathanassopoulos write in their book on the internationalization of television, this new breed of media tycoon is solely interested in high returns to stockholders and in the exploitation of their commercial strength.[17]

As Wald says, "Everybody always thinks you do things for the audience. That's relatively true, but not perfectly. Basically, what you put on the air is what you want to put on the air."[18]

The question is, will media professionals take the time and energy to learn to cover new areas of news and information? If not, it won't be the first time that people have failed to act in their own self-interest.

WHAT'S IN THE REST OF THIS BOOK?

The central question of the book is whether the new technology media will have a positive or a negative impact on the quality of life in the decades ahead. Dizzy from coping with technological developments and maximizing profits, media entrepreneurs pay little attention to the impact of these technologies. Even the viewers pay little attention to the impacts and become cooperative victims.

A unique window of opportunity is open—an opportunity to use these new tools to expand economic markets, stabilize democratic societies, and improve the quality of life on the planet.

The timing is perfect, at the onset of the cyclical swing of the pendulum into the next pro-consumer era. As in the 1930s and the 1960s, these periods prove to be times of high creativity, enthusiasm, and a fervent commitment to accomplish the seemingly impossible. So too, at the end of the 1990s, events mark the initiation of a new pro-consumer era. Just one example of this shift in public behavior was the massive outpouring of respect for Princess Diana at her funeral. It was a new "velvet revolution" against established institutions like the monarchy. It was a call for change.

This book consists of many interviews with the media and with the users of the new technologies from all across the globe. Together, they provide insight into the impact of these technologies, and they provide models for tomorrow's news standards.

As the reader explores the two parallel "media worlds" of the "haves" and the "have-nots," the book will examine the circumstances for creating both victims and victors. Is only the new technology global? or is how we use it global? As David Shields, a sociology professor at the Georgia Institute of Technology, stated, "All tools are socially constructed. They're shaped, that is, by an array of forces that includes tradition, politics, economic interests, history, and competing technologies."[19]

Will conscious decisions be made about how to use these technologies to shape the decade ahead, or will the industry and the consumers fall victim to the tyranny of indecision, infotainment, and ignorance that heightens tensions and instabilities between peoples?

NOTES

1. R. W. Apple, "Through London Streets the Sounds of Silence Toll." *New York Times*, September 7, 1997, p. 1f.

2. Reuters, "TV Audience for Funeral Estimated at 600 Million." *Boston Globe*, September 9, 1997; and AP, "50 Million Americans See Funeral Live on TV," *Boston Globe*, September 8, 1997, p. A5.

3. Joanne O'Brien and Martin Palmer, *The State of Religion Atlas* (New York: Touchstone Books, Simon and Schuster, 1993).

4. Graham Mytton, Head of International Broadcasting Audience Research, BBC World Service, *Handbook on Radio and Television Audience Research* (Paris: UNESCO and UNICEF, 1993), p. 2.

5. Carla Brooks Johnston, *Winning the Global TV News Game* (Boston and London: Butterworth Heinemann/Focal, 1995).

6. Max Frankel, "No Pix, No Di." *New York Times Magazine*, September 21, 1997, p. 53.

7. Warren Hoge, "Diana Buried as a Nation Mourns." *New York Times*, September 7, 1997, p. 1f.

8. Paul Schmollins, *Human Services in Contemporary America* (Monterey, CA: Brooks Cole, 1985), Chapter 1.

9. Associated Press Report in *The Herald*, Lima, Peru, June, 24, 1997.

10. Presentation by outgoing U.S. Secretary of State Warren Christopher, Kennedy School of Government, Harvard University, January 15, 1997.

11. Richard Wald, Senior Vice President, ABC News, 77 W. 66th St., New York, NY. Interview with the author in New York on May 20, 1994.

12. Religion Notes, "Survey: Media Edges Church." *Boston Globe*, March 19, 1994.

13. Everett M. Rogers, *Diffusion of Innovation*, third ed. (New York: Free Press, 1983), Chapters 1 and 7.

14. Wald interview.

15. Timothy Nolan, Leonard Goodstein, and J. William Pfeiffer, *Plan or Die!* (San Diego: Pfeiffer, 1993), p. 2.

16. Edith Weiner, Closing speech to the World Future Society annual convention, Cambridge, MA, July 26, 1994.

17. R. Negrine and S. Papathanassopoulos, *The Internationalization of Television* (New York: Pinter, 1990), p. 134.

18. Wald interview.

19. John W. Verity, "Introduction," *Business Week/The Information Revolution*, Special Issue, May 1994, pp. 12–18.

2

Free Press and Transparent Government

WHO'S AFRAID OF CHANGE?

Industry Decision Makers

The world is too complicated to pay attention to everything. By and large, journalists focus on telling the news, while media managers focus on growing corporate profits. Democratization in the abstract is a value to be upheld, like family and patriotism. In the concrete, democratization is left to the politicians, about whom it's popular to say bad things. People are generally too busy to think this through. Values—their real meanings—are on autopilot unless a sea change threatens the status quo.

For example, before Hong Kong was returned to the Chinese government on July 1, 1997, its residents and businesses wrestled with the question of whether or not their style of life and business would remain the same under Chinese authority. Should they emigrate? Thousands did. For another example, businesses wanting to operate in Burma must assess what damage would be caused by their inability to use a fax machine in Burma, where it is illegal to send a fax. Indeed, there is a connection between democratization and expanding a market economy.

Although decision makers would generally say that democratization is not an everyday concern for them, maybe that's because they aren't evaluating the real meaning of their routine market decisions. For example, dealing with a global market means reaching out to more of the globe's population—a form of democratization, depending on how that outreach is handled.

The potential for market growth in global television news and information is enormous. The world population is about five and one-half billion people. For that number, there are approximately one billion television sets. Indeed, distribution of sets is uneven. In some countries there are multiple sets per household; in other countries there may only be one set per one hundred people, but that's enough for a village viewing center. Not only is television accessible to virtually everyone, but the range of program options is growing rapidly. Barely a decade ago, government-owned station monopolies were the sole source for programs in many countries, including Europe. Now, satellite TV is crossing borders everywhere, and state monopolies are reeling from the pressures of cost and competition. Despite the booming computer industry and the Internet, global TV is the world's most influential transmitter of news and information.

As mentioned in Chapter 1, the rapid growth of the middle class in some of the globe's most populous countries means that an enormous market is waiting to buy advertised products or to subscribe to their favorite shows. What is the extent of this impact on the market?

The Future's Group, an American consultant to global business, studies this new middle class.[1] Of China's 1.2 billion people, there was, as of 1994, a middle class of 82 million people—less than 7%. Still, 82 million buyers is substantial for any industry. India, with 870 million people, has a middle class of 32 million. That is 3.6% of their total population, but a lot of TV subscription dollars. The territory of the former USSR is third in global population and promises an enormous market once the new economies stabilize. The United States is fourth and already a developed market. Indonesia, the fifth most populous country, has a middle class of seventeen million people. Brazil has a middle class of eighteen million. Japan has been highly prosperous for some time. Aside from these ten most populous countries, other countries are growing their middle classes. Mexico's middle class includes twelve million people. Poland has a middle class of four million; Thailand, seven million; and Turkey, six million. That's a lot of people to sell things to. It's also a lot of people to influence the level of freedoms across the globe.

The new middle class provides a point of focus for industry market growth. Second, focusing on this population bloc means that TV programming can no longer speak just to the elite of economic power brokers concerned about business and the market. Programming must democratize to meet the needs and interests of those who it hopes will buy the products and services that fuel the industry.

But, there's more. Opportunity for industry doesn't end at the front gate of middle-class homes. The middle class, while representing significant growth in numbers, remains a small fraction of the overall global population. Yet, the hardware investment for global communications covers the total planet's geography. It's good business to expand the middle class, because then the market expands even more. It's simple industry self-interest. Accomplishing this feat may not be impossible. It requires information, education, and access to jobs that lead to a better quality of life, translating into a position in the middle class where one can make choices (and purchases.) In fact, democratization can be linked to industry growth as well as to improvements in quality of life.

Growing the middle class and servicing the *new* class is not easy when the globe's population has such extremes of wealth and poverty. A report from the UN Earth Summit stated that in 1996 more than 1.1 billion of the world's population were living on less than $1 per day. This 20% of the globe's population, and the many more people who live within wealthier countries, disenfranchised because they are considered second class, represent the other media world. They don't make money for the industry because they can't pay. Their story isn't often told because they don't have the microphone. Sometimes news and information from the dominant media world are "about" them, but rarely from their perspective. But they certainly are getting to see TV, and on it they see how "the other half" lives. Is it in the self-interest of the dominant media industry to ignore them? If they are ignored, how can the middle class expand? Can the broad tent of democratization welcome these people under its flaps? If that doesn't happen, will their poverty (and the problems of poor health, crime, and lack of employment credentials) cause instability to markets?

Media Laws

Not only does market growth bring profit for the industry, market growth complicates the law of the press. We're now a global market, but our laws are not created for a global society. They are for nation-states.

To discuss democratization in a global marketplace, one must begin with the laws made by nation-states that either protect human freedoms or hamper them by placing restrictions of varying sorts on the press and the electronic media.

Within nations, it's long been accepted that democratization meant only passing laws and promulgating regulations that guarantee a free press and create the opportunity for balanced news coverage. In political and social circles, all too frequently the entire topic of democratization has been dismissed with the superficial notion that *being able* to print or broadcast news in itself guarantees democracy. But as is evident in many nations that still struggle with implementing democratization, the laws and regulations have little value, and the noble efforts of journalists and industry leaders fall on deaf ears if there is not an astute public prepared to ensure that press freedom laws are implemented on an ongoing and consistent basis.

For example, many countries with constitutional guarantees of freedom of speech and of the press have other laws used to stop journalists from saying anything critical of the government and its leaders.

Passing laws and the process of implementing them fit together like a hand and a glove. To be sure, in the coming decades we must leap from the old nation-state trapeze of believing that everything requires regulation to the trapeze swinging through cyberspace on which one must rethink whether it is necessary—or possible—to prevent free speech.

Some suggest that there's no need to deal with nation-state law and regulation because technology has rendered them unimportant. However, we live in two worlds in more senses than one; the transnational freedoms of communication are still fledgling compared to the billions of people whose freedoms to exchange information are limited by the laws of the nation in which they live. The American ideal remains a model for the world. As incorporated into the First Amendment of the Constitution, the law states, "Congress shall make no law respecting the establishment of religion, or prohibiting the free exercise thereof; or abridging the freedom of speech, or of the press; or the right of the people to peacefully assemble, and to petition the Government for a redress of grievances."

Many countries of the world have laws that control free speech. Erik Barnouw, media historian, describes a practice begun in Europe that continues in many countries:

> Under Henry VIII, as under other European kings, no one might operate a printing press without a royal license. Anyone wanting to advocate his ideas in print had to get such a license or get his words printed by one who had a license. But these royal licenses, holding a privilege that meant power and perhaps wealth, were cautious about what they printed. They quickly became gatekeepers of the society, helping the crown keep things under control.[2]

Even modern countries that have laws protecting free speech have difficulty implementing those laws, especially if political emotions reach a boiling point. Mordecai Kirschenboim, director general of the Israeli Broadcasting Authority, offers an example.

> You have to be very careful, especially in a state like Israel. These days [in 1994, when Labor was in power] I'm being attacked by the government, especially the Prime Minister, because I allow too many stories in the news of people who are against the peace process (with the PLO). So the government says now I service the extreme right wing. I explain that we operate by the law of broadcasting that forces us to bring all the news views that are being held by the public even if they are not convenient to the government, proportionally, of

course. In 1982 when the government went to war with Lebanon and the streets were full of demonstrators, I broadcast the demonstrations and then I was considered a leftist. Now I'm considered a rightist. We are democrats and we consider the broadcasting law a good law.

The government forgets sometimes that we are not a government station. We are being sponsored totally by the public. We don't relate to the government budget. The public pays for the broadcasts.

We work under a code that things always have to be balanced. Government doesn't have the only say. There is always an opposition. There is always a subject to balance.

Government nominates the IBA Director General in Israel. My board has members of all the political parties, but they reflect when they were nominated. Some have three year terms, and a maximum of two terms.[3]

Keeping the opportunity for free speech alive is a problem even when the laws say the right thing. Erik Barnouw notes that industry *practice* has been used to exert control contrary to laws. His example is from the United States. "During World War II the networks would only air documentaries that they themselves produced to guarantee 'professional standards and objectivity' which it implied was their bailiwick." The same phenomenon happened during the Viet Nam era. Barnouw warns of the limits to press freedom that can result from "network gatekeepers and licensing agencies."[4]

Barnouw further notes that Canadian author Harold Ennis once wrote that the very existence of a media monopoly controlling press freedoms serves to encourage new media to form on the edge of society and ultimately bring a realignment of power.

The global marketplace and the new technologies are bringing realignments of power in ways heretofore impossible to imagine. Nonetheless, as we seek to move into a cyberspace domain with First Amendment rights, we must work diligently to ensure that nation-states across the globe and the industries who want the patronage of their citizenry hold these principles. The price of compromise on free speech and democratization is too great. The disenfranchised know this. The rest of us must not take these freedoms for granted.

Nothing Is Neutral

The media is the megaphone that informs people about what's happening and helps them formulate their viewpoints. It can either be proactive in encouraging democratization, or it can mindlessly ignore whether or not the system works to the benefit of the overall society. Laws and regulations that protect a free press and electronic media are simply the first step. A democratic society requires ongoing participation in policymaking and on-going information about how one can participate. It is in the self-interest of the media, the policymakers, the economic leaders, and the public to be certain that everyone is included at the table. President Kennedy summarized this common self-interest in participation when he said, "Ask not what your country can do for you; ask what you can do for your country."

Regardless of content, any item of news or information can be evaluated in terms of where it stands on the spectrum of *values* shown in the following diagram. Does the media coverage

Enhance the Powerful—or—Respect the Citizenry

Lower Cultural Standards—or—Disseminate Information Needed for Choices

Create Hatred—or—Bridge Social and Economic Barriers

Encourage Cynicism and Superficiality—or—Provide Access to Opportunity?

SUBVERSIVE DEMOCRATIZATION

Program Content

Program content involves making value judgments. For example, Mary Roodkowsky, former chief of field operations, UNICEF, Dacca, Bangladesh, offers one example:

> In 1993, ITV news reported unprecedented floods in Bangladesh. Camera crews sloshed through the water shooting dramatic footage. The result was that our UNICEF office got telexes from N.Y. wondering why we were not asking for more emergency aid. They'd seen the flood stories on TV. In fact, the flooding was not worse than it usually is at that time of the year. The real problem is the sewage, and the disease resulting from it. But sewage isn't picturesque, so TV crews don't highlight that. And the public doesn't want to offer relief funds for that.[5]

Such value judgments tend to reflect the perception of the media industry decision makers. In the above case, the floods no doubt seemed horrendous to a person not accustomed to living in Bangladesh—and, besides, what great pictures for pulling on the heartstrings of viewers and, in turn, for pulling up the ratings that govern advertising profits.

Similarly, value judgments determine what topics to cover and what to omit. For example, Johan Ramsland, an editor for BBC World Service Television offers the following topic. "I think, in news terms, that economics and business is becoming of more interest to more people generally. Because of the level of communications now, what happens somewhere has an immediate effect on the other side of the world. It will continue to be important. I think business news is a real growth area."[6] That's a delightfully easy bridge from the era past to the one ahead because, before technology so expanded audiences, a major purpose of the news was to provide information to business leaders. The irony of the "privatization era" of the nineties is that while business is "downsizing" more and more, the general public has become aware of and concerned about business. In that sense, Ramsland's observation is accurate.

What about the topics that haven't immediately come to mind among those in the media industry? One, for example, that is important to reaching the newer audiences and to democratization is the topic of women. They do, after all, represent somewhat over half the population of the globe and an increasingly important block of decision makers in professional capacities as well as in consumer spending. Hillary Rodham Clinton. America's First Lady, addressed the Fourth World Conference on Women in Beijing on September 4, 1995, saying, "Tragically, women are most often the ones whose human rights are violated. Even in the late 20th century, the rape of women continues to be used as an instrument of armed conflict. Women and children make up a large majority of the world's refugees. And when women are excluded from the political process, they become even more vulnerable to abuse." Many aspects of this issue provide news and information program material as important to the self-interest of husbands and fathers as to women.

BBC's Ramsland had other thoughts on new programming: "I think we may get a lot more socially conscious programming. If one looks at the history of radio broadcasting, it started, I think, as a tool of education. [This approach] will be used more and more. You'll get programming that does aim at getting across messages—about better methods of agriculture in drought areas and things like this. I think (we'll see) more current affairs than hard news programs."

The range of topics for news and information program content evolves, as do the concerns of those who view the news. Some of these topics arise easily, because the professionals in the dominant media find, within their own experience, that these issues rank high on the agenda at the end of the twentieth century—AIDS, the environment, health, race, religion, genetics. Other topics may be less likely to arise, simply because they are not always priorities within the experience of the dominant media leadership. But, when examining a needs analysis of the global populations who rely on news and information, the following topics also rank high: poverty and the rich/poor gap, fresh water, cultural preservation, sustainable agriculture, renewable energy, educational and employment opportunities, transportation, discrimination, and consumer and worker health and safety.

It's always easy to say that news covers events, not issues. That simply provides a rationalization for selecting topics that "seem appropriate" according to the value judgments of the media professionals. It's easy to cover the latest shocking turn of events, far easier than to provide news that covers the real problem. For example, show pictures of the latest Bangladesh flood, but don't deal with the real problem of sewage control. Any of the topics previously mentioned offer rich potential for hard news events, soft news features, or public affairs commentary. Of course, covering new topics does require some extra effort initially to make the contacts and do the outreach necessary to reach the new audiences and new markets. The effect on encouraging democratization and a society less fraught with conflict might be impressive.

Program Format and Tone Choices

Format and tone have as much impact on democratization as does program content. Format is how the program is assembled—visuals, interviews, debates. Tone is how the program is projected—crisis, negative, positive, amusing.

In addition, presenting information within the experience of the audience is just as important as presenting it within the language of the audience. For example, take an incident of news coverage in the United States about the turbulence in Bosnia with the breaking apart of the former Yugoslavia.[7] Eyes glaze over. It's rather far from the personal experience of most people. But when a reporter told the story of Irma, one mute five-year-old victim of the civil war, people, for a moment, cared. One small child represents the symbol of hope, not despair. The story's narrative is the way people make sense of experience—with characters, a story, a climax. It becomes personal. That which was complex begins to take on meaning within the experience of the viewer. The Irma story is the strength and weakness of journalism. Policy statements and stories about institutional activity don't work. Bosnia by itself is not understandable. It can't be fixed. Events are not conclusive. But Irma can be fixed.

A skillful journalist could use the story to illustrate the larger decisions of the war. For example, the story might be linked with policy decisions about locations of safe havens or the decision to ban land mines. As with movies and sports, viewers often start watching because of a character's story or a particular hero. They move from spectators into participants and begin advocating for the resolution of a problem seen in a movie or for the prosperity of a sports league. The media does not become an advocate. It simply provides complete information.

Format can either grow the audience or contribute to anger and disinterest. Chava Tidhar, research director for Israeli educational television, got the following reaction when asking an Israeli news editor about the use of experts during the Persian Gulf War reporting, "If there is an enemy to proper journalism, it is the use of experts."[8] This came as reaction to the news reporting following two formats: (1) The news presented few facts and much commentary, usually by generals who didn't have frontline responsibility. People to be interviewed were selected from the station's "expert lists," mostly on the basis of personal acquaintance and preference. (2) The news reported the human side of the war. The analysis done after the war showed that the audience blamed the news programs for demoralizing people.

Had the media decision makers thought through what the audience might find useful, the emphasis might have focused to as great an extent as possible on the facts of hard news events. Certainly commentary of any sort could have been omitted from the news itself. Commentary is usually speculation, and it is a mistake to present it as news. Intelligent people resent the manipulation. Others find themselves frequently misled. In public affairs programming, it would better serve the audience, and consequently the station, to identify a cross-section of participants. They would more accurately be billed as persons with differing views, not as experts. Who is considered an expert frequently depends on whether his or her position is consistent with that of the person bestowing the label. In the interest of democratization, let the audience evaluate the material presented to assess how much of it is based in substance and to what degree the conclusions presented are warranted.

Humor is another important ingredient in presenting news and information. It's a powerful tool for communication. Whether part of the format or the tone of news and information programming, the use of humor requires thoughtful decision-making. Often, humor is omitted when it is badly needed, and it's used in silly superficial ways when it could provide a major contribution to enhanced understanding of the topic at hand.

One example illustrates how humor enabled people to mold a public policy decision into their personal experience and to think seriously about safety issues. In the early 1980s in the United States, the Federal Emergency Management Agency (FEMA) was getting increased federal budget appropriations to promote a program of protecting people from nuclear attack. Local government officials were supplied with camera-ready copy for newspaper articles to publish at the time of emergency to teach the public how this program worked. One article described how, at the time of a nuclear attack, people could hop out of their car, dig a hole under the car, stretch a plastic tarp from the car to the ground, jump into the hole, and be safe. The mental picture was so ludicrous that thousands of people used the materials in public hearings before local and state governments across the nation, demanding a change in FEMA policy. The meetings left people doubled over in laughter, able to deal with the unpleasant topic of nuclear attack; and they left the meetings having expanded their base of support to include police and fire chiefs, mayors, and legislators. They learned something. They became empowered. They changed FEMA policy.

No doubt an understanding of the power of humor lies behind the trends in some countries, especially the United States, to merge information and entertainment into the pathetic substitute for news called "infotainment." Unfortunately, it does not represent the best use of humor, because its approach often omits any topic that is important or serious and trivializes everything else. It's a weak alternative to an effective use of humor in the Greek tradition.

Coproductions

With the global technology revolution, it's not surprising that the definition of "newsmaker" is changing—as is the definition of a great many other so-called constants from the past. In the nineteenth and twentieth centuries, news was wanted by those who influenced the economy. They were the newsmakers, and they paid for that news. It was a circle for the power elite. Things have changed. While the rich-poor gaps are still great, technology and education have brought many more people—the globe's new middle classes—to the table of influence. They pay, and the elite rely on their money for industry prosperity. The same technology advances have brought the globe's poor to the table of influence. They watch TV and see what others have. If they're not given an opportunity to be included, they can create instability. They picket, they boycott, and they start militias, civil wars, and revolutions. The news is theirs too. In a few years, it's in everyone's interest for them to be able to pay for it, too.

The emerging democracies across the globe have been listening to the Western rhetoric of partnership. They're ready, impatient, to have it happen. "How would you like it if a film crew from Malaysia came to Germany and did a film for the world on German pollution problems? The third world is always treated as receivers, rather than producers, of material." That's a comment from a Malaysian professional to Meg Goettemoeller, president of the World Information Corporation, in a discussion about news production.[9]

Certainly there is a global media industry changing news and information delivery for the world's populations, but it's not globally based. Primarily, it's based in London—Reuters, WTN, BBC. Those whose principal offices are not in London are U.S.-based and have offices in London—CNN, AP. It's never clear where Rupert Murdoch's News Corp. is based, but its roots are definitely entangled with those of the British empire. This base is even more segmented in that it is predominantly affluent, male, Caucasian, and English speaking. To be sure, the contributions of this set have been enormous in making the dream of global communications a reality. But now that the reality is upon us, democratization is a necessity, not an option.

Everyone has news that is relevant to the well-being of others. It's time to consider as partners—as sisters and brothers, not as foster-children—those from the Middle East, Africa, Asia, and Latin America; those whose skin is of color, whose gender is female, whose religion is not Judeo-Christian, whose language is not English, who may represent communities living on $1 a day per person.

One move toward these partnerships is CNN's "World Report." Launched in 1987, it provided a forum for local broadcasters throughout the world to contribute their own stories for CNN broadcast. In return, CNN material could be shown on their local stations. Astute at understanding how to match self-interest and ideal, Ted Turner developed for himself an army of quasi news bureaus and scores of potential clients in the global marketplace, while responding in action to the UNESCO argument about a media monopoly that perpetuated an information dictatorship. The options for expanding this idea are enormous, as is its potential for good will and market growth for any industry entrepreneur.

Another foot in the door for democratizing news and information partnerships is the broadcasting unions that have existed for several decades. Among them are the European Broadcasting Union, the Arab States Broadcasting Union, the Asia-Pacific Broadcasting Union, and the Caribbean Broadcasting Union. They function largely as collaboratives gathering and distributing international news. They predate the global satellite broadcasters and have their roots in partnerships between member nations, many of whom operated government-owned broadcasting systems and did not have private stations. While they aren't as new or as affluent or as global as the new technology companies, the broadcasting unions offer one of the best resources for experienced media professionals, who can be brought on board as partners for democratized global news and information production. They can contribute to democratization because they know their members and can make the linkages between the newsmakers and the global media.

A more ad-hoc route to partnership building that can move beyond the information dictatorship is the field of coproduction. Coproduction is the collaboration of two or more parties engaged in either the content, the technical, or the financial aspects of making a program for broadcast. For example, the German media group Bertelmann's Ufa TV and Film division signed a coproduction agreement with Paramount and Procter and Gamble. The $90 million contract was to produce and distribute thirty-six English-language TV movies. Ufa produces and distributes them in Europe. Paramount distributes them elsewhere in the world. Procter and Gamble advertises on the programs.[10] Such collaboration is a "win" for everyone for two reasons. It costs each party less. It's a fast way to overcome the outsider stereotype as industry moves into new markets.

News features and public affairs programs lend themselves to coproduction. But, there are several critical ingredients for successful coproduction. First, the partners must be compatible in understanding the topic to be presented. While not always easy, given the cultural diversity across the globe, the exercise of determining a common mode of presentation is a useful test of whether prospective audiences from different cultures will understand it any better than do the producers from different cultures. Then, the partners need to find a mutually compatible mode of presenting the topic. This also is problematic. Different cultures approach the tone, message, and style of their productions differently. Some are more interactive and entertaining. Some provide lecture-style material. Some use a more linear logic. Some rely on a more spiral logic.

Critical to building partnerships in global news and information exchange is the concept of equality, which can exist only if the initiative comes from both sides of the partnership. This means that while the dominant media industry clearly needs to be receptive and to commit resources toward such an endeavor, those from the "other media world" should also be aggressive in taking the initiative to arrange partnerships. Without such assertiveness, the partnerships are unlikely to occur, in large part because the dominant media industry is unfamiliar with where to go, whom to contact, and how to forge agreements with those who have not previously been partners to agreements.

Another example of a coproduction is *Nova*, the American public television program that produces science documentaries and public affairs programming on topics of scientific import. It uses coproduction in a number of ways. Individuals with program ideas supply hundreds of unsolicited suggestions each year. In addition, the producers seek out people with ideas or with partially completed programs to buy. One method is to go to the major festivals. Marche Internationale de Programes de Television (MIP), the largest, is held in Cannes in the spring and is a great place to meet people and shop. Producers make contacts, with whom they later communicate directly. Unfortunately, the festivals are expensive, and a newcomer can get lost in the crowd unless exceptionally skilled at self-marketing.

Many other organizations exist in Europe and the United States to help producers find contacts. See Carla Brooks Johnston's *International Television Co-Production* for lists with many organizational contacts.[11]

Those who wish to become partners in newsmaking have options for action, in addition to having good ideas, assertiveness, and an articulate case statement. They can explore alternative forms of partnership that provide services that fit their strengths and offer alternative ways to meet the other needs. Alternative funding strategies are always a welcome topic, even for established production companies. Maybe it's possible to bring in money from a new sponsor, or goods or services in lieu of money. Sometimes foundations and wealthy individuals have funds, especially if the topic of the program fits the particular interest of the funder or corporate sponsor.

One entry-level step for new production partners in the United States has been available through a service provided by many cable companies in cities where they negotiated franchise agreements. A "community access studio" is a place where anyone of any age can be trained to use television production equipment. They then can produce and edit programs to be aired on designated local channels. Concurrently, on municipal channels and school department channels, people from the community access studio produce and broadcast programs about local government, education, and local sports events. This service has provided good will for the cable companies and career development for many a would-be newsmaker. With some understanding of the skills demanded and an accompanying education, the industry can have the next generation of camera persons, editors, and so on. When community access studios are located in localities where large numbers of economically, racially, and ethnically marginalized people are located, there's an added bonus in preparing for a more culturally diverse industry.

A final example shows how a good idea moved someone from anonymity to become a partner in newsmaking. A secondary school graduate photographer with some community access studio experience was able to borrow an underwater video camera. He had learned deep-sea diving and took the camera with him, just to experiment. Soon he was the only independent TV producer in the metropolitan Boston area able to shoot underwater video. He now works as an independent producer on a wide range of projects, on contract. When a news story breaks about the Boston harbor, he's called. He makes videos for government agencies about underwater environmental and wastewater problems. He works for those constructing bridges and tunnels, and he produces documentaries about fish species for the Discovery TV channel.

The decisions of media professionals indirectly effect democratization. They are like the incoming tide, lifting the bottom of society's boat to new levels of opportunity. They represent for the industry a merger of ideals and self-interest, as the results not only make a better quality of life, they bring market growth to the industry.

Media Literacy

This final indirect method for democratization, media literacy, is ultimately not the responsibility of the news and information industry. But it may be in the interest of the industry to help jump-start the larger societal interest in the topic.

Media literacy is basically the same as print literacy in that it means understanding the meaning of what one sees or reads and being able to offer an astute analysis of the validity of the material. This means understanding the bias, the omission, the subtlety of what one sees as a spectator. It means going beyond watching to interpreting. It also means going beyond interpreting to creating projects and initiating activity—becoming a partner in sending one's news to others.

For centuries, literate people have learned to incorporate print literacy into their ongoing assessment of the material presented to them. But we've been a visual society for only a few decades—in some parts of the world, for a few years. And no one is teaching people to discern the meaning of the images on the box in the living room.

Why should the industry care what the viewers understand? Surely, that they like it, watch it, and pay for it is what matters. In the short run, that may be true, but enough people have been watching TV news and information and TV entertainment long enough that the honeymoon may be ending. There's already evidence in the United States, with pressure from the public and their politicians, to add new rating systems for sex and violence.

In Zimbabwe, reporters were thrown in jail for filing news stories about the president having an affair. In China, persons who saw the 1992 Los Angeles riots on the news were fearful that all the city had burned down. People in the United States couldn't believe that it would be safe to go to South America, because surely the entire environment consisted of drug lords staging gun battles. Although most people lead normal lives, with all the variety of communities in any part of the world, the result of such misunderstanding and fear can be a public climate that fosters isolationism, parochialism, hatred, and cynicism. Such public opinion can translate into repressive laws that handicap or create encumbrances for the media industries.

Media literacy isn't just for the benefit of the public at large. It's for the benefit of the political, civic, and business leadership. Leaders in every arena need media literacy to be able to understand three things:

1. the extent to which the majority of people believe the news and information seen on television and the extent to which this medium is at least equal in importance to print and radio

2. the economic importance of being seen in a positive light by the rest of the world in order to attract new markets and to be a partner in the economic dialogues. In short, how economic and policy leaders are seen depends entirely on whether they are seen.

3. the advantages of multimedia journalism for print journalists and for broadcasters alike in an era where technology is converging and each format complements the other

Dr. Robert L. Hilliard, former chief of educational broadcasting for the FCC, said, "Until we require every student [and encourage every adult] to have at least as much academic preparation in analyzing, evaluating, and using the visual and aural media as we require for print, we are guilty of abetting the inability of these students to cope with the unethical influences of the electronic media."[12]

As ABC's Richard Wald noted, people don't take the word of authorities as absolute. Times have changed. Education, more information, and scandal have left many parts of the consumer market less trusting. I might add that if people misunderstand what they see, it only contributes to the unrest and cynicism. Indirect democratization results from thinking about decisions for program content, for program format and tone, for industry partnerships, and for fostering media literacy across society. All these efforts together combine to strengthen market growth and profits, both monetary and qualitative.

DIRECT DEMOCRATIZATION

Whose Government Is It, Anyway?

Perhaps the major problem faced by those engaged in business outside the major industrialized countries is a mindset about government. Democratization is based on the premise that people believe that they own government: its officials serve at their pleasure, its laws serve their interests. When government is viewed as "they" rather than "we," attitudes of apathy, cynicism, or antagonism become the norm. Decision-making then becomes more dysfunctional, to the detriment of the industry and the public alike. The market becomes less conducive to stability and growth.

Ownership of Government: Media Role

By holding to the mindset of a right to access and a right to register opinion, one turns the policy-making process into a dynamic participatory sport, rather than a spectator sport. News and information coverage of this sport can range from challenging to dangerous and has every reason to draw audiences because the events converge with audience self-interest. Unless the coverage is handled poorly, there's no reason for it to be boring.

The best coverage is done by those who abandon the gentle swing of the trapeze of reactive reporting that follows practices established by habit. A leap to the trapeze of proactive thinking is both critical for success and invigorating for the journalists and the industry involved. Proactive thinking means that the management and staff of a newspaper or station must develop models for their own coverage of policy-making. This may involve

- establishing criteria for coverage of topics that meet today's needs
- covering the story behind the headline (Who paid what? Who decides? When? What evidence supports each position? How can one register a position?)
- programming-in feedback mechanisms into the system
- determining criteria for assessing bias that excludes differing views
- finding mechanisms that separate commentary from reporting on events
- reallocating space and time in ways that foster inclusiveness

In order for news and information to evoke an interest in participation, rather than a spectator response, that news and information must do three things:

- speak to the self-interest of the person who hears, sees, or reads them
- provide adequate information for an informed decision
- identify what people can do to register their views and, if they wish, to become participants in the ongoing debate

It's easy not to think about democratized news coverage. However, gravitation away from covering news through and for the eyes and ears of the majority of the population is contrary to the self-interest of either the media or the government because it does not expand markets or constituencies. The media know that expanded markets increase their profits and their ability to negotiate favorably with would-be funders. Government leaders know that a broad base of support better enables them to deal with conflict and to resolve dissension.

Viewer Self-interest

There are several ways to link a story with that which is a priority for the viewer. First, people like news about themselves. Giving people a chance to hear their own voices—as partners, not spectators—is sound practice for a number of reasons. It reaches to the essence of democratization by bringing to the table a full range of voices. It is sound marketing for the media interested in larger audiences. It enables political leadership to take the pulse of their constituents, to prevent problems, and to respond to constituent interests. In fact, in some U.S. government programs, officials have found citizen participation so useful to preventing project delays and reducing dissension that they have mandated public involvement. Media coverage both provides good news and expands the viewers' sense that the news is theirs.

Second, take a tip from the ancient Greeks. They learned centuries ago to use comedy and tragedy to get the attention—and the involvement—of their audiences. What people heard or saw mattered. Comedy and tragedy evoke caring responses. The audience moves from spectatorship to the brink of participation, that is, doing something about it. Comedy has been used to make people think about topics they may not previously have given any thought. Tragedy has been used to evoke an emotion of empathy and concern. Handled carefully, simultaneous entertaining, informing, and educating can be effective. Yes, this is a vote for infotainment—if one can do it right.

Getting people to care and then not providing ways to solve the problems is risky. Such incomplete communication leads to frustration levels that often result in either anger or bitterness, which is not beneficial for anyone involved. This happens inadvertently when the news programs report (to the spectator) "just the facts." People need to know when, where, and how to make a point, if not a difference. That's not biasing the news; it's simply reporting the full story.

Accurate Information

An increasing problem is ensuring the accuracy of news and information, exacerbated by the speed required for "live news" and a base of knowledge so vast that no reporter can master all facets of a topic. The Annenberg Washington Program commissioned a study on this topic. Fred Cate, its author, noted that ending incomplete and inaccurate reporting is a two-part process. Specific journalists should be identified to specialize in news covering specific areas of communities. They should be provided extra training and access to local leaders. Concurrently, people must be trained to communicate with the media, to understand the importance of deadlines, concrete stories, and quality information. Cate notes that it is helpful when local spokespersons write editorials and letters to correct misleading stories and to compliment appropriate ones. People speaking to the press need to understand that concise phrases, if not "sound bites," will be selected from what they say. Otherwise, the story they tell risks being reported inaccurately because it was edited arbitrarily. This awareness could even the playing field somewhat for those who do not have the benefit of media consultants. Those not heard in the dominant media often don't understand these tricks of the trade.

Does journalism's watchdog role conflict with democratization? Not at all! Done right, it can strengthen the climate of democratization. However, U.S. journalists have had some problems with this in recent years. People across the globe have watched the trends in U.S. journalism in recent years and seen a diminished involvement in the democratic process. Steve Berg of the Minneapolis *Star Tribune* has an explanation. "One of the reasons that people are cynical about the process" and widely believe that government doesn't work is that "we tell them that every day."[13] We rarely tell them what works right, the positive new initiatives, nor do we show them the proper channels for correcting a problem.

There's a fine line between advocacy and disseminating information. In a free press, it's a line that only public opinion and the media can self-regulate. For government or industry to impose standards is to flirt with censorship. Advocacy means more than promoting one candidate or party as opposed to another. It also means promoting either complacency or cynicism, neither of which is healthy for the marketplace. The only advocacy appropriate for news and information journalists is advocacy for democratization, which makes possible media access and free speech. As American news commentator David Broder once said, "It's time for those of us in the world's freest press to become activists, not on behalf of a particular party or politician, but on behalf of the process of self-government."

Aside from its role as disseminator of information, the press in a democratic society has the task of keeping things honest—the role of watching what's happening and making certain that it is legal, professional-quality work that is fair to the overall electorate. It is not the role of the media to examine the personal lives of officials unless their behavior jeopardizes their ability to serve the public effectively. Tangential distractions are a disservice to the public, which is entitled to expect that both officials and their watchdogs focus on the policy-making work to be done.

Most journalists have not had the opportunity to evaluate how to effectively monitor performance without drawing conclusions that should be left for the public to determine or expanding their focus beyond the state of the nation. There are three areas for journalists to consider in dealing with their watchdog role while simultaneously encouraging a healthy democracy: value judgments, cheerleading, and prosecuting.

Value judgments are implicit in every decision about what is to be included in or excluded from the news, how it is to be presented, and what is to be emphasized. While this is inevitable, newsmakers can set forth criteria against which to measure their own or their station's/paper's level of fairness.

For example, take any story or situation. Substitute someone of a different background for the person about whom it is written. Then decide whether the story is presented without stereotypes, without labels, and without biases. In other words, can you take the facts of the story at face value if you substitute someone of another religion, another race, or another gender? After you apply this criterion, keep the substance of the story. Discard the biases and judgments.

Similarly, an item may be news because it is considered interesting. That works in general news and information coverage. But when there are public policy overtones, the inclusion of one news story and the implicit or explicit omission of another shortchanges democratization and can eclipse the concerns of a major population bloc.

Cheerleading is not watchdogging, it is advocacy. A press that is blindly supportive of the status quo is serving neither the status quo nor the process of democratization. Societies without democratization often have advocacy media whose function is to explain the wisdom of the establishment. Another variation is "protocol news": The leader got in the car. The leader waved to the people, and so on.

A cheerleading press does not really serve the incumbent political leadership or the process of democratization because it quickly loses credibility. The public is smart enough to know there's more to the story—the purpose of events. Consequently, they ignore protocol news as a waste of time. If synthetic praise is constant, how will the public know when real praise is deserved, and how will it be possible to rally an apathetic public for matters important to the common well-being?

In the same manner, prosecutors are not watchdogs. Journalists shift from watchdogging to prosecuting when they believe that their professional careers require discrediting almost everything. Prosecuting creates scandal. Scandal sells. Whether or not a story is true can be irrelevant to journalistic self-interest, although it may be enormously relevant to disrupting the viability of governmental decision-making.

Opposing authority is seen as an easy route to popularity. Attitudes take on their own irrational momentum, and thinking is abandoned. Incumbent political leaders, whatever their party or persuasion, become targets of attack for its own sake, but blind destruction is no more responsible or honest than is blind support.

How Do I Know How to Be Heard?

Covering public policy decisions requires widening the angle on the transmission of information. The audience needs to be informed about how to make a democracy work. How is a decision reached on a certain issue? Which elected body or official or which appointed official is in charge? Must this person act concurrently with some other entity? When will a decision be reached? Is it decided within a prescribed calendar for the budget deliberations? What are the milestones in that sequence of decisions? Is this matter decided annually or at some other interval at specific meetings, or is it decided in an election? Does it depend on the inclination and timetable of a particular funding grant?

When news and information coverage does not foster democratization, things happen as they did in Bolivia in the 1997 national elections. Over the early 1990s the economy in Bolivia had begun to stabilize. Living standards began to increase a bit. The rich-poor gap was still enormous. Multinationals began to move into the country to engage in a range of industries, from oil to mining. Then, the campaign of Banzar, campaigning against Duren and others, painted the walls of every building in every neighborhood pink, with enormous signs suggesting that the public should elect Banzar. They did. In doing so they elected as president a man who had ruled as dictator for many years, a man whose administration was responsible for "disappearances" of his opponents, a man who promises a heavy hand with everything—global business included. Since life expectancy is not long in Bolivia and the birth rate is high, many young voters went to the polls without any memory for what had happened in earlier years. Any debate on the issues or expectations for reputable democratic government were, at best, a thin veneer. One newspaper, reporting the election, stated that the new president was "a former dictator" who now believes in democracy!

Trickle-down news can't help either the public or its institutions in such a situation because the public has never had occasion to learn how to build the foundation for democratization. Where would they learn this? How can the media industry facilitate an exchange of news and information to lead people to expect to be included? Aside from earlier examples, several program models exist, as shown in the following four discussions.

Space Bridges

The series of TV programs that linked the United States and the former Soviet Union through a "live" satellite hookup were an early model for global TV news access. They provided participants the opportunity to question each other on air, and they provided the audience an opportunity to view their "enemy," thereby discovering that people's hopes were similar. "That's a major breakthrough in Soviet TV," observed Dr. Leonid Zolotaravesky in 1991, when he was the director of the Department for International Programming, USSR National State Broadcasting System (Gosteleradio) and Sovtelexport, the self-financed distribution and coproduction arm of Soviet Television. "For the typical citizen who has felt disconnected from the policy decisions that affect his or her life, this 'Space Bridge' means that the views of all sides are debated on TV by those who actually make national policy. One can see them. Television is the most efficient medium for establishing direct contacts between people of different countries. It's not purely business; it's something more. It's not purely political; it's of a humanitarian nature. A devotion to humanitarian aids and ideals is the most important thing to begin with."[14]

Talk Television

CNN's "Larry King Show" is a successful model for allowing anyone, anywhere, to call in to a news show and speak with policymakers or candidates. Some media industry professionals are reluctant to endorse such programs because they say that leaders have a limited amount of time for doing things other than their jobs. What they fail to grasp is that all public leaders in democratic societies thrive on the opportunity to solidify and strengthen their constituencies. They make time for such appearances.

The print media version of this is the opportunity to have a letter to the editor or "op-ed" article published on the editorial pages. Other variations include "off-air" audience opinion solicited by both radio and television newsmagazine programs. The producers then select viewpoints representing different positions on an issue and either tape the voice of the letter writer or just read the response on the air. Similarly, journalists sometimes stop people on the street to tape-record or videotape their answers to a common question.

Gavel-to-Gavel Coverage

This is another news format designed to bring the consumer to the policy table. For example, in the United States, the cable TV industry established C-Span, a network devoted to covering the transactions of government bodies making and carrying out policy—without editing and without commentary. To provide this service, its programming includes gavel-to-gavel coverage of the U.S. House of Representatives and the U.S. Senate proceedings, aired without commentary, analysis, or interruption; coverage of candidate speeches, appearances, and events leading to the next presidential election; interviews focused on the issues currently being debated by the U.S. Supreme Court; live viewer call-ins; deliberations of legislative bodies in other countries, like the British House of Commons and the Canadian House of Commons; and news from other places, like the evening news from Russia. C-Span transmits to some ninety countries via Worldnet. It offers a television service; a radio service; opportunities for direct audience contact via its school bus, which tours the country; and incentives for educators to teach democratization policy-making techniques using their materials.

Videoconferences

Technological advances now make possible other opportunities for audience involvement and response. For example, a White House Conference on Aging was televised to auditoriums across the country, where senior citizens could join in the discussion via closed-circuit television. The media sometimes offer audience response polls, admittedly unscientific, whereby a person can telephone a certain number and register a viewpoint by pushing a button.

Let the Sun Shine In: Sunshine Laws and Transparent Government

Sunshine laws across the United States protect the dynamic exchange that invigorates our democratic process. They contribute to fostering honest government, an educated, involved citizenry, and an informed policy debate in the media.

Whether sunshine laws work to accomplish these ends depends in large part on the media and how the media use these news and information sources. How fertile the fields are for the media to provide quality news and information programming depends on the extent to which these laws exist and are used.

Four types of sunshine laws operative in the United States are (1) open records laws, (2) laws on campaign finance reporting, (3) open meeting laws, (4) open planning and policy development laws—public participation mandates.

While these laws are especially important to media, they also impact government officials, industry and business, non-governmental organizations (NGOs), and the civic community. They provide the media with access to government operations. In the United States, fortunately, the debate is about how to strengthen sunshine laws, not whether to have them. They have made a difference in a number of situations over the years.

Many of the sunshine laws that exist in the United States came into being in the 1960s and 1970s. They are a product of an era when substantial controversy existed about the integrity of government at the level of elected legislators and reinforced by enormous popular support. This was a volatile time. In the early 1960s there were massive civil rights protests, new laws, and a commitment at the federal level to undo the racially discriminatory laws and practices operating at state and local levels. By the mid-1960s, as more and more young Americans came home in body bags from Viet Nam, the public increasingly raised questions about government foreign policy. The "Pentagon Papers" reached the press, describing how government had lied about the extent of U.S. involvement in Viet Nam. In 1968, the incumbent president, Lyndon Johnson, declined to run for a second term because of the overwhelming opposition to U.S. involvement in Viet Nam. A few years later, in 1973, another president, Richard Nixon, was forced to resign from office over lies about the administration's role in the Watergate scandal. Without this climate of concern, which led to forging a consensus among those who often were political rivals, sunshine legislation might never have gotten the needed votes from Congress and from state legislatures and city councils.

While such laws might hamper business as usual, incumbents believed that voting for them was essential. It would have been hard to do otherwise and face an aroused public in upcoming elections. Opponents would be out of office, and indeed, in 1972 many were. In addition, many political careers were built on championing such laws as ways to prevent or root out waste and corruption in government.

Let's look at the four types of sunshine laws:

Open Record Laws

There are a series of laws in this category that allow anyone access to a wide range of information.

The U.S. Freedom of Information Act

Act 5 U.S.C. Section 552, FOIA, is one of the best known of the U.S. sunshine laws. It was first passed in 1966 and later strengthened in 1974.

The law created a specific procedure for requesting the records of a particular federal government agency. FOIA defines "agency" to include agencies, offices, and departments of the executive branch of government and those agencies called independent agencies. FOIA does not apply to Congress, the federal courts, or those units within the executive office whose sole function is to advise and assist the president (like the White House chief of staff). It gives access to materials created or obtained by an agency and, at the time of the request, in the possession and control of the agency.

One can obtain material on a wide range of topics—public health, consumer safety, government spending, civil rights, business, taxes, history, foreign policy, national defense, and the economy.

The request can come from "any person"—including noncitizens, corporations, associations, universities, other levels of government, and members of Congress. The agency can charge direct costs but not time costs, but the fee can be waived if the request is deemed "in the public interest." The agency has ten days in which to provide an initial response, twenty days for an administrative response, and an added ten days for unusual circumstances. After that, the request can be taken to court.

There are nine statutory exemptions under which the agency can refuse to release material:

- classified in the interest of national defense or foreign policy pursuant to an Executive Order. Courts have upheld the right of the CIA to neither confirm nor deny the existence of material.
- agency internal personnel rules—example, certain law enforcement manuals
- specifically exempt from disclosure by statute
- commercial "trade secrets" or critical financial information
- "interagency" or "intraagency" material not available by law other than when in litigation
- personnel and medical files that constitute an invasion of personal privacy
- law enforcement investigatory records that might impede a fair trial
- records prepared by an agency for use in supervision of financial institutions
- geological and geophysical information concerning oil wells.

These exemptions are discretionary, not mandatory. The person who could be damaged decides.

In addition, organizational practice within the United States is that anyone requesting FOIA material can solicit a member of Congress and/or an NGO advocacy organization for assistance in making the claim.

A wide range of examples illustrate how FOIA has been used: (1) Small Business Administration documents obtained through FOIA proved that $60 million in government-insured surety bonds had been granted to a Chicago organized-crime figure. The result was a grand jury investigation. (2) Food and Drug Administration documents obtained through FOIA proved that over 600 licensed prescription drugs were proven ineffectual. Congress then refused to allow Medicaid or Medicare payment for them. (3) The Governor of Utah used FOIA to request Nuclear Regulatory Commission documents proving that in 1950 government officials knew the health hazards of atomic testing in Nevada, but lied to the public. Congress and the president have now approved a special fund to compensate victims.

A list of over 500 FOIA successes for the public interest can be found in materials gathered by the American Civil Liberties Union. Requests for information are submitted daily. Pressure on Congress and the president is also constant from special interests seeking to exempt their areas of specialty from compliance with the FOIA law.

State Information Access Laws in the United States

Most states have their own versions of FOIA. In Massachusetts, for example, the Massachusetts General Laws Chapter 4, Section 7 defines public records as all books, papers, maps, photographs, recorded tapes, financial statements, statistical tabulations, or other documentary materials or data, regardless of physical form or characteristics, made or received by any officer or employee of any agency, executive office, department, board, commission, bureau, division, or authority of the commonwealth, or of any political subdivision thereof, or of any authority established by the general court to serve a public purpose, unless such materials fall within certain exemptions—similar to FOIA exemptions.

It should be noted that municipalities and counties are generally considered subdivisions of the state and that they operate in accord with state law, by and large.

Community Right-to-Know Laws

MGL Chapter 111f is a law that permits a Massachusetts citizen to find out what toxic or hazardous substances (which might be a public health or safety problem) are being stored by companies in a given community. Companies are required to file "Material Safety Data Sheets" with the state Department of Environmental Programs in the Executive Office of Environmental Affairs. The public can inspect these at will. A similar right-to-know law requires employers to inform employees if they are working with hazardous substances.

Required Notice for Government Meetings

Laws requiring notice seem insignificant, but they are crucial to access to information about policy-making. Look at a Massachusetts state law, MGL Chapter 30, Section 11. Such events as meetings of legislative bodies, government boards and commissions, and public hearings require a stated public notice a given number of days prior to the event. This notice is usually published in papers and posted in government building lobbies. The meetings could concern pending legislation, all matter of permits for building, or rate increases, for example.

The disadvantage of such a law is that it may cause delay in holding a meeting. The advantages exist for those on the industry side, the nongovernmental organization side, and the government side of an issue. If it's someone else's meeting and it affects you, you want notice to attend and perhaps to prepare to speak or to contact the principals. If it's your meeting and people complain about the decisions after the fact, there is a certain satisfaction in saying that there was a public meeting with a legal opportunity for them to make their case.

What's the verdict on the FOIA and similar access to records and laws? Legislators have no problem, by and large, unless they are trying to do favors for particular business or industrial entities. Legislators are exempt, and their careers are embellished by holding the executive branch accountable. Executive branch officials have mixed feelings. If they are populists and don't like being pressured by legislators or by special interests, then the sunshine law provides them a useful shield. It provides a way to avoid doing something one would rather not do. On the other hand, it's a pain to find, make available, and defend one's own past—depending, of course, on what that past involves.

Industry and business use the law to obtain information about others that helps their endeavors, but they dislike it when others try to hold a magnifying glass to them. Making proprietary product information exempt has provided some assurance that one's competition can't steal the product. Of course, the debate will be eternal regarding what is proprietary and what is not.

Interested citizens, nongovernment organizations, and the media are generally supportive of open record laws. Openness guarantees that they can obtain information needed to make their case about a product or action that they believe is wasteful or corrupt. Their dissatisfaction is generally that there are too many exemptions to the law. Of course, that complaint will vary depending on who is making the claim.

The bottom line is that access to information means that it is very difficult for history to be changed or misconstrued from either inside or outside government.

Campaign Finance Reporting Laws

Public reports of campaign finances are another form of open records law. Candidates for all federal offices must file reports at prescribed intervals before and after elections as required by the Federal Election Commission (FEC). Anyone has the right to call the free telephone at the FEC and request printouts showing who has contributed to a given candidate's campaign or to a political action committee (PAC). Anyone can also request copies of reports on the allocation of campaign expenditures.

State and local laws requiring access to campaign finance records generally parallel the federal law. In Massachusetts, for example, all candidates for state or local offices are required to file their financial income and expenditure reports at regular intervals before and after the elections.

What's the verdict on laws requiring access to campaign finance records? As with all the sunshine laws, they can be perceived as a double-edged sword. A campaign may find it a bother to file the reports and to verify data to be sure it is in compliance with the law. It requires careful record keeping not only on amounts but on the employer information for major donors, and it requires detailed expenditure records. But, on the other hand, it is always useful to see who is contributing to one's opponent, to identify future contributors for one's next campaign, and to evaluate where a candidate is spending funds and whether that might lead one to alter one's own strategy.

Business and industry are generally neutral on campaign record laws. After all, the candidates want the money, and how they record it is their business.

Interested citizens and nongovernmental organizations are usually positive about such laws. If they want an official's support and can find a friendly contributor, it's a route of access. If they want to prove that an official is biased toward a special interest, they can look for contributors from that special interest. One good example is the public interest group listings of those members of congress receiving support from the gun lobby, the National Rifle Association. On the other hand, this access to information can be used as a shield for a politician wanting to refuse a special interest contribution.

For the media, a smart journalist knows that the money trail tells a great deal about who a candidate is and to whom he or she is beholden. Campaign finance reporting laws make it possible for journalists to do their job.

How campaigns are financed and laws circumvented remain matters of urgent discussion in the United States. While there is some evasion of the law, much must be recorded for the public. Without the sunshine laws, violation of public trust could more easily occur. The checks and balances of the democratic system of one candidate on another would function less rigorously. Public scrutiny of the entire process would reach new lows as ignorance and rumor replaced information and records. The principal problem regarding campaign expense in the United States is not primarily about open record requirements, but about the high cost of campaigns, wherein two-thirds of expenditures go to media advertising on public airwaves that should provide free air time before elections as a service to preserving democracy.

Open Meeting Laws

This third category of sunshine laws takes access to government one step further by allowing anyone to observe the deliberations of government bodies as they wrestle with various ways to solve problems.

U.S. Sunshine Act of 1976

This law provides for open governmental operations at the federal level of government. It applies to the full range of government agencies and boards.

State and Local Open Meeting Laws

The laws at lower levels of government tend to follow the federal lead. For example, in Massachusetts, MGL Chapter 30A, Section 11A, covers state administrative procedure for open meetings and MGL Chapter 39, Section 23A, addresses open meetings at the level of municipal government. In both cases, all meetings are open to the public, and governmental bodies with a quorum present are prohibited from meeting in private for deliberation of any except a few stipulated reasons. However, a person is permitted to speak only at designated points of a meeting and only with the permission of the presiding officer.

Any gathering that wishes to retire into executive session (closed session) must first convene in open session. There are basically seven areas where closed sessions are permitted:

- to discuss the character or health of an individual, unless the individual requests an open meeting
- to consider dismissal of an individual, unless the individual requests an open meeting
- to discuss a collective bargaining or litigation strategy
- to investigate criminal misconduct or discuss filing of complaints
- to discuss deployment of security personnel or devices
- to discuss purchase, exchange, or lease of real property if discussions could be detrimental to negotiating
- to comply with provisions of any law or grant

Executive sessions must have written records, and votes must be roll-call votes made part of the record. No open meeting votes may be secret. The court can require that these records be made public.

What's the verdict on open meeting laws? This type of law can also be a double-edged sword. The disadvantage for a public official is that items one would rather not have aired in public are sometimes aired in public and sometimes not dealt with at all. The fact that the law requires a majority of the members of a board to go on record requesting an executive session means that such decisions are not made lightly. Rounding up sufficient votes may be a problem for an official or may protect the integrity of the open democratic process.

On the other hand, if an official is to be the topic of a board's executive session and politics has replaced reason, the official can use the open meeting law to mandate the group to meet in public, in front of the press— thereby depoliticizing the discussion somewhat. If one is in an executive capacity and is having difficulty implementing a program that requires board approval, one's constituents can, by attending an open meeting, see clearly where the problems lie.

Business and industry, interested citizens, and nongovernmental organizations generally favor open meeting laws because, to influence someone, there's nothing like looking her or him in the eye while he or she is forced to cast an open vote on a policy decision. It is also an opportunity to better comprehend the extent to which officials understand a matter one thinks important and to examine the arguments and the positions taken by various camps. One should note that public officials at one level of government often like an open meeting laws, because it provides them an opportunity to send someone to report on the state of affairs at another level of government with which they might need to engage in a business arrangement. For the media, these events are the actual news. It's been somewhat more difficult with TV than with radio and print. For the latter genres, words mattered. For TV, the news needs exciting pictures, and unless a meeting results in a major altercation, there aren't many exciting pictures. Nonetheless, the thorough journalist will use the actual decision-making event as the base for the story and edit in pictures that describe the topic at hand.

Media and Public Access to Decision Making

This last category of sunshine laws brings the public into the process of policy development and execution.

Transportation Planning Model

The Federal Highway Act of 1962 requires a "continuous, comprehensive, and cooperative" planning process. This is a good example of statutes mandating public participation.

Over the years, the participatory requirements in this law have been strengthened. The present legislation is titled the Intermodal Surface Transportation Efficiency Act of 1991 (ISTEA). It requires public involvement in decision-making from the beginning of long-range planning. The emphasis is on process, not projects. Regional and state transportation agencies must establish this process and operate it, and use public dollars to pay for the work elements that support it.

In addition to examining alternative transportation options, the process requires examination of the social, environmental, air quality, and energy impacts of transportation decisions. It is required that funding sources for proposed projects and activities be identified during the process, at both metropolitan and state levels. Project selection is the outgrowth of the planning process.

One method for conducting this process is to establish Citizen Advisory Committees or Technical Advisory Committees. However, these tend to be less functional and more problematic in the long run than do established task forces. They tend to have too few members to represent a full cross-section of interests and constituencies. In addition, their small size or appointed structure allows them to become elitist. The result may be confrontation—not over issues, but over who's in charge. They tend to forget that those officially elected have a legal mandate that carries more weight than does their committee.

A viable alternative is the task force approach. While everyone will admit that task forces are cumbersome, everyone can conclude that they are fair and a collegial way to tackle some very complex problems of allocating resources. A task force can include a fixed representation from every sector of the interested or impacted community. The membership can be elected annually by those who want to attend the election of their constituency. Sectors might include state and municipal government agencies (usually all with a mandate are automatically included), business and industry, environmental groups, unions and labor, citizens, or NGO groups.

For example, a task force established in metropolitan Boston was called the Joint Regional Transportation Committee. It coalesced diverse groups, enabling the mayors and the governor to approach the federal government to successfully change federal law on allocating federal transportation tax dollars. The force of this lobby not only convinced those in federal government to approve something unconventional—allowing highway money to be reallocated for public transportation—but it provided those same federal officials with a shield and a base of political support when the critics of their decision emerged.

The National Environmental Model

In the environment area, also, public participation is mandated. It generally takes the form of preparing a lengthy report on all conceivable impacts any new construction project might have on the community. In concert with this report, the National Environmental Policy Act (NEPA) requires public hearings that take recorded testimony from anyone who wishes to speak. This material is tallied for use by the decision makers.

Facility Siting Laws

At the national level, regulations govern the siting of facilities such as nuclear energy plants. At the state level, in Massachusetts, for example, regulations require that the government involve the public in determining the location of major public facilities such as power plants or waste disposal sites. A written record of such involvement is required.

What's the verdict on open planning and policy development laws? The major benefit is that this type of decision-making minimizes complaints or opposition. The premise governing successful citizen participation is inclusiveness. While the process can be time-consuming and irritating, the rewards are significant. Officials frequently find that part of the battle was won just by getting people into a room with each other. Many had vehemently disliked others because they felt that their own viewpoints weren't heard. To get them to listen to each other, then to address collaboratively the same issue, was a major step toward resolving major irritants to public officials and citizens alike. For the media, this process made government transparent, providing better materials for more, and more interesting, news stories.

Broad participation in a controversial decision helps to prevent public dissatisfaction, legal challenge, and stalemates. Occasionally, the best ideas emerge from such a process. For example, after months of internal government debate about where to locate a subway station, someone at a task force meeting made a helpful new suggestion to transportation planners that seemed an obvious solution. Everyone wondered why no one else had thought of it.

Similarly, concerned citizens and public officials often find that this open planning and policy development process becomes a forum for constituency development. When a consensus emerges within a task force, that view is carried back to membership constituencies, and the political leadership charged with executing a plan has the mechanism for strengthening constituent support. The open planning process also makes accepting decisions one doesn't like easier—for example, a sequence for construction that postpones one's project for five years is harder to fight when one is part of the decision. As a task force in Pennsylvania put it, "Tell me, I forget. Show me, I remember. Involve me, I understand."

Task force members were generally pleased to be considered colleagues in the process, and everyone treated everyone else as important to the decision-making. However, the staff hired to coordinate a citizen participation task force must work effectively with task force members, with the media, and with government officials to make sure the process is "continuous, comprehensive, and cooperative" and that decisions are in fact made in a timely manner. That staff must provide everyone with needed information, to insure that all parties are talking together, to catch conflict and bring it to the table before it becomes hardened into "political camps" and before it goes underground and sabotages the process. The staff's job is to make sure the hard issues are debated fairly and to make sure consensus is reached. It's job is also to make sure those from other sectors of society understand the reasoning and the pressures on the elected policymakers when certain suggestions are made. Dissension must not become so adversarial that it becomes impossible to make constructive policy decisions that carry public support. The media must be provided ample access to report on the actions debated, the impact decisions will have, and the deadlines for input. Believe it or not, with careful staff selection, it works—for everyone.

The Verdict on Sunshine Laws

Sunshine laws don't turn the political process into a "love-in." The stakes for winning in decisions involving power, money, and prestige will never disappear. What sunshine laws do is to protect the dynamic exchange that invigorates democracy by enabling journalists to provide essential news and information to the public. They set a benchmark for honest government, an educated and involved citizenry, and an informed debate, facilitating the best possible decisions for difficult issues. Sunshine laws are voted in and supported by the very officials who are inclined to find them irritating because, at the end of the day, these officials too have benefited from the existence of such an insurance policy for democracy.

Do the Media Control Elections?

At election time, providing adequate information takes on particular importance, because covering elections can easily degenerate into covering a horse race. Unfortunately, election coverage isn't usually as thorough as the coverage of a horse race, in part because journalists haven't had the opportunity to examine what fosters democratization in election coverage. Consequently, the coverage is often reduced to announcements of someone's view of who is ahead. In sports coverage, great care is taken in reporting the capabilities of the horses, enumerating their past performance and analyzing the competition. The coverage is both exciting and substantive to those who follow sports news. In election coverage, it would be helpful to the selection of able leaders for the media to provide news and information about what's required to do the job effectively, what are the candidate's past experiences are, and for what attributes or skills each candidate is known (for example, executive skills in delegating and decision-making or legislative skills in organizing support and negotiating).

Reducing election coverage to reporting poll results usurps the democratic process, in which the only poll that is valid is the one cast by all voters on Election Day. As Margaret Douglas, chief political advisor to the

BBC, says, "When you report on the polls you must bear in mind that all they tell you is what someone said they might do yesterday. They never tell you what they will do tomorrow."[15]

Participants in a democratic society need to evaluate the candidates' capabilities. For example, if they are electing someone for an executive job, they should know how well the candidates can administer and delegate. If they are electing someone to a legislature, they should assess which candidate can best build a consensus and work as a team player. Past performance matters. For example, which candidate has demonstrated an ability to accomplish the kinds of tasks that will confront him or her in this particular government job? What are each candidate's philosophical viewpoints, and how might they affect his or her policy decisions?

Election results determine how we live our lives, and the media determine the results of a great many elections. Look at the different aspects of electioneering used in the United States. Their effectiveness is a topic of frequent debate in other countries across the globe. Three topics warrant discussion: (1) the dynamic, among candidates, the media, and the voters, (2) how technology is changing coverage of U.S. elections, and (3) the decisions facing journalists and media managers.

Candidates, the Media, and the Voters

For democracy to survive, capable leaders representing the views of the majority must be able to be elected. Turning this ideal into concrete reality isn't easy. Candidates, the media, and the voters each follow a course that serves their own self-interest.

The Candidate's Agenda

The candidate's agenda is simple: get enough votes to win. To get these votes, candidates need name recognition and a favorable image. Consequently, the candidate has little choice but to follow the customary formula: raise money to buy advertising, rely on advertising to bring name recognition, and hope that name recognition leads to decent ratings in the polls. Decent ratings in the polls often bring more free news coverage. (Although, perhaps, free coverage should be equal for all constitutionally qualified candidates, so that credentials, not money for advertising, propel name recognition.) The free news coverage brings more campaign contributions, and the cycle begins again with a broader base.

The pressures on candidates are enormous. Without amplifying their message, candidates can't get enough votes. Without free access to the media, huge sums of money are necessary to buy access. Such contributions are often available only from those who expect favors in return.

Candidates, consequently, try to manage their media coverage. In fact, today, the media is the campaign. In the United States, the "campaign trail" has been replaced by the media superhighway. To maximize their coverage, candidates do things such as:

- stage events for the press. For example, George Bush held a press conference in a flag factory to suggest that he was the patriotic candidate.
- use "sound bites" to get headlines. For example, Ronald Reagan in Berlin shouted, "Take down that wall."
- cultivate unforgettable images. For example, the Kennedy family's activities perpetuate an American "royal family" image.
- arrange for "spin doctors" to talk with the media. Find those who are sympathetic to offer commentary immediately after a candidate debate, telling the public how to interpret who won or lost.

The candidate's objective is to avoid events that may be uncontrollable and to complement this managed coverage with advertising, which becomes a form of political theater. For example, a powerful thirty-second revolving-door advertisement showing criminals being furloughed was used most effectively by the Bush campaign to create a negative image of opponent Michael Dukakis as soft on crime. Being effective is the object. Fairness and honesty are often left for someone else to determine.

The Journalists' Agenda

Journalists' profession places them within a different paradigm. They've learned how to make a headline—to sell papers or to capture media ratings that increase the value of the station's advertising. Nowhere in journalism school have they been taught anything special about the difference between covering an election and covering any other news story or horse race. They know about grabbing headlines. They know about assuming a watchdog role. But some journalists aren't clear about the fact that election coverage means something other than being either cheerleader or prosecutor. Many journalists have never had the opportunity to think about carrying out their responsibility as a voice enabling democracy to function. In addition, on the electronic information superhighway the journalist is sailing the same uncharted waters that the rest of us sail. The practices of democracy are changing more in the current decades than they have changed since the earliest practices in ancient Greece. We've only had nine national elections since television was first seriously used in the 1960 Kennedy-Nixon race. It was only in the 1970s that reliance on computerized polling became commonplace. We've had only one presidential election, in 1996, since the paving of the electronic superhighway. Making intelligent decisions about the impact that these addictive new technologies have on electing capable leaders is difficult. There's no precedent.

Journalists have, however, consistently followed some specific practices:

- Use "horse-race" coverage. Focus the campaign on whoever a specific poll says is ahead. All too often, media-designated "winners" win.

- Make the sound bite the headline. It saves time and conserves space, while allowing room for the journalist to editorialize.

- Take advantage of "photo-ops" staged by candidates. While journalists know these are designed to make the candidate look favorable, they use photo-ops because they define election news as "events" rather than as "ideas" or "credentials." Photo-ops save the journalists time.

- Find a catchy angle. Since the American experience with Viet Nam, press about elected leaders has seemed to require either scandal or cynicism to bring approval from peers. To be sure, this watchdog reporting keeps democracy honest and keeps a society free. But fast-paced deadlines and headline-driven reporting can result in bending the truth to satisfy media or political self-interests. That may be forgotten as reporters seek their own fame.

- Remember the audience. The audience is treated as spectator, as consumer, not as participant. Herein lies the most important difference between reporting typical news or sports and reporting the news and information necessary to a functioning democracy.

The Trapped Voter

In the dynamic between candidates and journalists, the voters, the public, are caught in the middle. It's true that who's elected affects individual lives, but the typical voter is busy with her or his own life. In addition, unless one has experienced a loss of freedoms or services, elections, like democratization in general, can be taken for granted. The barrage of advertising images hurled at the public daily can numb people to the importance of elections. The barrage of media cynicism eclipses the reality that some public officials work hard to do a decent job and that a society can't work if it can't rely on some decent public officials. Many members of the public suffer from what a computer calls "internal stack overload." The barrage of "factoids" that have little context make it easy for the busy person to ignore the political process. The media coverage frequently doesn't invite involvement. It isn't even coherent. The attempt to cover elections like horse races wouldn't be a bad idea, if the political reporters provided as much information on the offices sought and the candidates as a sports reporter provides when covering a real horse race.

One example of confusing election coverage is the U.S. 1994 midterm Congressional elections. The media resoundingly proclaimed a "mandate" claimed by the winning Republican majority. In fact, the outcome was the result of a vote of about 1/6th of the adult population going to the polls. Actually, "none of the above" won. In fact, of those who voted, only 4.5% more people voted Republican than Democrat: 51% of the votes for Congress were Republican and 46.5% were Democrat. This perception of an overwhelming "mandate" isn't quite accurate, but the Republicans certainly did a fine job of getting the spin of the media in their favor.

Another area of confusion comes with the emphasis placed on certain issues and the exclusion of other issues. While candidates seek to focus the coverage on their priorities, the journalists usually win out in choosing the topics to emphasize.

For example, crime has been a critical issue in U.S. campaigns in the 1990s. It's a fine example of the media setting the public agenda. Public officials and candidates are outdoing each other to demonstrate a commitment to curb violence in America, a fine objective. However, it is interesting to note that the Center for Media and Public Affairs issued a report in 1997 saying that between 1993 and 1996 the homicide rate dropped 20%, but the media coverage of homicide increased by 721%. In addition, they noted a 1994 *Los Angeles Times* poll indicating that 65% of the public say their feelings about crime are based on what they get from the media, while 21% base their feelings on personal experience.[16]

All sides of issues need coverage, both between elections and at election time. All legally qualified candidate views must be presented. The public needs information for democracy to work. How and where can citizens who care register their views? What's the process for selecting the candidates who will run for office? How can citizens become involved in a candidate's campaign? How can they question a candidate about a concern? Between elections, how can they lobby officials on behalf of or in opposition to issues?

Changing Coverage

Election coverage is changing in the United States mostly because of the new technologies and partly because of general media dissatisfaction with the 1988 presidential campaign coverage. Thoughtful people were offended by the finding that less than 10% of the campaign coverage in 1988 addressed key substantive issues facing the country. Most of the coverage focused on the horse race (someone's view of who's winning), subjective commentary by "analysts," and stories about the polls. In addition, "none of the above" won in 1992, with 50% of the voters voting. George Bush won with 26.95% of voters, and Michael Dukakis lost with 23.05%.

In the 1992 election, the decline in voter turnout reversed, slightly. Some 90 million people voted in 1988 and about 103 million in 1992. By 1992, leading U.S. journalists began to initiate some changes in election coverage practices:

- More network-sponsored debates occurred.
- Debate formats reduced opportunities for grandstanding by questioners or by studio audiences.

- Print journalists launched "ad-watches" to critique the content of candidate TV ads.
- Greater journalist skepticism reduced media reliance on candidate-produced releases or photo-ops.
- On some occasions, longer segments of candidate presentations replaced the sound bite—that is, 15–18 seconds rather than 9 seconds.

The candidates, too, changed their approach to campaign coverage in 1992. Basically dissatisfied with the fact that the voters heard more *about* their campaigns than *from* their campaigns, candidates set out to avoid the Washington journalists. Candidates encouraged the satellite media tours whereby local journalists would ask them questions about local concerns, unhindered by a Washington press corps. Candidates, for example Ross Perot in 1992, bought time for direct-broadcast satellite transmission to bring their campaigns into voters' homes without any journalistic filtration. Perot's campaign used print media to announce the exact satellite coordinates for receiving his programming. Campaigns duplicated candidate presentations and mailed the videotapes to thousands of voters, bypassing the media. Candidates became guests on radio and television talk shows, accepting voter calls and answering questions on-air without editing. Other imaginative high-tech techniques were used for the first time. Candidate Perot established a computer database for telephoning up to 30,000 voters at once, and voters could use their phone keypads to agree or disagree with his comments. Candidate Clinton held an online forum, answering voter questions on a computer bulletin board.

These changes, propelled in large part by the new technologies, became commonplace for the first time in the 1996 campaign. That campaign not only made use of the new technologies, it was required to operate in a new environment created by the same new technologies—the change of pace of news. For example, White House press secretary Mike McCurry observed that the impact of the speed of these technologies meant there was increasing reliance on commentary and analysis to fill the gaps while waiting for more news.[17] In journalists' jargon, the who, what, when, and where have taken a back seat to the why. He points out that this change in structural flow results in a decline of civil discourse and pushes us toward a point where there's competition for the nastiest commentary as the way to make the headlines needed for the ratings.

Against this backdrop, several interesting changes occurred in 1996:

- The public began to react negatively to the negative campaigning. Always before, nasty comments left some mud on the person toward whom they were hurled. Probably the best example was the Dole response to a question asked by an elementary school teacher about instilling idealism in the young. In a tried and true classic response, Dole "spoke through" the question to make his point about an untrustworthy Clinton. He wasn't even aware of the enormous negative reaction from the audience. The public seems to have a saturation point when it comes to hurling dirt for the sake of dirt.

- Clinton mastered what Bush had initiated—the "message of the day" approach. While any intelligent taxpayer would hope the enormous U.S. government is acting on many fronts every day, the media of TV and sound bites can't handle complexity. One theme a day—simplified—is what works. The question is whether that's an asset in that it might educate a marginally interested public, or whether it's a problem to oversimplify essential business.

- Clinton also demonstrated an understanding of the difference between the narrowcast cable TV appearances and the broadcast network appearances. For example, eighteen- to twenty-seven-year-olds voted in the highest numbers since eighteen-year-olds got the right to vote in 1966. Many think it was because Clinton spoke at length to them on MTV. Similarly, he addressed and answered questions from the African-American community on the Arsenio Hall show. Cable has air time to fill. Talk is cheap. The messages got replayed recurrently. Newt Gingrich did basically the same thing a few years earlier on C-Span. His nightly appearances making impassioned speeches to an empty chamber were dinner-table video across the country, building him a national constituency.[18]

- In the spirit of broader audience outreach, President Clinton spent a half-hour with a group of children who asked him questions on the air. Not only useful for political purposes, the program served to educate those who'll be the new voters in the next election cycle about the debate and their role in it.

- In 1996, the first experiment in the United States of free prime-time TV air time occurred. This practice has existed for many years in other countries. For example, check election laws in Australia, Denmark, Finland, France, Japan, the Netherlands, and Turkey. Rupert Murdoch initiated an offer of ten free prime-time spots in the U.S. market—one minute each and half an hour of free time on election eve. The other three American networks, PBS, and CNN joined in—not to be outdone by Rupert. The experiment did provide less negative content on a broader range of issues, but the placement of the spots and the uncertainty of what would happen if such spots were on election eve—when there was no chance to correct any errors—meant the test of free TV got off to a limping start. It's an enormous problem because the TV networks are receiving enormous amounts of money for the ads—two-thirds of it coming from the public finance matching share for presidential candidates and less than 30% from campaign contributions and PACs. They have no incentive to change the system. Congress, which makes the laws, benefits from industry campaign contributions and has no self-interest in leveling the playing field for potential opponents.

- The Internet is the newcomer in campaigns. Each candidate and the parties had web pages from which the public could get enormous amounts of information. But there is not yet the sophistication about tailoring or updating this information, nor is there a scheme for using the two-way capability to enable the average citizen to engage in a dialogue with the candidate. Clearly, this technology will increase in importance rapidly over the next decade. What isn't clear is whether this will be to the advantage of the elite, thereby widening the chasm between its members and typical citizens who will have fewer opportunities to be part of a democratic society, or whether it will expand democracy.

Decisions Facing Media Managers and Journalists

What is clear is that journalists, candidates, and voters are all embarking on an era of election communication that involves much more flexible communication than was customary just a few years ago. This will likely have the greatest impact on the journalists because both candidates and voters are working to reduce the filtering role of the middleman. The technologies are helping them succeed. In this environment, what can the journalists and media managers do to enable election coverage to strengthen democracy?

Media managers make choices that effect election coverage. They could:

Establish a Policy Framework

A media policy framework could be a guide for campaign coverage. If it is possible to cooperate with other media or to secure legislation, such a policy might establish the beginning date of a campaign. It might designate an end date, say, twenty-four hours before the voting begins. This practice is followed in a number of countries. Such policy might agree to honor the campaign laws that determine if someone is a candidate by agreeing to provide equal access to the media and equal coverage for all legally qualified registered candidates. A policy might include prohibiting the publication or announcement of poll results during the last day before the election and during the hours that the polls are open. The media and the pollsters would not preempt the voters' right to decide who is to be elected.

A policy might include a decision to regularly provide analysis of candidate advertising to document how performance compares to promises.

A policy might include a statement that all debates will occur even if one candidate makes a tactical decision not to participate. It might allocate reporter time between following the campaign trail and engaging in substantive investigative reporting on candidates' records. Allocation of time might also include choosing candidates, debates, voter questions/talk shows, candidate-initiated releases and speeches, commentary, and the present-day requirements to carry out the job a candidate will fill.

Train Journalists

It would be useful to quality reporting and to the democratization process if reporters understood the difference between news coverage and campaign coverage. It would also be useful to their coverage if they understood the difference in skills needed to fulfill different electoral positions. For example, a legislator must be able to build consensus. An executive must be able to administer. These are very different skills.

A reporter should know where to access information about a candidate's prior job performance, about campaign contributions, about the pros and cons of an issue. It's important that a reporter understand how to prepare a story for a participant in a democratic process, rather than for a spectator. That includes so many of the things discussed in this book. Finally, a reporter must be able to distinguish between personal views and fair coverage of a story.

Establish Unbiased Tone

Fair reporting requires understanding bias. Reports should not imply bias. It's best to avoid labels like "front-runner" or "unimpressive." Avoid discrimination that categorizes by ethnic or gender stereotypes. Avoid being deferential to glamor and wealth.

Provide Context

Confusion and misunderstanding arise without context. For example, George Bush promised to ban chemical weapons from the face of the earth in 1988, but in 1983 he had cast the tie-breaking vote in the Senate to renew chemical weapon production and in 1986 he did the same on a vote to allow development of the Big Eye nerve gas bomb. By 1988, he may have viewed the situation differently, but the journalist could provide the voter a context for the statement—especially now that computer banks can archive data.

Report on the Money Trail

Nothing could be more important. Candidate financial obligations frequently influence loyalty. In the United States candidates' campaign reports are public information available to anyone who calls the Federal Election Commission's free telephone number.

NOTES

1. The Future's Group, Glastonbury, CT, "Where in the World Markets Are the Emerging Markets?" Paper distributed at World Future Society Conference, Cambridge, MA, July 1994.

2. Erik Barnouw, media historian and author, "Testimony: Advocacy Video and the Documentary," presented at Advocacy Video Conference of the Benton Foundation in Washington, DC, on May 21, 1993. Interview with the author in Cambridge in Fall 1996.

3. Mordecai Kirschenboim, Director General, Israel Broadcasting Authority, Khalal Building, Jaffa Street, Jerusalem, Israel. Interview with the author in Jerusalem on January 19, 1994.

4. Barnouw, "Testimony."

5. Mary Roodkowsky, Regional Program Officer, UNICEF Regional Office for Middle East and North Africa, Comprehensive Commercial Centre, Jabal Amman, 3rd Circle, P.O. Box 811721, Amman 11181, Jordan. Interview with the author in Amman on January 10, 1994.

6. Johan Ramsland, Editor, BBC-WSTV, Television Centre, Wood Lane, Lon-

don W12 7RJ, United Kingdom. Interview with author in London, January 27, 1994.

7. Robert Feranti, Executive Producer of the morning news on National Public Radio, *Talk of the Nation*, Washington, DC, August 16, 1993.

8. Chava E. Tidhar and Dafna Lemish McCan, "Israeli Broadcasting Media Facing the SCUD Missile Attacks," in Thomas A. Styles and Leonard Styles, eds., *The 1,000 Hour War: Communication in the Gulf* (Westport, CT: Greenwood Press, 1994), pp. 117–118.

9. Margaret E. (Meg) Goettemoeller, President, World Information Corporation, New York. Interview with the author in Brooklyn on December 6, 1990.

10. Erik Kirschbaum, "Rising Costs Co-production UFA into Para/P&G Pact." *Variety*, 362, no. 13 (April 29, 1996): 42.

11. Carla B. Johnston, *International Television Co-Production* (Boston and London: Butterworth Heinemann/Focal Press, 1992).

12. Robert L. Hilliard, "Ethics, Education and the Necessity of Media Literacy," *Media Ethics*, Fall 1988, p. 7.

13. Paul Starobin, "A Generation of Vipers: Journalists and the New Cynicism." *Columbia Journalism Review* March/April 1995

14. Dr. Leonid A. Zolotaravesky, Director, Department for International Programming, U.S.S.R. National State Broadcasting Company. Interview with author in Moscow, Russia, on June 13, 1991.

15. Margaret Douglas, chief political advisor to the BBC. Presentation at election coverage workshop for East European journalists conducted by author through New Century Policies, in the Netherlands, 1991.

16. Howard Kurtz, "Murder Rates Drop, but Coverage Soars." *Boston Globe*, August 13, 1997, p. D8.

17. Mike McCurry, White House Press Secretary, Presentation at RTNDA–Poynter Institute event. C-SPAN, June 15, 1996.

18. Henry Jenkins, MIT Director of Film and Media Programs. Speech at the MIT Communications Forum on October 31, 1996.

3

Global Village Media

THE COMMUNICATIONS REVOLUTION

Today's communication technologies leave no further excuse for restricting democratization and access to partnership in the global TV news and information exchange. It has now become a self-interest priority of the companies in the high-tech communications business to expand their markets—in part by gathering news and information relevant to a whole new cross-section of clients.

Tomorrow, among other developments, Teledesic, a system of 840 satellites, will beam voice and the Internet anywhere in the world—even to places without ground lines. Leapfrogging generations of technology will be possible in developing countries. In fact, leapfrogging country borders will also possible, making laws regulating free speech even less relevant. Bill Gates, CEO of Microsoft, and Craig McCaw, founder of cellular phones, are basing their new venture in Seattle. The FCC granted them a U.S. license for it.[1]

In the nineteenth and twentieth centuries, most global news came from England and the United States. BBC World Service Radio was the premier radio service, and remains so, among the many sponsored by countries across the globe. Shortwave radio was unchallenged as a method of transmission to every corner of the globe until the 1990s. Newspapers carried detailed wire service stories across the globe, but only reached those in cities and those who can read. Until the last decade of the twentieth century, people in most parts of the earth had only one or two national television channels. Television, in many places, was three decades old at the most. Some countries didn't have any television until the 1990s.

At the end of the 1980s and the beginning of the 1990s, technological developments, combined with the vision of Ted Turner, who founded CNN using the new technologies to bring the world "live" news, changed everything. World leaders and typical TV viewers alike suddenly had global TV and were able to watch events as they happened. George Winslow wrote for *World Screen News*, "Tiananmen Square television footage, the Berlin Wall falling, and the Persian Gulf War coverage convinced broadcasters that international news could be a 'ratings bonanza.' These events and similar forced news organizations to beef up their global coverage."[2]

Global broadcasters emerged. CNN, BBC's WSTV, Reuters, and Murdoch's News Corp. were well ahead of the big three American networks and the major national and regional television stations across the world.

Within nations, things changed too. At the end of the 1980s, European countries began to expand upon their limited public broadcasting and offer commercial television stations. Public TV companies that never worked overnight or in the morning couldn't compete. Everything changed.

As Robert E. Burke, president of Worldwide Television News (WTN), put it, "There's a large part of the world just peeking out from under government regulation, a huge number of people who speak many languages. In 1989 and 1990 when eastern Europe began to open up, business for us changed overnight. It used to take six months to get a visa to do a story for a week, now, we set up permanent bureaus. That's good news for a news agency. Those people are well-served."[3]

Now, as we enter the twenty-first century, much of the world is reshaping itself into global village neighborhoods connected by the information superhighway. A small number of TV news agencies and TV broadcasters have spent a lot of money to make satellite TV distribution available to totally new areas of the globe. Entrepreneurs in local communities are producing handmade satellite receiver dishes and stringing cable around the neighborhood so programs can reach into homes that never before had TV. Television set ownership in countries across the globe is escalating at unprecedented rates. Technology continues to advance, and digital television makes possible scores of new channels—channels that need programming.

With these technological changes and the growing consumer interest comes an opportunity for more newsmakers and more programmers of all sorts. For the first time, it is becoming in the self-interest of global media owners to hear from those previously not heard. There are two reasons for this new interest: First, their investment in the hardware for global TV distribution can be successful only if it attracts the interest of new consumer markets. Second, a lot of channel space needs programming—inexpensive programming that appeals to the new markets.

The window of opportunity is open. As soon as the global video business fills the channels with programs, secures the subscribers and the advertisers, this opportunity will disappear. As soon as the Internet settles into a pattern of operation, there too the opportunity for creative planning about widespread exchange of news and information will become more limited. There is a greater possibility for the multidirectional flow of news, information, and other programming now than ever before. It's time to examine the avenues for such access.

SATELLITES, FIBER OPTICS, AND DIGITAL COMPRESSION

Satellites

When publics across the globe watched the television coverage of the Falkland Islands War in 1982 and later watched the end of the Marcos regime in the Philippines, in 1986, the world got its first glimpse of how direct broadcast satellite (DBS) technologies would revolutionize the news-gathering business. Satellite pictures could be transmitted "live," and they were universal. That is, they could be sold anywhere, and local broadcasters could put on a soundtrack giving the news item the locally acceptable spin. Or, global broadcasters could transmit the pictures directly to people's homes, putting a global spin on the stories (see Table 3.1).

Initially international TV and data communication was carried on IN-TELSAT satellites and relied on COMSAT earth stations in the United States and on government-owned earth stations in other countries. INTEL-SAT is a system of satellites owned by a consortium of 119 countries.[4] President John F. Kennedy created the Communications Satellite Act passed in 1962. The alternative satellite network was the INTERSPUTNIK, created by the Soviet Union and used to reach Soviet allies. It began service in 1974.[5] In recent years, many countries and corporations have launched their own satellites. It's estimated that by the year 2000, the Asia/Pacific basin alone will be served by 790 commercial satellites with over 500 transponders, making possible some 2,000–3,000 television stations offering programs. How common news—the news we all should hear—will reach the majority of the globe's population remains a challenge. When do many become no one? One hopes these questions are also in the minds of those proliferating channels. Could racing for technological progress become racing like lemmings toward oblivion?

While the initial satellite use was primarily for military purposes, scientific exploration, and meteorological use, the civilian communications industry soon began growing at a previously unimaginable pace. As computer and video technologies begin to merge and as cellular phone use expands, it will be increasingly difficult to segregate visual transmission from voice and data transmission.

Robert Lovell, visiting professor in the Department of Aeronautics and

Table 3.1
Turner International Worldwide Distribution

Geography	Satellite
North America except north of Hudson Bay and Greenland, Central America to Nicaragua, the Caribbean	Galaxy 5, 125'W Spacenet III, 87.5'W
Mexico and Central America to Colombia	Solidaridad 1, 109.2'W
South America, the Caribbean, Mexico and eastern USA, eastern Canada except northern Quebec	Intelsat VI F1, 27.5'W
Brazil	Brazilsat, 70'W
Central America, the Caribbean, South America except southern Argentina and southern Chile	Panamsat 1, 45'W
England, Ireland, western Europe except northern Sweden and northern Norway, not Finland, part of western Germany, northern Italy, Spain, south to the Canary Islands, none of Africa	Astra 1B, 19'E Astra 1C, 19'E
Scandinavia, Estonia and part of the Baltics	Thor, 1'W
Central Europe, north to the Baltic Sea, west to French border, south to Cairo and Jerusalem, east to Turkey and Poland	Eutelsat IF4, 25.4'E
North Africa and the Middle East, east through Pakistan, Afghanistan, Uzbekistan, the Balkan countries and Rome	Arabsat 1C, 31'E Arabsat 1D, 20'E
All of Africa, the Middle East through western Saudi Arabia, western Russia, all of Scandinavia and western Europe	Intelsat VI,
Turkey, north into Russia, the Central Asian Republics, south to Saudi Arabia and Somalia, Australia, North Island in New Zealand, Japan, Korea, Mongolia	Apstar-2
Eastern India north into China, east through Japan, south through Indonesia	Apstar 1, 138'E
Bangladesh, north into southern China, east through New Guinea, west of Sumatra, Thailand and Burma	Palapa B2P, 113'E
Southeastern Russia in Siberia, Japan, North Island of New Zealand, Australia, through Bangkok, into China	Intelsat V F8, 180'E
Japan	Superbird B, 158'E
North into Southeastern Russia through parts of Siberia, Mongolia, east through Japan, south through all of New Zealand and Australia, west to Burma, Bangladesh, Tibet and China	Panamsat 2, 169'E

Source: CNN.

Astronautics at the Massachusetts Institute of Technology, gave the following background on the communication satellite industry and some indication of its direction in the late 1990s:

In the 1970s, one to five communications satellites were launched per year. In the late 1990s, seventy to eighty will be launched in one year. By 2011, there will be about ninety-five launched that year. The industry is dominated by three main companies: Lockheed, Lorrall, and Hughes.

The newest emphasis is LEOS—satellites that operate in non-geosynchronous orbit and are used for cellular phones. They must deal with power limited down-link and a diameter limited up-link. This market was totally new in the mid-90s and has a big future. Motorola alone will have 66 mobile satellites in flight. LEOS require less power than Direct Broadcast Satellites.[6]

Those who wish to broadcast television by satellite, if they don't have their own satellite, will need to buy or lease satellite transponder space.[7] A transponder is the unit within the satellite that receives and transmits signals. Each transponder handles a single program. When purchasing satellite time, the buyer must decide on several things. Do you want protected, unprotected, or preemptable time? Protected time provides a backup satellite or transponder in case of service interruption. Unprotected time has no backup. Preemptable time allows the transponder to be taken when needed as a backup for someone else. Prices vary as expected. You also need to consider the period of service—an hour occasionally or a long-term regular period. The long-term rates are better. Or, perhaps you want to purchase the transponder or part of a transponder. Finally, you need to decide on the scope of service purchased. Does it include only the transponder, or does it also include the uplink and downlink services? One can buy time or hire someone like WTN to do it.

Fiber Optics

Fiber optic technology was first tested for video transmission in 1980. Utility companies began, by the late 1980s, to replace the traditional co-axial cable with fiber optic cables. By 1991 some 300 cities in the United States were connected by fiber optic cables, and many specific corporate, government, and communication routes throughout the world were similarly wired. The rest have followed rapidly. In developing parts of the world, technologies were completely bypassed as whole countries went from virtually no telephone system to fiber optic systems. At the end of the twentieth century, this installation is still in process, promising big changes in eastern Europe, Africa, and South America.

Fiber optic technology can transmit high-quality voice, data, image, and video in two-way communication at a cheaper rate and in a more accessible, more flexible manner than relying on satellite transmission. In addition, privacy of transmission is possible. The customer using fiber optics for video transmission won't have the mechanical worries of arranging the location, the equipment, and the satellite time; these mechanics will be built into the system.[8]

By the early 1990s, video producers were beginning the new technology transfer:

- TV studios were directly linked to satellite ground stations. No extra transport is required.

- Studios were linked with other studios in a point-to-point communication enabling a video back-and-forth that is helpful for business and helpful for the video producer collaborating with others.

- Television stations began to regionalize their program and advertising distribution to provide more flexibility for themselves and to create new revenue opportunities. This capability made it possible for producer products that have a specialized appeal to be shown to segments of the general audience, rather than being rejected.

- Full broadcasting-quality videoconferencing occurred between national or international sites via telephone company equipment, with no need for special equipment. The material was transmitted via fiber optics or, if technology required, via videocamera tape or satellite up/down link.

- Instant video was transmitted back and forth between wired locations without the need of a microwave truck. For example, TV stations can be wired directly to sports arenas, state capitols, and other locations to which they regularly send television crews.

- In some places, "video dial tone" service became a reality. One could simply go to a pay telephone, insert the payment required, and plug in one's camera to the jack provided. The picture will be transmitted to the intended party. Imagine the uses for unscheduled news events, for live entertainment interviews, for production crews, for videoconferencing and corporate training.

- Academic institutions were able to use fiber optic loops for distance learning—bringing one expert into a number of classrooms simultaneously, bringing a classroom into a museum or laboratory, or enabling several classrooms of students to participate simultaneously in a common discussion.[9]

By the early years of the new century, installing fiber optics will be history, and the techniques used by video producers in the 1990s will be quite outdated in many parts of the world. This pace of developing technology infrastructure still depends more on financial and political decisions than on technological ones. For some decades into the twenty-first century parts of the world will not be able to use the new technologies. Why? Those places have no priority either for government policymakers or for business and industry. They don't have a large enough middle class who will buy products and services. In the Central American rain forest, in Tanzania, in rural Peru, rural China, and the Central Asian republics the telephone lines don't exist. On the other hand, the new Bill Gates global phone system may hasten the process of technology access, at least for the affluent.

Digital Compression

Other technological development is contributing to the communications revolution. Digital compression tops the list. As explained by John Forrest, a British communications expert, digital electronics arrived with the home computer and CDs, in the layperson's view.[10] TV is a heavy user of the radio frequency spectrum, with each channel occupying the space of several hundred radio channels. Much of this space is wasted because the signal is highly repetitive. Digital consolidates space and makes it possible to have more channels in the same space. TV picture frames are sent each 1/25th of a second, with the space in between containing only minor movement modifications. Similarly much of the picture (sky for example) doesn't change from one frame to the next. In fact, as much as 98% of what is sent can be redundant. To sift out what's not redundant is called compression and can be done digitally with silicon chips similar to those used in a high-speed computer. To send a program by satellite is very expensive because of the cost of transponder space. If the signal is sent digitally, one can sent eight or more times the number of channels over one transponder, thereby greatly cutting the cost.

Forrest explains that digital television transmitters operate at lower power levels than the traditional sets and that therefore more integration of mobile communications with terrestrial radio or TV is possible. The present palm-top computer will evolve to the point of having telephone, fax, and data connections to cellular telecommunications networks and will also receive digital radio and television broadcasts. As the technologies merge, so will traditional industry lines. For example: (1) hardware vendors will merge electronics and computer companies; (2) distribution companies will blend telecommunications, cable, and satellite companies; (3) software companies will include broadcasters, narrowcasters, production companies, games, and software experts; and (4) transaction collectors will include subscription TV companies, payment card companies, and telecommunications and cable companies.

One view of the impact of digitalization is that there will be so many television channels that common news—information that is useful for everyone who is a citizen of a country or region—won't be possible. Another take on this is that at last there will be an opportunity for those in the "other media world"—those who have been excluded. Democratization may in fact be happening. The argument hypothesizes that the diversity of channels presents opportunity for niche programming because cable channels don't need to satisfy large audiences, creating a point of entrance for those excluded from mainstream media. However, problems remain. One is a lack of money. Another is that this outlet may further isolate mainstream audiences from the thinking of minority audiences, meaning an absence of democratization.[11]

Enrique Jara, director of Reuters Television, raises important questions about the uses of digitalized television—the ethical considerations.

> Does that picture made out of a number of frames of the moving pictures have the same value as the picture that you just get with a still camera? I think that has debatable points. People are putting on the table mathematical arguments that the still picture is only a virtual representation of reality because there are certain times where you need to get the image chemically represented. Therefore, there are many many seconds' difference between a few frames so the integrity of the content, rather than being based on a time consideration, is based on the freedom of the operator to change the reality. Anyway, it may take some time to clarify the ethical limits, the quality of the final product, and the spread of the technology worldwide.[12]

A major change in communications of news and information will come when the fiber optic telephone companies deliver customized programs. Will people find it a problem to receive selective information? How do you know that you've missed something if it's not available? Even if one has the power to do the selecting, might the information received have gaps? Add to this the integrated-services digital networks and the technological capabilities of digital television, where camera angles and images can be manipulated. Will we know what's real and what isn't? Will it matter? How?

GLOBAL TELEVISION NEWS

In less than a decade CNN, BBC's World Service TV, and Murdoch's B-Sky-B and STAR TV have reached into living rooms across the globe with "live" news. Simultaneously, the traditional wholesalers of news and information, Reuters and AP, have joined Worldwide Television News (WTN) to sell wholesale video to broadcasters.

CNN launched the global TV news era. Ted Turner had the vision to jump in in the early 1980s. Whether accidental or intentional, Turner's timing was brilliant. The BBC's World Service TV (WSTV) was launched in 1991. WSTV was propelled by the impact CNN was having as result of its unforgettable Gulf War coverage—Peter Arnett showing the world live missile attacks over Baghdad. Rupert Murdoch's B-Sky-B news coverage in Europe also began on the heels of the Persian Gulf War in 1991. In 1993, Murdoch solidified his northern hemisphere coverage with the purchase of the controlling interest in STAR TV in Asia. In less than a decade a revolution had occurred.

These newsmakers are well aware that in many parts of the world a picture is, indeed, worth a thousand words. Together, these half-dozen global media giants (and some powerful regional partners) are shaping the world's view of what is news, what is worthy of the attention of political and economic leaders.

Now, even more than in the past, how the rest of the world sees you will depend on whether the rest of the world sees you. It's important to take the initiative to become a partner newsmaker—not just a news receiver. Let's examine the companies responsible for this change.

Cable News Network (CNN)

The traditional American networks called CNN "the chicken-noodle network" when it began its 24-hour news programming in 1980. But by 1989—two years into Ted Turner's program of personally giving satellite dishes to world leaders—the Cable News Network was seen in 120 countries. By the early 1990s, during the Gulf War, at the fall of the Berlin wall, and at the Tiananmen Square prodemocracy demonstration in Beijing, CNN upstaged all its rivals. By the late 1990s, CNN was broadcasting to over 200 countries using some twelve different satellites. It is seen in 16% of the globe's 800 million television homes—that's 128 million locations. By the late 1990s they also broadcast in Spanish. They have become the place where all the world's leaders can share a common base of information. CNN claims about 67 million subscribers.

CNN's success was in large part due to its quickness to adapt to the new technologies. Satellite news gathering (SNG) technology was not new at Tiananmen, but CNN pioneered the use of "fly-away packs," portable SNG gear packed in crates and set up anywhere. CNN also pioneered the use of cellular phones. Also, CNN used "handicams"—miniature 8mm cameras that one could use while on a bicycle and not be as prominent as with big equipment.[13]

CNN's record is outstanding in attempting to provide news without a political bias—news that some say the West shouldn't broadcast—news that many say the West needs to hear. Why not? On a democratized globe, we need to expect people to make their own sound judgments. The CNN policy is articulated by Peter Vesey, former vice-president of CNNI:

We can't deal with cultural concerns in that we are probably seen in 150 to 160 countries. That represents all the world's cultures, religions, value systems and political systems. There is no convenient way to accommodate cultural, political, ethnic concerns which are mutually contradictory. I think our role is to become ever more sensitive to them and to represent all different points of view reflecting cultural and political concerns whenever possible and appropriate. I think we've made great strides. For example, during the Gulf War, I think we won points with skeptical audiences around the world by including in our comment, expert guests, interviews, and other elements of our stories covering the war—the full range of Arab opinion—not just Saddam versus U.S.A. A number of states in the region have a number of cultural and political concerns but weren't protagonists. There were about six or eight protagonists in that dispute and we went out of our way to make sure they were all represented.

We also do stories to show how the Moslem view might differ from the Western view in terms of value systems. While we can improve, and we hope to do so, I think people were impressed that our approach is correct, if not flawless. Nevertheless, our main goal is to report the news as factually and accurately as possible. We're not to advocate a point of view, a special political or economic agenda. Our standards of journalism also indicate that we're not advocates; that also helps us to overcome these cultural and political barriers.

Our kind of journalism is often not practiced elsewhere in the world, even in very sophisticated Western democracies. TV frequently is used as a social or political instrument, and, of course, our goal in the news business is to make it an instrument solely devoted to information that is accurate, timely, factual, well-balanced, absolutely up to the minute. I think that helps us overcome some of the natural barriers that exist—that we're Americans or represent Western cultures. That approach is [the] only one we can maintain. There's no way to cater to one or another group.[14]

In new markets, CNN offers free to-air service. In some places, like China, they sell their service by barter, providing news to China Central Television (CCTV) in return for access to CCTV footage and the right to sell two minutes of advertising space on CCTV. In early 1997, CNN broke through one of the last remaining global walls—the one that exists between the United States and Cuba. CNN is the first outside global broadcaster allowed to set up a bureau in Havana. Why CNN? Because Ted Turner worked to establish a good relationship with the Cuban leader Fidel Castro. CNN takes great care to broadcast all sides of issues.

Probably the best entrée to CNN for new newsmakers is through a program initiated in 1987, *World Report*. This is more than a program. It is a mechanism whereby CNN cooperates with local broadcasters who agree to contribute material to CNN and who in turn are able to broadcast CNN material. There is no need for a regular contract to purchase from CNN. The material contributed must be shipped by the donor to CNN where it can be used on any of a number of CNN programs. CNN provides periodic opportunities for its contributors from across the globe to meet to discuss issues of concern. The benefit for CNN is that it has access to a network of local newsmakers who can become partners when it's important to cover breaking news. Between 135 and 150 countries now participate in *World Report.*

The BBC's World Service TV (WSTV)

WSTV was created in 1991. It was designed to build on the BBC radio service, which had 130 million listeners in 1993. WSTV is a separate company that commissions its TV product. According to WSTV editor Johan Ramsland,

> We are a small company of 30 people commissioning from within the BBC the product and resources that we need to meet the needs of our partners. We are, therefore, responsible for delivering into the marketplace the channels that we think the market needs. In order to do that, we agree on costs with our partners whom we get to cover our costs and, then, using that money, we commission from within the BBC to specifications set down by us. We decide what the programs should be, how they should be made and how they should be scheduled. We leave the day to day editorial responsibility and management of the program groups to others. We don't concern ourselves with that. In that sense we're very like Channel 4 in this country which is also a commissioning agent rather than a direct broadcaster. WSTV is a commercially funded company that seeks to promote through television the values and principles of the BBC for which we now believe there is a worldwide audience.[15]

WSTV began with some 1.25 million viewers in Europe, but moved rapidly to expand. In October 1991 it contracted with Hong Kong-based STAR TV and expanded its audience to 38 countries with 2.7 billion people, stretching from Israel to Taiwan and from Mongolia to the Philippines. The viewership is estimated to be only about 2% of the population; but those 45 million viewers certainly influence the economic and political priorities of their regions.

Ramsland describes how global radio became global television.

> The greatest spread for WSTV with the picture gathering has been making use of Hi-8 [a broadcast format that works with small portable cameras] with the reporters and training them in the use of it. Some take to it. Some don't. Most journalists have an inquiring mind and they take to it fairly well. It's been very successful. It's convenient. It's considerably cheaper, and it gives you much easier access to places

where you want to get to. There are still quite a few places in the world that you can't get into with a full television crew. But, just a video camera, well every tourist's got one. We've done a lot in Burma with Hi-8 where we know we wouldn't have gotten in a crew. In other places, it's not a political problem to get a crew in, but the terrain and logistics make it very difficult. For example, It's been a bit rough in Kabul in Afghanistan, we'll shoot in the countryside with Hi-8 and then stick it on a plane, or good old DHL shipping, or something like that. It's core material we can use today or in a month.

WSTV continued to expand. In 1992 it entered into an agreement with South Africa's M-Net to provide satellite service throughout Africa with rebroadcast contracts signed with national terrestrial broadcast systems. Their entry into North America comes through agreements with the Canadian Broadcasting Corporation and cable service.

WSTV sees its role as quite different from that of CNN, believing it important not only to show what's happening in the world, but to tell why it is important or interesting. In October 1997, WSTV expanded its formula into a twenty-four-hour news station. In doing so, it affirms the movement to ending "news by appointment." It also affirms its view that news cannot be only instant pictures without context and analysis. The question is, when does content and analysis become commentary that spins the story with an editorial bias?

Rupert Murdoch's News Corporation

Rupert Murdoch is one of the Hannibals or Horaces—depending on your view of his style of operation—of the next decade to watch extremely closely. The reason is not so much that his communications empire has tentacles into every corner of the globe. The reason is that he's not known for respecting anyone who gets in his way—business leaders, workers, prime ministers. Early in his career in Australia, his press coverage of Australian elections destroyed the incumbent prime minister and elected one who would change the law Murdoch wanted changed. In England, his headlines shifted the blue-collar vote toward the Tories, enabling Margaret Thatcher to win the election for prime minister. In New York City, his tabloid headlines elected Koch as mayor. In 1987, he brought 6,000 new workers from places across the globe to run the London *Times* in order to evade the unions. The Congress of the United States passed a special law to allow Murdoch to become an American citizen and thereby legally own media in the United States. To win favor with the Chinese for broadcasting STAR TV over China, he dropped BBC news and made it possible for the daughter of the supreme Chinese leader to get her book published. He published it. This is not unlike his 1994 move in the United States, when a publishing house he owns, HarperCollins, gave the new Speaker of the House, Newt Gingrich, a book contract. The issue this time was Murdoch's Fox television. Would the Federal Communications Commission permit a United States network to be financed with foreign money? In sum, a PBS *Frontline* documentary calls him "very careless about democratic institutions," noting that his only interest is profit.[16]

Over the 1990s, Murdoch has moved rapidly to turn his print news empire into one that uses television and multimedia technology. His B-Sky-B began offering satellite news and information in Europe in 1991. Now he's building on this accomplishment to present A-Sky-B to U.S. audiences as an alternative to cable.[17]

In 1993, Murdoch acquired STAR TV in Asia. In this predominantly British and American global industry, STAR was really the first really global service started by a businessperson whose roots are grounded in another of the world's cultures. Richard Li, son of Hong Kong billionaire Li Ka-ahing, at age twenty-three started STAR TV in 1990; it was on the air in 1991. STAR (Satellite Television Asian Region Ltd.) started as a free satellite service delivering five channels twenty-four hours a day, including BBC News, MTV, and other entertainment. It carried four channels in English and one in Mandarin Chinese. Initially 38 countries from Turkey and Israel to Taiwan had access wherever a small satellite dish could be hooked up. The potential audience surged 279% in the first ten months of 1993 to reach more than 42 million homes. That year, he sold a majority interest to Rupert Murdoch for $525 million U.S. For Li, it was a sixfold return on his investment. For Murdoch, it was the base for delivering satellite TV to the majority of the globe's population. By 1997, Murdoch owned it all.

Murdoch owns TV property in Latin America. He owns the Twentieth Century Fox film studios in Hollywood. He owns 50% of CBS/Fox Home Video, the world's largest distributor of videocassettes. He has joint ventures with companies on every continent. His most recent partnership is with MCI Communications in a move to make possible electronic delivery of films, TV, and computer data to dozens of countries. MCI fiber optic telephone cables and satellites already serve over a hundred countries. In 1996, a plan was announced for the new A-Sky-B, with a twenty-four-hour news network for the United States. Murdoch named as chairman Roger Ailes, former president of CNBC and a principal political strategist for right-wing Republicans. The news feeds will come from Reuters, WTN, and B-Sky-B in Europe. The network will get Washington news as a one-fifth partner in the news pool with C-Span, APTV, Reuters, and Conus. The plan included signing with Telecommunications, Inc. (TCI) (10 million subscribers), Continental and Comsat (600,000 subscribers), MSO, Cablevision, and DBS operator DIRECTV (3.5 million subscribers). Initially Time Warner (which acquired CNN in 1995) refused to carry Murdoch.

CNN's founder Ted Turner is now a Time Warner vice president. While it won't be easy to build A-Sky-B from the spotty news services currently within News Corp. television operations, Murdoch's plans draw on his global resources, not just his U.S. holdings. Neither Murdoch nor Turner should be underestimated in this competition to provide news.[18]

Murdoch's hardware acquisitions multiply constantly, but his ultimate success depends on how fully the hardware is used. To illustrate the point, take STAR TV in Asia. Until 1995 it was building a market with five channels. At that point, it expanded to 114, which can't all be programmed with imported American video. Access will depend on personal contacts to deliver proposals to produce something that it finds appealing and cheaper than the alternatives. Murdoch is investing in production studios in Bombay and elsewhere to accomplish this.

His accomplishments are indeed remarkable. The question is, will he respect democratic institutions? Or will they all take second place to greed? It will take a vigilant public and political and business leaders with spine to be sure that Murdoch's programming is balanced. The world doesn't need another Mussolini or Hitler, whose news messages on radio solidified fascism in Europe in the 1940s. Is anyone watching?

Reuters

Reuters is the first of the globe's big-four print journalism news agencies to incorporate TV into their work. Associated Press (AP), United Press International (UPI), and Agence France-Presse (AFP) all had other concerns. Because the British empire covered 20% of the globe and one-quarter of the world's population, the English language became important across the globe and Reuters gained early influence in the news business. Reuters operates under a 1941 trust agreement specifying that "Reuters shall not pass into the hands of any interest group or faction, that its integrity, independence and freedom from bias shall be fully preserved, and that no effort shall be spared to expand, develop and adapt the business of Reuters."

Serious moves into television by Reuters began in the early 1990s with the hiring of Enrique Jara to head that operation and the incorporation of Visnews as a part of Reuters. Reuters has a base of 120 bureaus, 400 camera crews, and a comprehensive satellite network. They serve 200 broadcasters and affiliates in eighty-four countries. With the transition, Reuters now expects both its print and video journalists to become multimedia journalists. Reuters doesn't see itself as a traditional broadcaster.

According to Jara, by 1994, Reuters had started a narrowcast financial service, accessible on PCs, that includes digital video, audio, and data; planned a joint-venture Spanish cable news channel; launched three U.S.-based video on demand experiments; and begun producing a public affairs program for a Russian TV network. In a 1994 interview he told the author,

> The central objective from a strategic point of view is grounded in the reality that Reuters television is a news agency. We'll provide television pictures doing very much the same thing we do with text, still pictures, and graphics for the traditional media and for the new media. We'll provide natural raw material as wholesalers to the media outlets, broadcasters, newspapers, radio stations, correspondents, institutions, etc. We see an existing market. . . . We are very strong in Europe. We are less sophisticated in other markets including the United States. Now, we are expanding very quickly our news gathering capability, simply by providing television capabilities to the 123 Reuters bureaus around the world.[19]

Part of this expansion included a deal Reuters concluded in 1994 with the second-largest Spanish language network in the United States, Telemundo, and with minority partners Antena 3 (a Spanish television channel), Artear (the television arm of the largest publishing company in Argentina), and a consortia of independent cable operators in Mexico with about one million clients. In 1994, these companies launched "Tele Noticias," a Miami-based twenty-four-hour news channel in the Spanish language targeted to 2.3 million homes in Latin America and Spain, and to Spanish-speaking cable households in the United States.

The other change Reuters television made in the early 1990s was to change staff contracts, providing access for people with multimedia skills and challenging those unaccustomed to the new technologies. Says Jara,

> We expect journalists interested in operating or ready to grow themselves in terms of multi-media journalists. That move has actually been preceded by the structure that we adopted in Moscow where we opened a Broadcast Center the middle of 1993. Actually that bureau has been quite significant as a symbol of the cultural change within our organization, a company that has always been dominated by the textual journalist. The head of the Moscow bureau is a television man. It symbolizes the idea that we no longer believe that the boss will always be someone who got their experience in textual journalism. The boss is going to be the best. That's a significant move.

> We are doing the same in Washington with a Broadcast Center so that all the textual and pictorial operations are in one place with a clear indication that we are going to work in multi-skilled environments. Actually another very important step in this direction is the development of a new generation of media editing systems. Of course,

they are digital. But they are digital in a way that incorporates, now potentially, later on actually, the capabilities of editors of any kind handling textual, alpha-numeric and pictorial material in one terminal. So all the functions and scripts and texts and the introduction of coding or items to facilitate the next step which is the storage with elements imbedded to create navigation tools that will allow the access to the information.

The bottom line is that Reuters sees itself as a content-focused news agency. It doesn't plan to be involved in the utility end—laying cable or buying satellites. The focus is on increasing the skills and abilities to develop program capability.

Reuters's principal emphasis remains that of a news wholesaler, with a strong emphasis on providing information to participants in the global financial markets. Its products begin to blur the line between raw material and finished programs. They offer

- news feeds at fixed times—ninety-second bulletins with regional interests
- world news services—immediate access to timely news events available in Europe, the Middle East, parts of Africa, Asia, and the Americas
- a comprehensive video archive (from 1896) incorporated into a multimedia base
- a desktop news library (stories since 1963) able to be loaded into IBM-compatible PCs
- news feature programs such as five- to fifteen-minute segments on topical news events or hour-long documentaries and packages featuring significant historical events
- satellite and news production services including crews for hire, satellite news gathering setups, and dedicated transponder space
- visual business news whereby the computer screen shows actual business leaders as announcements are made, adding to the appreciation of what is going on because it's possible to perceive meaning in the voice, or the pronunciation, or the stress, or whatever characteristics of their counterpart are relevant to their way of appreciating the market

How is Reuters unique in the global news arena? Jara speaks to the point.

We do believe a lot in putting together competitive advantages. We have no internal expertise in programming, or very little. We have not a great internal expertise in advertising. Also, we do believe in the diversity of the world—the global village. We don't think that that is a winning formula to create a program together with someone in Atlanta, London, or wherever and expect to make it attractive for everybody in the world. We think it has been a very interesting starting up formula. . . . The idea of creating universal platforms ignoring babel is something to pursue with caution. We would like to go for coherent markets that can express something in a commonality of language and culture.

One very interesting and complex issue is copyrights. An issue that is in evolution these days. We are carefully looking at this to ensure that our basic right on every piece of information that we acquire is satisfactory for these new uses—the contracts with the people that we employ, the contracts with the sources that we are in contact with and ensuring that we have a clean portfolio of material that we own from A to Z. We must establish in our contracts with our customers exactly what we are selling—usage in real time, no distribution, no electronic storage, or if electronic storage, control of the reproduction and the copyrights.

Reuters's product line includes a vigorous mix. At present their services are delivered worldwide in fifteen languages. It's an expanding news market from the Reuters perspective. Jara comments on the mid-1990s:

A 29% revenue growth indicates that the market is still there to pay for the news. I think that you can agree that there is a significant market growth as result of deregulation. Europe has been a star in the last few years with deregulation happening. Independents are now much more significant than public broadcasters. That is now being very actively followed by Asia—Japan. So the deregulation of the broadcasting industry is creating an opportunity for growth of pure news activity. We don't see, however, that this opportunity is going to last a long time.

APTV

The Associated Press (AP) is one of the four major print wire services. In 1994, APTV was launched to move AP into the international video news-gathering business.

As the director of the AP Broadcast Division, Jim Williams, said,

We are going to be different in several ways. First and foremost because we have so many bureaus in so many locations. We will have more focused regional coverage. We'll be able to cover international news with AP's proven news judgment. AP's been in business since 1848. We've been established in these countries with professional journalists. We have a reputation for fast accurate and reliable news coverage.

You look at the broadcasters—CBS, ABC, NBC—I think they have anywhere from 6 to 12 bureaus. CNN has around 18–20 bureaus. For them to open up a bureau it's very expensive. Broadcasters find themselves competing more and more with other broadcasters for their core business, their broadcasting channel. As they find more competition for advertisers and viewers, they will focus, I think, on making their product distinctive and unique in a competitive market. They'll rely increasingly on companies like Reuters, WTN, and APTV to gather news for them because that's what we do for a living. It's our core business.[20]

AP already has 3,100 full-time employees in seventy countries. They see the pictures as simply complementing the traditional job of gathering news in words and marketing them via news wire to papers, stations, and database companies. Basically, AP is providing Betacam SP and Hi-8 equipment to existing bureaus, preparing for the convergence of existing media into a multimedia news product. They have video, words, still pictures, graphics, and audio and offer a complete product to TV, newspaper, radio, audiotext, fax on demand, or a multimedia database platform.

WTN

Worldwide Television Network (WTN) has been evolving for decades from its newsreel days and its international news film services under the name of UPITN in the 1960s. Now, WTN is 80% owned by the U.S. network CC/ABC. "WTN is unique," says Robert E. Burke. "We have to go to the site. We have to do in broad daylight what other people only have to describe. Counting our contacts aside from the listed bureaus and crews, we have people with whom we can work in over 400 locations worldwide. WTN serves as an agent. We find the coverage that already exists that is authoritative and we acquire it rather than waste our customers' money by covering something that's already available through a good source. WTN operates to access copyrights for video material directly through the broadcaster."[21] WTN is a clearinghouse for material shot by others as well as by WTN's own crews. WTN is a wholesaler to broadcasters, who subscribe to various WTN services. Broadcasters find it cheaper to buy these services than to produce original programming. Burke continues, "You cannot buy a story from us; you must buy a subscription service. And there are different echelons of service you can purchase based on which satellite services you wish to receive. We sell programs largely exclusively because that's how broadcasters want them. We have the run-of-program contracts, a series. The subscription business is a good business." WTN sells

- News Packages, a general news service with up to twenty news stories with up- dates and background and a features service with about thirty pieces, each an hour long. WTN aims to sell factual programs with a "documentary flavor" that a broadcaster can reversion as deemed appropriate.
- Satellite Services, offering a news-gathering service with fixed and mobile links, booking services, conferencing, and a range of other services.
- Video News Releases, developed for clients interested in reaching key audiences. WTN helps clients identify the right angle on their story and then helps with distribution.
- Special Program Productions, including current-affairs magazines like "Earthfile," a series about humans and their environment; "Healthfile," a series about global health issues; a series on entertainment news; one on sports; another on the in- ternational criminal world; and a newsmagazine for youth called "Hands across the World."
- WTN also is expanding its Commercial Directions Services to provide TV services for institutions that need or want to report to the public, for example, the World Health Organization. WTN's broker services make it possible for the client to produce material suitable for the target audience and to increase the chances for broadcast.

WTN has archive materials, provides crews for hire, and offers satellite media tours for stars. The diverse offerings of WTN could provide any number of opportunities for new parties to provide TV program material through WTN.

For WTN the greatest growth is coming from the demands for new broadcasters. "Since the mid 1980s, when commercial licenses began to be issued, especially in Europe, but also elsewhere around the world, the growth in cable and now satellite television, and the number of people who require news gathering to make news programs has expanded exponen- tially," Robert Burke noted. Established broadcasters fill more program- ming slots with news. In past years there were no breakfast programs, late-night programs, and frequent news bulletins throughout the day.

MSNBC

At the end of 1995, Microsoft made the first move toward merging com- puter and video technology with its joint venture with the U.S. network NBC. The venture offers an interactive computer news service and a twenty-four-hour all-news cable channel. CNN, of course, already offers its own online service. In order for the MSNBC venture to succeed, the technology must advance to the point where the bandwidth used to trans- mit data will change to accommodate the transmission of high-quality video images to a home computer user. Cable modems and fiber optic cable will upgrade the speed of transmission greatly. Eventually, the idea is that viewers will be able to watch a newscast in the corner of their TV screens while working with computer data at the same time. To accomplish this Microsoft paid NBC to convert NBC's America's Talking cable channel to an all-news format and rename it MSNBC, effective July 15, 1996. As of late 1996, it had 24 million subscribers. Try it on <*http://www. msnbc.com*>. Its web site presently includes expanded versions of news coverage seen on TV.

THE INTERNET

History

The revolutionary technology of the Internet has changed global communications in countless ways in less than a decade. The following chronology summarizes its evolution.[22]

- 1969—Bolt Branek Newman creates a network called ARPAnet for the U.S. Defense Department Advanced Research Projects Agency.
- 1973—The network now has 35 nodes and is renamed DARPA.
- 1976—Email is tested by Queen Elizabeth.
- 1979—The Internet Configuration Control Board is established by DARPA.
- 1983—The name "Internet" is used to describe the linked networks.
- 1985—There are 100 networks linked.
- 1989—There are 500.
- 1990—There are 2,218.
- 1991—There are 4,000.
- 1993—British researcher Tim Berners-Lee invents the World Wide Web, and it becomes public with 1,313,000 nodes having access. It carries 5.5 terabytes (i.e., million million bytes) information per month.
- 1995—By July, the Web carries 22 terabytes per month.
- 1995—By April, the Internet is turned over to the public as no longer useful to the Defense Department.
- 1995—By July, there are 6.6 million hosts to carry 22 terabytes per month.
- 1996—In February, AT&T promises customers five free hours per month on the Internet and unlimited access for $20 a month.
- 1996—In December, America Online, a flagship ISP (Internet service provider), experiences such a rapid growth in subscribers at $19 a month that its lines overload; it shuts down briefly to reconfigure its service.

The Internet of the late 1990s is a collection of over 30,000 computer networks, and growing rapidly.

Internet Users

The public are very rapidly adapting to the Internet. By August 1997 there were forty million users online worldwide and twenty-four million in the United States. According to the information Larry Landweber released at the Internet Society Annual Meeting in Kuala Lumpur in 1997, 195 countries out of 237 countries, territories and jurisdictions have email access and 171 countries have direct Internet access.[23]

The Net started as an English-language system of communication, but it is rapidly adapting to global users (see Table 3.2). Use is the heaviest in the Western industrialized countries (see Table 3.3). Yahoo, one of the major search engines on the Internet (*http://www.yahoo.com*) originated in Sunnyvale, California. By spring of 1996, it had expanded to Japan (*http://www.yahoo.com.co.jp*). It became the first Internet guide produced by an American company that localized language and content for an international audience. Yahoo has also been usable in French and German since 1996. In addition to language accommodation, it has provided localized search items for the United Kingdom. Yahoo's offerings include the news headlines from Reuters.

Lycos, another search engine, has been available in German since 1996 and has a localized version for Sweden.

The search engine Infoseek (*http://www.infoseek.com*) launched its multiple language service in late 1996. It's available in French, German, Japanese, and Spanish. Robin Johnson, president and CEO of Infoseek, indicated that at that time 10% of the users were from outside the United States. Other countries have their own localized services. For example, in Japan, there is a customized directory as well as news and entertainment. Infoseek is establishing partnerships with advertising representatives in eight European countries and in Israel.[24]

It was estimated that 69% of users in 1996 were from the United States, 28% from Europe, and the remaining 3% from other parts of the globe.

To look more closely at North American use, examine the results of a Nielsen survey done in late 1995.[25] There were at the time twenty-four million Internet users in the United States and Canada. Note that this figure is less than 10% of the population of the United States. Two-thirds of all North American users are male, and they account for 77% of the time online. Over half of the users are between sixteen and thirty-four. One-third of the users log-on daily with a total average use of five hours and twenty-eight minutes per week. One-quarter of the regular users have an income of over $80,000, placing them well into the top 10% of U.S. wage earners; 64% have a college degree, whereas only 28% of the general adult public has that much education.

Vice President Albert Gore, in 1991 when he was a senator from Ten-

Table 3.2
Internet Use, in Rapid-Growth Countries (over 500 Internet hosts)

Country	July 1996	July 1997	%Growth
Malaysia	8,541	40,533	374.6%
Turkey	7,743	22,963	196.6%
Peru	2,269	6,510	186.9%
Former Soviet Union	13,601	38,363	182.1%
Venezuela	1,679	4,679	178.7%
Korea	47,973	132,370	175.9%
Croatia	2,480	6,705	170.4%
Russian Federation	32,022	81,104	153.3%
Bulgaria	2,254	5,515	144.7%
Ukraine	4,499	10,513	133.7%
Japan	496,427	955,688	92.5%

Source: Network Wizard *<http://www.nw.com>* compiled by Akio Sugii *<TGD56490@biglobe.ne.jp>*.

nessee and chairing the Senate Subcommittee on Science, Technology, and Space, commented, "We are witnessing the emergence of a truly global civilization based on shared knowledge in the form of digital code. The ability of nations to compete will depend on their ability to handle knowledge in this form."

Indeed, by 1995 a global information infrastructure (GII) had become a reality.[26] The chair and chief executive of IBM Europe, Lucio Stanca, noted in 1995, "On the campuses of major corporations, large research universities and government laboratories, broad-bandwidth pipelines for carrying digitized information are already commonplace."[27]

The question now is how to transfer sprawl into infrastructure? How can the user be sure that the information and its source are accurate? How

Table 3.3
Global Internet Use, by Population

Country	# Hosts July 1997	%Growth in One Year	Hosts per 100,000 People
Finland	335,956	21.2%	6,581
Iceland	14,153	30.9%	5,236
Norway	209,034	73.1%	4,768
U.S.A.	11,829,141	43.8%	4,439
New Zealand	155,678	99.9%	4,388
Australia	707,611	78.0%	3,875
Sweden	284,478	52.7%	3,196
Denmark	137,008	78.0%	2,610
Canada	690,316	62.7%	2,395
Netherlands	341,560	59.1%	2,194
Singapore	60,674	58.1%	1,786
Israel	61,140	54.4%	1,128
Hong Kong	48,660	101.6%	772
Japan	955,688	92.5%	762
Korea	132,370	175.9%	291
Malaysia	40,533	374.6%	203
Taiwan	40,706	32.8%	190

Sources: Network Wizard <*http://www.nw.com*> compiled by Akio Sugii <*TGD56490@biglobe.ne.jp*>. Population from CIA FACT BOOK.

can the marketplace gain, not lose, jobs? How can the exacerbation of a two-tiered "have" and "have-not" society be prevented?

Economic and Social Limits to Access

Dr. Howard Frederick, executive director of Germany's Saxony Telecommunications Development Corporation, is one of the early Internet educators. He is most enthusiastic about the democratization potential for the Internet. He compares the Internet with television as a form of communication. TV he calls centralized, a medium with little opportunity for feedback, one requiring lots of capital and trained personnel. And, he says, TV is susceptible to outside manipulation. The Internet, on the other hand, he says, is decentralized, has huge interactivity, no ownership, a short learning curve. And, he says, it resists control by outside forces.[28] Is he right?

Certainly we are witnessing a major shift in the ability to share information across the globe. Indeed, the Internet has liberated the individual from media imperialism by providing access and choice in securing whatever news one wants whenever one wants it. But it's not so simple.

Aside from the problems of a niche information society where people can isolate themselves from exposure to common news, from which they might learn something they had not thought to look for or something useful across society, there *are* access problems. If one doesn't have a telephone line, what good is the Internet? If one doesn't have the money for a computer, and one's school or library hasn't invested in computers, how can one access the hardware needed to use the Net? If one hasn't been privileged to have the education required to use this new technology, how can one access the Net? True, the Internet can provide a doctor with critical health-care information, and it can facilitate business operations, but it may have little effect on the socially and economically marginalized. Simultaneously, people with disabilities have gained new opportunities because the technology doesn't care about their handicap. People can use the Net to find jobs, even to find romance. It is an equal-opportunity platform for those who have access, in that it masks race and gender and other characteristics used to discriminate among people.

But, this sprint forward in global society may simply widen the "have" and "have not" gap. If that is of no concern to the "haves" on moral grounds, then it should be a concern on political grounds. Terrorism, wars, and a long list of market-destabilizing events can result when this gap generates real hostility. Such instability can happen even more rapidly now than in the past because, thanks to the new technologies, it is a lot easier for people to see how good life is on "the other side of the tracks." It remains to be seen whether on not the global satellite phone system now under construction will reach anyone other than the elite. Bill Gates, CEO of Microsoft, and Craig McCaw, cell-phone pioneer, are financing Teledesic's development of a system of 840 satellites circling the earth. They will beam voice phone calls and Internet services anywhere in the world. No ground lines will be required.[29]

Within the United States this is a problem. In late 1993, the Census Bureau indicated that fewer than 14% of adult African Americans and Latino/as have a home computer compared to 26.9% of whites. While minority-owned equipment has increased since then, the gap still remains.

Some efforts are beginning to correct the imbalance.[30] Los Angeles Councilman Mark Ridley-Thomas started a computer bulletin board enabling South Central's African American residents to contact each other. Sixty-five terminals are available. In the end of 1994, LatinoNet was created to connect this community for communication around common interests. UCLA Chicano Studies Research Center and UC Santa Barbara's Linguistic Minority Research Institute started Chicano/Latin Net. Elder advocate groups started SeniorNet in Los Angeles. In Ohio, Ameritech, the regional phone giant, funded fourteen computer centers in low-income parts of Dayton. Ameritech will spend $2.2 million to build the centers and set aside $18 million for school systems to buy equipment and wire schools to networks.

To look more closely at the disparity between population groups, the writer Matthew Scott analyzed how the black population might fare in terms of securing a proportionate share of any economic opportunity resulting from the information superhighway.[31] African Americans own two hundred of the ten thousand broadcast stations in the United States. That's about 2% of the whole, and the population group is 12% of the U.S. population. By 2000, it is estimated that the Internet and related industries will produce 300,000 jobs and generate $1 trillion in revenues, forming one-sixth of the U.S. economy. At this point, it doesn't look as if those economic benefits will be available proportionally to the black community. In Africa, 80% of all the information about Africa is generated outside of the continent. All African countries have some ability to use the Internet, but coverage is jeopardized by poor or nonexistent phone service and by lack of access to equipment. In 1995, only eleven of the forty-three countries in Africa had full Internet service: Algeria, Botswana, Egypt, Kenya, Morocco, Mozambique, Namibia, South Africa, Uganda, Zambia, and Zimbabwe. Politically and socially the continent is ready for this economic growth, but it is short on infrastructure and on interested investors.

There are many more issues about Internet access. Coralee Whitcomb, chair of the Boston chapter of Computer Professionals for Social Responsibility,[32] noted that as ownership of the Internet passes from the National Science Foundation to individual companies, the public sector may be shortchanged. She raises a number of questions: Will cable companies, phone companies, and television networks maintain public space for dialogue? How much space will be available for nonprofit purposes? Who will pay for the equipment and training costs for low-income people? Will there be electronic redlining? Who will have the ability to publish as well as consume? Whitcomb cautions that it is important for providers to adhere to the common-carrier regulations that enable anyone to put any information on the Internet. Owner control of content would be a major problem in limiting the Internet's potential.

Across the world, especially in developing countries, the principal problem is access to adequate phone lines. For example, in China one may have to pay over $600 to get a phone installed and then wait many months before it happens.[33] Further, the Chinese government has tried to channel all Internet use through the University of Beijing.

SRI Research observes that we may be moving into an era where a new class structure evolves based on education rather than on economics.[34]

Government Regulation

The overwhelming self-interest of legislators is to legislate, and the self-interest of regulators is to regulate. They're trying very hard to curb free speech on the Internet.

Some of this activity comes from countries with limited individual freedoms. For example, in South Korea in December 1996 a warning was issued to Internet users not to put on the Net anything that might violate South Korean national security law, that is, any information that the North Koreans might find interesting.

Even in open societies, efforts to control are surfacing. The U.S. Congress tried to control pornography on the Internet through the Communications Decency Act (CDA) of 1996, but the U.S. Supreme Court found the law unconstitutional. Prior to the Department of Justice's appeal to the Supreme Court, the federal court in Philadelphia issued a preliminary injunction against CDA as a violation of the First and Fifth Amendments to the Constitution. The case was brought before them by the Citizens Internet Empowerment Coalition, including the American Library Association, Internet servers, and civil liberties groups. One key argument, for example, was that if it became illegal to discuss the human body, it would also be illegal to discuss breast cancer. The Philadelphia court ruling said content-based regulation "could burn the global village to roast the pig."[35]

The list of attempts to regulate grows longer daily.[36] Germany, Iran, and Singapore are all among those trying to limit content on the Internet. An Internet access provider in Germany wants to block a Canadian neo-Nazi group. Major governments want to break codes used on the Internet in order to track criminals. Corporations want to limit how their employees use the Net while at work, and they want "firewalls" to protect their own proprietary information. The Electronic Privacy Information Center in

Washington, D.C., monitors these efforts to help protect privacy. Compuserve, a U.S. ISP, has tried to eliminate sexually explicit bulletin boards in response to a child pornography investigation launched in Germany. Viet Nam won't allow Internet use to begin until regulations are established determining what's allowed and by whom. The Chinese explore a digital wall to cordon off part of cyberspace so they can communicate with each other but not with the outside world, unless so authorized. In Saudi Arabia, the minister of interior approves opening email accounts, and one can be jailed for accessing *Playboy*.

These regulatory methods are only deterrents and can mostly be circumvented. Not only is it very expensive to implement censorship, but it results in loss of business. In addition, in today's world, limiting the use of new technology means limiting the overall economy. In February 1996, Frederico Mayor, the director of UNESCO, called for drafting a global agreement to protect cyberspace, citing the issues on the table as copyright matters and banned materials. In the United States there's an Internet Law Task Force that is evolving into a global watchdog on these matters. It's too soon to know how free global free speech will be.

News on the Net

"I'm an international student attending a college in America," said Guney Keser. "Now, with the Internet, I am home. News from my country is only a click away. I have access to most of the country's newspapers, magazines, radio stations, news agencies and television stations."[37] That's a good illustration of using news online, but it's just the tip of the iceberg. One can access so much specialized news that, depending on one's objective, it's either enormously helpful or enormously confusing.

Newspapers, Magazines, and Radio and Television Stations

Many publications and stations now have their own Web sites, and there are specialized news source Web sites. The following are a few examples.

- The Electronic Newsstand *<http://www.enews.com>* (ENEWS) has four levels of content—urgent news flashes, fresh news, current briefings, and archive handbooks and manuals.
- The Newsroom *<http://www.auburn.edu/~vestmon/news.html>*. This site contains material from Reuters, *USA Today*, and television networks. Its advantage is that it can be delivered in flexible formats, either continuously or on-demand, and customized for the reader.
- *The International Herald Tribune* *<www.iht.com>*. This is among the best papers for global news.
- For lists of newspapers across the globe, see *<http://www.newslink.org/>*. Also see *<http://www.newspaper.com>*.

- For wire service news, see *<http://www.clarinet.com>*. This site is the first and largest electronic newspaper. Its subscribers include global businesses and hotels that provide summarized material for busy professionals. It also provides users with new insight into the news. Guney Keser, the Turkish student, noted, "I found out that recent news about a fight between Israeli soldiers and the Palestinians was described in some of these news stories very differently from the way it was described in *Zaman Gazatesi*, a Turkish fundamentalist Muslim newspaper."
- *The Wall Street Journal* *<www://wsj.com>*
- *The New York Times* *<www://nyt.com>*
- East Africa's largest newspaper *<http://www.africaonline.co.ke/AfricaOnline/east-african.html>*
- England *<http://www.yahoo.co.uk/headlines/european/>*

The print media are experimenting with alternative ways to use the internet.[38] For example, *The Atlantic Monthly* has an interactive feature called "Executive Decision," where a user addresses a problem that the U.S. president may face. The best answers are made available online for other users to read. *Foreign Affairs* has an email notice system where users fill out forms indicating interests; they get a message when a news issue of the magazine is available or when the Web site has new information on those selected areas of interest. *The New York Times* and National Public Radio in the United States joined forces to cover U.S. elections with an online talk and discussion.

Broadcasters of both radio and television are using the Net. One sad note is that the Internet has caused a number of shortwave radio stations to go off the air. It is simply cheaper and easier to communicate on the Internet. For some. For those who live in a part of the world without adequate phone lines or where political and economic problems prevent access, the loss of shortwave radio means a loss of their connection to the outside world.

The following are a few sites for obtaining radio and television information.

- Information about television *<http://www.television.com>*
- The BBC *<www.bbc.com>*
- Hong Kong programming *<www.cuhk.hk/rthk>*
- Canadian television on ATV *<www.atv.ca>*
- Channel Africa from South Africa *<http://www.rtvf.nwu.edu/links/broadcasting.html>*

Most broadcasters deal with the Web through their own Web sites. MSBC was created as a dedicated technology mix. NBC plans to spin off other Web sites as a program strategy to supplement its on-air programming. WCBS news in New York City has up-to-the-minute news on the Web and a provision for allowing users to email the mayor and other politicians.

Such sites not only enable people to obtain and react to the news, they also offer possibilities for people to be newsmakers. For example, Meritxell Vila Grau, a mass-communications student from Spain studying in the United States, notes, "On the Internet, I contacted TV 3 Televiso de Catalunya, which is my television station at home. It made me very happy because I felt as if I were at home. And I have the option to send them story ideas by email."

Obtaining personalized news is becoming popular for those interested in investment news. At *<http://www.dowjones.com.pj.html>* is the Dow Jones subscription service that allows users to get breaking news only on those items they have selected.

General Research News

Whatever region of the globe or topic of interest concerns a user can be accessed on the Net. The following are some sample Web sites for this kind of research.

For an introduction to resources, try the WWW Virtual Library *<http://www.analysys.co.uk/commslib.htm>* This references communications and journalism entries. It also has information on practically anything listed from A to Z. There's a vast listing of nonprofit organizations, listed by category of work. There's also a listing of business and industry. The WWW Virtual Library lists ninety-one email newsletters under a wide range of topic headings.

Government sites are extensive. In the United States, *The National Journal* publishes a directory of them. Here are some government listings or information sources on selected countries for news research.

- The United Nations *<gopher://gopher.undp.org>*
- The U.S. government *<www.fedworld.gov>*
- Voice of America (the U.S. international service) *<gopher:gopher.voa.gov/voa.news>*
- European news from U.S. embassies *<gopher://smile.srce.hr/english/subject/news/>*
- Russia *<www.russiatoday.com>*
- Singapore *<http://www.gov.sg/>*
- Hong Kong *<http://www.ofta.gov.hk>*
- Asian countries *<http://www.asiaonline.net>*
- African countries *<http://www.afrika.com>*
- Latin America *<http://latin-america.com>*

Human Rights and Public Interest Advocacy News

Human rights groups are online in force. Not only do they publish information, they have a wide range of opportunities for two-way communication. Their enthusiasm about the Internet is not surprising, for two reasons. First, many of the individuals concerned about these issues are highly educated and are skilled in use of the new technologies. Second, often their concerns are either not addressed or minimally covered in the dominant news media, where news and information tend to focus more on the economic and political concerns of the powerful.

Usenet, described in the next section, is mostly for academics and activists. Browse the "alt" groups on Usenet to see the range of topics, See <soc.rights.human.newsgroup>. Specialized topics can be found like <talk.politics.tibet>. One can also search Usenet groups by "keyword." For example, once connected to its Web site, one can locate a regular newsletter called "This Week in Haiti." It is posted to the group whenever it is published, according to Internet researcher Douglas Gray.[39]

The Association for Progressive Communication (APC) is the premier site for a wide range of public interest news. See <http://www.apc.org/>. It consists of twenty-one international member networks linking 40,000 NGOs, activists, educators, policymakers, and community leaders in 133 countries.[40] APC associations include:

- PeaceNet <http://peacenet.org/peacenet/>. Organizations involved in peace development. Also see <http://www.igc.apc.org/interact/Peacenet.html>.
- EcoNet <http://econet.apc.org/econet/>. Organizations working for sustainable environment
- ConflictNet <http://www.igc.apc.org/conflictnet/>. Organizations working on conflict resolution methodology
- LaborNet <http://www.igc.apc.org/labornet/>. News and information for the democratic labor movement
- WomensNet <http://www.igc.apc.org/womensnet/>. Resources for women

In addition to the APC networks, many other human rights organizations use the Net. For example, the Anti-Defamation League <www.adl.org> deals with human rights to eliminate bigotry. Fairness and Accuracy in Reporting <www.igc.apc.org/fair> monitors the media. Project Censored <http://zippy.sonoma.edu/ProjectCensored> cites news not told. The Center for Democracy and Technology <www.cdt.org> examines when technology use undermines democracy.

News Groups

These groups provide a way for individuals across the globe to join ranks with others with similar interests. They are either a replacement for the community organizing of past generations, or they are a diversion side-tracking people from actual engagement with the institutions that solve problems. Probably they are both.

Usenet, sometimes called Net News, is the premier cooperative information exchange service. It is accessible internationally and has several thousand "newsgroups," each with a specific topic. Most are interactive, like electronic bulletin boards. This concept was created in 1979 by two Duke university graduate students. Most of the newsgroup services are free.[41]

Internet Relay Chat (IRC) is a chaotic site that is not well known, according to Internet researcher Douglas Gray.[42] This is the place to observe how racial stereotyping and bigotry appear online. It has small groups of people known as channels, like "#whitepower" or "#rapesex" and can be really harmful to those unaware that it is "Real Time Chat." That is, in real time, when the Enter key is pushed, every user group sees the message. IRC is structured in a hierarchy, with a "channel operator" or "op" and other users. If the "op" doesn't like a user, he can "kick" the user off of the channel, even when it's on a mainstream channel like "#politics."

Personal Publishing

If not satisfied receiving other people's news, create your own electronic newspaper. One way to do this is through the Electronic Newsstand's (<http://www.enews.com/zones/news/>) CRAYON ("Create Your Own Newspaper"). CRAYON is an email news provider where a caller can create her/his own newspaper and it will be sent free to his/her email addresses. This opportunity provides yet another way to have a voice on the Net. It may provide a forum for new ideas and creative thinkers, or it may put more words on the Net to add to the confusion. Probably, personal publishing will do both. That's the price of free speech. People have to think and make intelligent judgments about what they hear.

In simpler times, one assumed that once a story appeared in print, that was it. Now, it's just the beginning. That can encourage democratization, chaos, and inaction. The question is, how can society encourage using these online technologies to accomplish democratization? The answer to that question might become even more complicated once we accomplish the next technology advance—convergence.

Technology Convergence

As is evident from projects like the Bill Gates's venture to link Microsoft with NBC and with cell phone technology, these once-separate technologies are rapidly merging. In 1996, several manufacturers began promoting a big-screen TV that is also a big-screen personal computer. With it, one could receive a TV program, play a videodisk, or access the Internet. The handheld remote includes the hardware needed to enter a credit card and make a purchase. PC makers have the capability to feed a digital signal from satellite services like DirecTV or from a DVD player directly to a big digital screen.[43]

Television broadcasters and computer buffs alike are not interested in recreating TV on the Net. They're experimenting with more. For example, when NASA, the U.S. space agency, repaired the Hubble Space Telescope in early 1997, Discovery TV <www.discovery.com> had audio and video with the text so that viewers could follow the details of the repairs. Another experiment was to enable a subscriber to watch someone explore the Dead Sea area with a digital camera mounted on a bicycle.

By April 1997, Microsoft announced it was buying WebTV, a California company that makes a set-top box for browsing the Internet via a TV set. Craig Mundie, Microsoft vice president in charge of convergence, said, "Computer technology is the underlying technology base for digital television and video-based communication. Whether you call it a better PC or a better TV, we think you're going to need to do both."[44] The idea is to integrate Microsoft's broadcast architecture for Windows, including Netshow, to allow PC users to access digital video and audio signals from cable, broadcast, and satellite with a computer no faster than 133 mhz.

Testing this new service has already happened. National Public Radio uses Microsoft's Netshow server for its "Radio Expeditions," an audio excursion illustrated by National Geographic. Audionet uses Netshow to offer C-Span, the gavel-to-gavel coverage of U.S. government in action, online. Audionet plans live event programming with London NewsDirect and others. Taggeshau, a one-hour daily German newscast, uses VDO-Live.[45]

Other convergence projects began in the summer of 1997. Microsoft is delivering video-enhanced Web sites in conjunction with DirecTV, that is, its satellite-delivered Internet. NBC, USA Network, IBM, and Sony and others have joined with Microsoft to deliver Web content to desk tops.

The Oracle Corporation and CNN introduced a free personalized Internet news service called CNN Custom News. It will carry articles from about 150 sources and, on a dozen of them, it will have real-time news with pictures. Reuters, AP, Bridge News, and CNN will contribute.[46] See <customnews.cnn.com> or <cnn.com/customnews>. This service will carry advertising from Citibank, among others. It's not a totally new idea, as *The New York Times, The Wall Street Journal*, and CNN already have similar services. But the key to this one is whether the indexing will make it possible to select preferences quickly.

Convergence will have other impacts for the public. For example, in the United States, since the Telecommunications Act of 1996, video dialtone makes it possible for telephone companies and cable companies and even utility companies to offer visual, voice, and data transmission. This could enable more people to be newsmakers, that is, give them access to an audience. On the other hand, it could restrict access, because only the original cable companies were required to provide public access production studios and local channels for public use. Will this very useful public service continue?

In 1997, the FCC responded positively to Apple Computer's petition to release a portion of radio frequency spectrum for unlicensed wireless digital communication and an NII Band, or national information infrastructure band, is being created. Such a bandwidth could be worth tens of billions of dollars. It can accommodate schools, libraries, and health facilities. One issue is whether it will accommodate institutions only, or be "outdoor" and accommodate a community. Can this be the twenty-first-century equivalent to cable access? Who has the right and the equipment to initiate news and information?

A major issue is copyright. Copyright owners including software industry, publishers, and film, music, and video producers have a lot at stake regarding how a converged technology uses their materials. Another issue is, what's educational in terms of "fair use"? What happens to materials used in digital format?

Internet researcher Dana Sanders summarized the impact of these changes when he said, "The Internet is its own conquering nation."

Global Sales and Advertising

For these new global news technologies to be successful, global sales and advertising must develop to the point of producing revenue to reduce subscriber fees. In fact, while it is discouraging to those of us who hope that substantive thinking will govern global communication, the purpose of these enterprises from the perspective of industry is to make money. The objective is to reach the right demographic with the advertisements in order to sell product. The content of material is secondary.

The U.S. video and film entertainment business is leading the global expansion. In 1989, global trade in TV programs produced $2.4 billion, of which 71% was for U.S. exports. At that time, Europe imported half of all global exports and three-quarters of U.S. exports. By 1995, the dollar value of the market was three times what it had been six years earlier. But the market share changed because western Europe began exporting television programs. Europe was investing a lot in coproduction. In 1992, Europe spent $2.8 billion on coproduction and $2.15 billion on imports. By 1995, $5.3 billion was spent on coproduction, and a far smaller percentage of the whole, $2.7 billion, was spent on imports.[47] By the mid 1990s, U.S. sales globally were increasing at a rate of 15% per year.

If your business is advertising, global TV advertising is just beginning to assume a life of its own. Global Net advertising is at a very infant stage. Global advertising is difficult because of language and cultural differences. For example, an American automobile called "Nova" has had trouble with marketing in Mexico because "no va" means "doesn't go" in Spanish.

Look at one of the success stories in global advertising—Coca-Cola. Fernando Perez, marketing director of Coca-Cola in Venezuela, says, "Coca-Cola has been doing an 'always Coca-Cola' campaign for years. It's the same commercial used across the globe and all that changes is the language in which the jingle is sung. There's no person or characters so it's not necessary to insert a Chinese, a Latin, or an African person to link it to a culture." Coca-Cola's 1995 annual report states,

> Some of our individual operating groups outside of North America now generate income equal to that of our entire company in the mid eighties. . . . Currently 60% of the world's population lives in markets where the average person consumes less than ten servings of our product per year, offering high potential growth for our company. The emerging markets of China, India, Indonesia and Russia represent approximately 44% of the world's population, but on a combined basis, their average per capita consumption is approximately 1% of the United States level. As a result we will continue aggressively investing to insure that our products are pervasive, preferred, and offer the best price relative to value.[48]

In 1996, Coca-Cola's advertisement to accomplish this objective was an Olympics advertising theme used in over 135 countries—in eleven spots with the same idea, same images, and different languages.

Another example of global advertising success is Pepsi Cola, which sells its products in nearly 200 countries, with retail sales of $52 billion in 1995. Gustavo Ghersy, chief operating officer for Pepsi Latin America, says, "Emerging markets may well be our greatest opportunity of all. In the last three years, we've invested more than $500 million to develop markets such as eastern Europe, China, India and Russia, which include more than one third of the world's population and offer tremendous long term growth potential. In Hungary and Poland, we regained the cola market share. In India, our total market share jumped to almost 40%. All together, more than one third of our 1995 international volume growth came from emerging markets."[49] Ghersy describes one advertising approach—global branding, or providing a common name, look, and quality. "Global branding gives us enormous economies of scale and a competitive edge in purchasing and marketing."

One thing Pepsi has done is sign a three-year contract with MTV to make the two companies partners throughout the world, except in the United States. This paves the way for cross-promotions, event marketing, and jointly developed programs. Pepsi's global theme is to "paint the town blue," using landmark billboards and neon signs in key places like Picadilly Circus in London. It's also launching a space marketing program and linking it with the Russian space station Mir to do a promotion around the space station. In the summer of 1996, two cosmonauts walked in space with a replica of Pepsi's new blue can. Video was shot for 1997 ads. Ghersy summarizes, "We're globalizing. It's a major breakthrough. Just one commercial for all these different cultures." The commercial will air in Europe, the Middle East, and Southeast Asia. Another part of Pepsi's television advertising is to sponsor a "Global Dance Connection," Europe's largest interaction dance party with one million people in televised events in Barcelona, Berlin, and Amsterdam.

Never underestimate the ability of one communications industry to find a way to make money from another. Reuters figured out a way to assist advertisers and make money. "Another acquisition we completed in 1994," said Enrique Jara,

is a company called Ad-Value that developed a very interesting transaction platform in advertising. Because advertising, at the end of the day, is a product, a commodity, it works. When you want to buy a page in the *New York Times* in, let's say, July, you can book it very comfortably in January. But advertising agencies buy a block of space to keep the rates down. It may happen that you have space and no customers. On the other hand, it may happen that you have customers and no space. So you get a clear imbalance between demand and offer, which is very common to what happens in the currency markets or the equity markets. Reuters has a great expertise in these areas. So, for us, entering the advertising market on a transaction basis is another hook into the learning curve in advertising.[50]

Summary

Somehow, we must pull ourselves free from the tangles of wires of all these new technologies. We must find the time to examine how to use them wisely for the improvement of the global quality of life and for the advancement of democratization so that the industry marketplace can expand and thrive and our children can thrive.

In the words of the former South African president Nelson Mandela, "It's our responsibility to give them [our children] the skills and insights to build the information societies of the future. The young people of the world must be empowered to participate in the building of the information age. They must become the citizens of the global information society. And we must create the best of conditions for their participation."[51]

The new communication technologies are changing everything; maybe they will even change the way we think. It's a volatile market. At most, the globe has two decades experience with satellite television, satellite cell phones, fiber optics, digital compression, global "live" TV broadcasts, and the Internet. It's enough time to move beyond the euphoria surrounding our love affair with these new inventions. It's time we examine how to use them effectively, to provide access and opportunity for ourselves and for those heretofore marginalized. What's the likelihood of this happening? Who must take the lead? How?

NOTES

1. Del Jones, "FCC Clears Line for Global Phone System." *USA Today*, March 17, 1997.

2. George Winslow, "Global News Wars." *World Screen News*, April 1993.

3. Robert E. Burke, President, WTN, The Interchange, Oval Rd., Camden Lock, London NW1, United Kingdom. Interview with author in London on January 26, 1994.

4. See <*http://www.intelsat.int/cmc/bcaster/bc0996.html*>.

5. Raymond Akwule, *Global Telecommunications* (Boston and London: Butterworth Heinemann/Focal Press, 1992), p. 72.

6. Robert R. Lovell, Visiting Professor, Department of Aeronautics and Astronautics, MIT. Minta Martin Lecture, "Issues Affecting the Future of Commercial Space," April 27, 1995.

7. Carla B. Johnston, *International Television Co-Production* (Boston and London: Butterworth Heinemann/Focal Press, 1992), p. 57f.

8. Presentation by Mitch Abel, Director of Video Transfer Services, New England Telephone Company, to the seminar sponsored by the Society of Motion Picture and Television Engineers and the Society of Broadcast Engineers, New England Telephone Company, October 9, 1991.

9. Ibid.

10. John Forrest, "Views of the Future," *Spectrum* (London: Independent Television Commission, Autumn 1993), p. 14f.

11. Patricia M. Rodriguez, "The Globalization Issue in Cultural TV." Unpublished paper, Emerson Program in Mass Communications, October 30, 1996.

12. Enrique Jara, Director, Reuters Television, Ltd., 40 Cumberland Ave., London NW107EH, United Kingdom. Interview with the author in London on January 28, 1994.

13. Carla Brooks Johnston, *Winning the Global TV News Game* (Boston and London: Butterworth Heinemann/Focal Press, 1995).

14. Peter Vesey, Vice President, CNNI, One CNN Center, 4th Floor, North Tower, Atlanta, GA 30303. Telephone interview with author on November 21, 1991.

15. Johan Ramsland, Editor, BBC-WSTV, Television Centre, Wood Lane, London W12 7RJ, United Kingdom. Interview with the author in London on January 27, 1994.

16. PBS profile on Rupert Murdoch, Boston, Channel 2, November 7, 1995.

17. Heather Fleming, "Hill Limiting Murdoch's Vision," *Broadcasting and Cable*, April 14, 1997.

18. Bill Carter, "Murdoch Joins a Cable TV Rush into the Crowded All-News Field," *New York Times*, January 31, 1996, p. 1; and Jim McConville, "Fox Ready to Roll Dice in All-News Gamble," *Broadcasting and Cable*, October 7, 1996, p. 52f.

19. Jara Interview.

20. Jim Williams, Vice President and Director of Broadcasting, APTV (Associated Press Television), 1825 K Street, NW, Suite 710, Washington, DC 20006. Telephone interview with the author on June 22, 1994.

21. Burke, interview.

22. *New York Times*, March 4, 1996, p. F25.

23. <*apowellfreedomforum.org*> August 18, 1997 distribution regarding Larry Landweber's "purple map."

24. Anna Matsuzaka, unpublished paper, "Internet Growth," Emerson Program in Mass Communications, Fall 1996.

25. Nielsen, "Commercialization of Internet Expands with New Product Services," *Boston Globe*, October 31, 1995.

26. For information, contact the U.S. National Telecommunications and Information Administration, 202–482–1840.

27. Lucio Stanca, CEO and Chair, IBM Europe, "Building Global Infrastructure for a Real Information Society," *International Herald Tribune*, February 21, 1995.

28. Dr. Howard Frederick, Executive Director of Germany's Saxony Telecommunications Development Corporation, lecture in Boston and interview with author on September 1996.

29. Del Jones, "FCC Clears Line for Global Phone System," *USA Today*, March 17, 1997, p. 31.

30. Jube Shiver, Jr., "Altering the Face of Cyberspace: Activists across the Country Urge More Minorities to Get On-line," *Boston Globe*, April 2, 1995.

31. Matthew S. Scott, "Quest to Own the Information Superhighway: How Much of It Can Blacks Realistically Expect to Own?" *Black Enterprise Magazine*, 25, no. 11 (June 5, 1995): 55–57.

32. Coralee Whitcomb, Chair, Boston Society of Computer Professionals for Social Responsibility. Speech at Internet conference, Boston, January 18, 1995.

33. Chris O'Malley, "Connecting China," *Popular Science*, August 1996, pp. 77–87.

34. SRI Research, *SRI International* at <*http://www.future.sri.com/valssurvey.results.html*>.

35. Jill Lesser, "Federal Court Affirms First Amendment Protections on the Internet," *American Way*, Washington, DC, Summer 1996.

36. "Fences in Cyberspace: Governments Move to Limit Free Flow of the Internet," *Boston Globe*, February 1, 1996, p. 1.

37. Guney Keser, International Communications student, Emerson Graduate Program in Mass Communications, Fall 1996.

38. Douglas F. Gray, "The Current Status of News and Information Available on the Internet." Unpublished paper, Emerson Program in Mass Communications, Fall 1996.

39. Gray, "Current Status."

40. Guney Keser. Unpublished paper, "Internet Opportunities," Emerson Graduate Program in Mass Communications Program, Fall 1996.

41. Keser, "Internet."

42. Gray, "Current Status."

43. Christian Hill and Jeffrey A. Trachenberg, "When a TV Joins a PC, Will Anybody Be Watching?" *Wall Street Journal*, April 3, 1996.

44. Steve McClellan, "Microsoft Buying Web-TV," *Broadcasting and Cable*, April 9, 1997, p. 11.

45. Richard Tedesco, "Netshow, VDOLive Gain Clients," *Broadcasting and Cable*, April 14, 1997, p. 71.

46. Mitchell Martin, "Oracle Unveils CNN Service," *International Herald Tribune*, June 5, 1997.

47. Richard Parker, "The Future of Global Television News," Shorenstein Center, Harvard, Research Paper R-13, September 1994.

48. Shanni Tozzi. "Selected Developments in New Communications," Emerson Graduate Program in Mass Communications, November 4, 1996.

49. Tozzi, "Selected Developments."

50. Enrique Jara, Director, Reuters Television, Ltd., London, England. Interview with the author in London on January 28, 1994.

51. Nelson Mandela, speech at TELCOM 95 Conference, *Trotter Review*, October 2, 1995.

4

The Americas

CANADA AND THE UNITED STATES

It's What Sells

In a capitalist system, profit is essential to stay in business. Beyond that, the frenzy over profits and the defining point whereby profit and greed become one wax and wane depending on the people involved and the mood of the times. The end of the twentieth century, rather like the end of the nineteenth century, brings a period of intense profit-seeking activity. The politics of the era were built on the Republican themes of Reagan's and Bush's rugged capitalism, not tempered by concerns about overall social well-being. All will be well, they insisted, because profits will trickle down to everyone.

This climate has resulted in the widest gap between rich and poor the United States has known in a century. In fact, the change was dramatic in even the fifteen-year period between 1980 and 1995. In 1980, the salary of a company chief executive was, on average, forty-one times greater than that of an average worker. In 1995, the gap grew to the point where a CEO salary was one hundred seventy times the pay level of the average worker.[1]

In 1994, 10% of the population held 72% of the country's wealth, leaving 90% of the population with just 28% of the wealth.[2]

Simultaneously, the new technologies expanded the national and regional markets into a global marketplace. Profits soared. Mergers consolidated the biggest companies and abandoned the smaller ones. The stock market soared to record levels, and the workforce experienced "down-sizing" and the inability to find replacement jobs at the previous skill level.

In this climate, the communications industry has been no different from the others. Local programming declined. Expensive programming declined. The irony is that this resulted in increased news and information programming, because it's cheaper to produce news than a major entertainment program. The problem is that the value corporate executives placed on news was redefined. Less and less emphasis was placed on a thoughtful assessment of what news was important to the well-being of the society. More and more, the policy became focused on selecting news that would escalate the ratings. More and more the news content became infotainment—the mix of information and entertainment.

NBC senior vice president Preston Beckman said, "I don't want to sound cheap or anything, but this business is about buying into success and reducing the cost of failure."[3] What happened to the idea that it was about delivering a service to enhance the public's quality of life? That concept coexisted with capitalism for many decades.

Much of the major U.S. network news became the coverage of scandal involving the rich and famous. It could, in some perverted way, be called investigative reporting, but it certainly wasn't in the Edward R. Murrow tradition. And, to save the money that would be spent on new newsgathering, the news became heavily repetitive. The rationale is to be sure viewers are able to see a story.

The profit-driven economy strikes at the news programming in yet another way. The journalists in the newsrooms and the news-gathering agencies are certainly not responsible for all the content decisions, but they have important roles to play. To do their jobs well, it's helpful if their knowledge goes beyond the technical to some ability to make intelligent decisions to assure that their stories are done accurately and that they reflect the place of the story within the larger society. If educational institutions cut corners to save money, how can people preparing for these important jobs learn to understand the issues of the larger society? For example, should the public understand the value judgments made by the media in deciding how to cover elections? Is that important to keeping a viable democracy? Another example: Does the media or the public know what is American society's median income? When reporters say that a tax bill will affect the "middle-class" household and describes that class as earning incomes over $100,000, the reporter grossly distorts reality. People earning over $100,000 are not in the middle class. They're in the top 10% of wage earners. The median income is around $36,000. The most important thing that could be provided in educating new journalists is to enable them to understand why this kind of background is important and to know where to quickly find the necessary information.

By the mid 1990s, critics increasingly questioned the trends in news coverage content. Richard Zoglin in a *Time* magazine article noted that the explosion in news programming was not accompanied by an equivalent increase in news gathering.[4] What's exploded is not news, but talk about news, or commentary. He observed that the trends gave birth to a "civic" journalism movement aimed at reconnecting journalism with its community by conducting polls and forums to determine community concerns and focusing on solving neighborhood problems. Critics say this turns the media into advocates instead of journalists.

Global News

Technically, North America has been on the forefront of communication satellite technology. In 1965, the United States took the global lead in establishing INTELSAT. In 1973, Canada launched the world's first domestic synchronous-orbit satellite system using low-cost earth stations and low-power transmitters to send facsimile, voice, video, and data on Westar I.[5]

However, the U.S. consumer receives very little international news in comparison with the European consumer. Ostensibly, American viewers are not much interested in global news that doesn't directly affect them. That argument is difficult to defend. When 7.2% of the American public are first-generation immigrants with family in other countries, global news affects them. Another 1.5% of the public is in the military. Triple that number to conservatively reflect their immediate relatives, and it's evident that global news affects about one-third of the U.S. population personally. That doesn't include the top 10% of the American public, consisting of multinational corporate executives and globe-trotting vacationers. Of course, any Americans concerned about their wallets should be concerned about the enormous sums of tax dollars that are invested in, borrowed from, and spent on the military defense of other countries. Is the public so isolationist that it doesn't care about global issues?

The result of policies invoked by the nation's leading news media is that there is much one doesn't easily learn if one relies on the major U.S. media. Traditionally, that's whom the U.S. public has relied on—in part because of very sensible prohibitions on foreign ownership, because we are isolated from most terrestrial cross-border news broadcasts except for Canada and Mexico, and because the technology hasn't caused us to invest in satellite TV.

Canada has, for years, dealt with issues of cultural imperialism. Most of its population lives near the U.S. border and is the recipient of cross-border viewing. Canada's CBC, a broadcasting system based on the BBC, has provided excellent news and information and quality programs that many in the United States would like to watch. In addition, in 1993, the CBC signed an agreement with the BBC to provide the first transoceanic TV in North America.

In the United States in 1997, there were 98 million households with TV,

27 million people had only broadcast TV, and 65 million subscribed to cable TV (see Figure 4.1). Satellite services, which had just really begun in 1996, reached a small percentage of households. DirecTV had 2.4 million households. Primestar had 1.7 million. USSB had 1.4 million, and Echostar and Alphastar were the smallest, with 400,000 households and 40,000 households respectively.

In 1997, the United States learned that it's about to have what countries around the globe have known about for nearly a decade—foreign programs. Direct satellite broadcast (DBS) has been insignificant to the U.S. market because of its reliance on well-developed cable. Rupert Murdoch, the foreigner who isn't a foreigner, plans to expand his European satellite TV, Sky, to the United States through a partnership with MCI in a new company named A-Sky-B.[6] Existing U.S. satellite services for TV— DirecTV, Primestar, and USSB—use only from one to three satellites to beam programs to pizza-sized dishes in subscriber homes. They're all very new and not much of a threat to the well-established cable market. But Murdoch will use at least seven satellites for A-Sky-B and thereby bring more channels, to create the first 500-channel service. Opponents within the cable industry have nicknamed the project "Death Star." It may well have that effect on cable. Current DBS subscribers don't get any local programming, meaning that the current service is simply a supplement to cable and/or broadcast TV. Murdoch promises to carry local programming. In addition, there'll be programming flexibility with channels to have "video-on demand" movies. The cost will be about the same as cable. This is a totally new game for the U.S. communications industry. It's so new that many of the issues weren't even addressed in the major revision to the U.S. Telecommunications Act just passed in 1996.

For the first time, the United States faces the prospect of dealing with media that are hard to control with national laws—a situation familiar to other countries for nearly a decade. For example, issues that need resolution include:

- U.S. cross-ownership rules prevent cable stations from owning broadcast TV or newspapers in same city. The idea is to ensure that one owner's political biases don't monopolize access to news and information and silence the healthy debate that diversity brings. Murdoch's satellite company will broadcast to markets in which he already owns newspapers and terrestrial stations.

- There are global satellite ownership laws where the United States controls only three orbital slots—areas of space—from which satellites can transmit. This is to protect space for other nations who have not yet embarked on satellite ventures. The licenses for these three spaces were auctioned off by the U.S. FCC, which said that a single company couldn't own more than one of the three slots. A-Sky-B, through its partners Echostar and MCI, would control two of the three orbital slots.

Figure 4.1
U.S. TV Set Use, by Type of Service, 1996

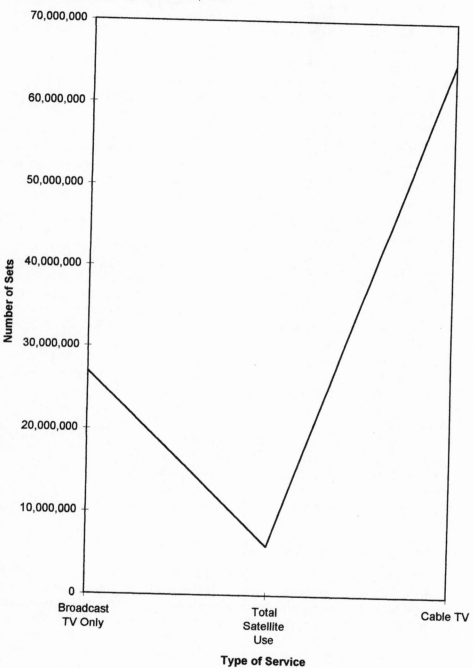

- The U.S. laws relaxed foreign ownership of U.S. TV stations in 1996, but the FCC has said that this doesn't apply to satellites. What happens as satellite and domestic offerings begin to merge? Will there be a new interpretation of limits on foreign ownership? A-Sky-B has MCI, the 10% partner, which is now owned by British Telecom and News Corp, the 40% partner, based in Australia.

- There is a set of laws associated with whether or not A-Sky-B must legally carry local TV broadcast stations. First, will Sky have to pay fees to program producers to retransmit their programs on countless numbers of local stations, as terrestrial broadcasters and cablecasters do? Then there's the "must carry" law. Can Sky choose, when cable companies cannot choose, which local stations to carry and which to exclude? This provision protects local broadcasters, to prevent audience loss. If the "must carry" law is found unconstitutional, the rules could change again.

   While Murdoch is starting his A-Sky-B from scratch, without subscribers, he can easily promote it on services he owns that already operate—Fox TV, sports networks, 20th Century Fox studios. And, he plans to team up with regional phone companies to enable the phone company to offer both phone and TV, with the quid pro quo that Murdoch inherits the workforce and equipment needed to install satellite dishes.[7] If Murdoch finds his way around the laws, as he always does, then the only slowdown might be cost—to Murdoch and to the customer. The phase-in of A-Sky-B is planned to happen during 1998.

   It won't be long before the U.S. viewer is able to tune into WSTV news brought by the BBC. It's a logical extension of the WSTV agreement to provide a half hour of WSTV every night in Canada. Since that agreement was signed, WSTV now has available a twenty-four-hour news service in Europe.

   While the United States hasn't imported foreign programming, it's a major exporter of programs—mostly entertainment, but some news. Even the entertainment contributes to the news and information transfer. Just one example occurs when the person arrested in Turkey asks, "When do I get read my rights? Where is the jury in this courtroom?"

Profile of the U.S. Media Market

   The U.S. Census Bureau demographic projections estimate that by 2050 the population will reach about 400 million and that the major areas of increase will be among elderly and Latin/a persons.[8] By then, it is projected that 25% of the population will be Latino/a, up from 10.7% in 1995 and about 9% in 1990. In 2050, 4.6% of the U.S. population will be over age 80, whereas in 1995 only 1.4% of the population was in this age category. By 2050, those over age 65 will be 29% of the total population.

   The growing wage gaps are evident when looking at the range of family incomes.[9] U.S. Census Bureau figures indicate that 80% of all households in 1979 earned less than $63,0000, whereas in 1994 the 80th percentile was $70,000. The median household income in 1979 was about the same as in 1994, in the $36,000 range. On the lower income end, in 1979, 20% of the U.S. population earned less than $20,000. In 1994 they earned less than $19,000.

In 1995, women in the United States still made only seventy-one cents for every one dollar a man made in the same job. In 1995, 13.8% of the population or 36.4 million lived below the poverty level which was set at $15,100 for a family of four; a family of one mother and one child had to earn less than $10,300 a year to be eligible for poverty programs.[10] Most poor are women and children. In fact, 40% of all poor in the United States are children, a disproportionate number since children are only 25% of the total population.

In 1995, 82% of adults over 25 in the United States had a high school degree, while 23% had a university BA or more. Both statistics are record highs for U.S. education levels.

The mass media news staffs don't yet mirror the population. Women and all minorities together still are less visible in TV newsrooms than in the public. In fact, in the late 1990s, efforts to mirror the market have slipped. The CBS track record for women in the newsroom increased to 34% of its on-screen employees by 1993, then dropped; and by 1996 it was only 14%. On CBS minorities also gained steadily, to 24% of the on-screen employees in 1993, and then dropped by 1996 to only 8%. NBC, on the other end, peaked with women handling 25% of the news reporting in 1994, but slipped to only 10% by 1996. At NBC, minorities peaked at 9% in 1994 and slipped to 6% by 1996. The ABC record is best at sustaining on-air news staff, who reflect their market. Women news reporters peaked at 24% in 1995 and, in 1996, were still 23% of the total. Minorities reached a level of 12% of this staff category in 1994 and in 1996 are still at 12%.[11] Nationally, women represent 51% of the total market, and minorities (African American, Asian, Latino/a, Pacific Islander, and Native American) total about 24% of the population.[12]

Another interesting look at the overall market is to examine where the new technologies are used on a regular basis. As we move into convergence of computers and video, this will provide some sense of how quickly the entire country will buy in. In early 1997, it was reported that the New York University Taub Research Center had found that 50% of all Internet host computers in the United States are in just five states—California, Massachusetts, New York, Texas, and Virginia. Of all Internet users, 90% are in just twenty-one states, mostly on the east and west coasts and in a midwestern belt. Clearly, usage is spreading rapidly, but the numbers give a sense of how rapidly and where.

The United States is not the stereotypical demographic grouping of the postwar period familiar to older professionals in the nation's leadership positions in industry, government, and communities. It's the sixth wealthiest country in the world, with a 1993 GNP per capita of $24,750. It's much more a place called home for people from non-European backgrounds. This should be no surprise, since for over two hundred years we've been a nation of immigrants. Immigration has been our principal method of nation-building. There has been in the 1980s and 1990s some animosity toward the latest wave of newcomers. The question is, how will the media portray newcomers? Will it be inclusive and focus on those hardworking community people who are "just like us," or will it sensationalize by focusing on the smaller segments of every population group whose behavior doesn't measure up to society's expectations? Will it differentiate between poverty and criminality? Will it tell people that, statistically, the largest number of people on public welfare are white skinned? Will it ignore the subject, thinking that somehow its programs don't have underlying messages?

Every few generations, the country seems to undergo a readjustment as a response to the discontent of a significant block of the population. At those times, the democratic process is more responsive to the influence of the *vote* (i.e., the population) than it is to *money* (the influence of the wealthiest 10%.) An example is the swing of the pendulum back from the "robber baron" era at the end of the ninteenth and start of the twentieth century to the self-protective rise of labor organizers in the 1920s and 1930s. Labor became active to protect themselves against the exploitation of the worker by the robber barons. The Palmer raids, where the Attorney General arrested labor organizers as possible subversives, and the execution of Sacco and Venzetti, who were labor organizers, the force of populism became united and a more consumer-oriented era occurred in the 1930s. Then, the pendulum swung back again in the 1940s and 1950s, the war years and the prosperity following, when suburbia was created. Again, in the 1960s, a readjustment occurred. The ban-the-bomb movement of the early 1960s followed by the civil rights movement, the women's movement, and the anti-Viet Nam War movements all were the manifestation of this 1960s and 1970s "readjustment." Except for the nuclear freeze movement in the 1980s, the decades of the 1980s and 1990s can be described as a renaissance for the robber baron.

But, now, at the start of the twenty-first century, we're overdue for another such readjustment. The result will likely be a pendulum swing to a more "pro-consumer" period, during which there is some curb on benefits to those whose currency is financial campaign contributions in deference to those whose currency is votes.

It's worth examining the readjustment of the 1960s and 1970s to note what happened. The 1960s outcry had an effect on communications in that the FCC localized radio through its allocation of regional, nonmetropolitan frequencies. Before it had been mostly network based. This decision coincided perfectly with the "empowered" 1960s generation. "Drawing on their 'can-do' parents' belief that anything is possible, and driven by their own anger about shattered dreams, these young people saw no problem in recreating radio in their own image."[13]

The news and information coming out of these radio stations, the civil rights movement, and all the other consumer movements fueled each other and influenced media across the United States—both in news content and in management regulation and practice. First, outrage ultimately resulted in the sunshine laws discussed in Chapter 2. It also influenced local government officials to insist that provisions for cable public access and local access channels were written into cable franchise agreements. The timing was perfect because the first cable franchises were being awarded during this period. Further, media management across the United States for the first time focused on covering a cross-section of the American public and having the coverage done by a cross-section of Americans. The FCC required ascertainment of community needs and affirmative action plans for station license renewal, and the stations complied rather than wasting time and money on court battles. This was the period of major strides in diversity.

The 1960s and 1970s consumer movements differed from earlier movements in that they were more broadly based. The Nuclear Freeze movement in the 1980s again broadened the base for consumer movements. It provided a test run for millions of middle Americans who had never before been activists. They were motivated to action by President Reagan's statement about firing nuclear "warning shots" over Europe to let the Soviets know that we "mean business." Now a whole new generation knows how to build a national movement. Others are beginning to speak out with the environmental protection movement, tax limitation ballot initiatives, or extremist groups resorting to militias and bombings. This is middle-class discontent. It's joined by the displeasure of lower-income workers, who galvanized the U.P.S. strike to protest the failure of business to hire full-time workers, winning labor's first major victory in decades. Another parallel theme is the discontent in minority communities and among the very poor—people who think their opportunities are not equal. These protests have a common theme—threats to quality of life, anxiety about the globalization of the marketplace, and outrage about the extent to which the leaders of business and politics ignore the public good.

Overlay these reasons for unease with trends in household income, where lower-income and middle-income people have found themselves either static or losing ground. It sets the stage for the next pro-consumer swing of the pendulum.

To be sure, the discontent in the United States seems trivial when compared with the economic difficulties and political problems of people in many other parts of the world. Opportunities for even those in bad situations in the United States are so much greater than in most other parts of the world. But U.S. consumer-market expectations have always been high, as are its industry expectations. America is the place where amazing things have always been possible. What happens in the United States has often set a benchmark for global expectations. Will the remarkable opportunities coming because of the new communications technologies improve the quality of life for everyone and bring stability in the decade ahead? Or will it improve things for only a few and result in social, political, and economic instability? To be too busy, or too lazy, or too self-confident, or too insular, or too uncertain to think in proactive ways about the decade ahead is a mistake. Media access for divergent groups and diverse opinions is a crucial step toward solving problems before the level of discontent causes societal instability.

Types of News and Information

Major Television Networks

NBC

The NBC network is owned by General Electric. Its major move into the global market, at the level of the convergence of video and computers, came with the creation of MSNBC, discussed in Chapter 3. In addition, NBC has a number of global television involvements. NBC owns a majority interest in the Superchannel, a pan-European satellite service that is seen in sixty million homes in Europe. It carries a lot of NBC news programs—by and large, the same as those aired in the United States. In some cases programs are translated and efforts occur in conjunction with NBC's European bureaus, to provide some local news.

Bill Wheatley, vice president for international development at NBC, describes the company's partnership approach. "We have a long-term relationship with Nippon TV in Japan. We work with the CBC in Canada. We work with the BBC and we work with ITN in Britain. We work with a lot of people. We do work with other broadcasters, and we've met with some success in doing that. One of the great challenges ahead for everyone—to work in a way so that whether you do it yourself, or more likely, you work with partners, your programming is relevant in those countries, and that it not be news from nowhere."[14]

CBS

CBS, one of the U.S. big-three networks, is owned by Westinghouse. Its international programming is handled primarily through CBS International. According to Rainer Siek, senior vice president of CBS International,

CBI is part of CBS Enterprises, which is a division of CBS. CBS News is another division of CBS. CBI is the sales arm for all other news divisions, include CBS News. We have virtually a contract with 80% of all the European broadcasters. It's difficult to define that because of the proliferation of broadcasters in Europe at the moment. The same applies, I would say, in Asia and Central America. Apart from the news agency business—selling the raw material, we sell news programs. We sell news feeds, and we give access to our news feeds in the United States. We host foreign correspondents both at our news bureaus in New York and in Washington, and so on. Our overnight news service is "up to the minute." It is all sold in English. We do our own news gathering. We sell the pictures of CBS News. CBI doesn't do any news gathering.

The current affairs programs, *60 Minutes* and the likes, are being sold by our regional offices. The Pacific is more or less done from New York. Otherwise, we have offices in Canada, Miami, and London. They sell mostly output deals. You can either do an output deal for all current affairs programs that are on CBS network, or you do a *60 Minutes* deal where you give them access to all *60 Minutes* segments during the year for which they pay a fixed price. Or, what we've been doing recently, is to sell the format of *60 Minutes*. So in Britain, you'll have a British *60 Minutes*. You have a Russian *60 Minutes*. You have an Australian *60 Minutes*, New Zealand *60 Minutes*. They buy the clock. They buy segments from us, but they do their own segments too. When they start off they do one segment and take two from us. That's how Australia started. They started about fifteen years ago, and it's the strongest current affairs program in Australia.[15]

CBS has other partnership arrangements. As part of a news-gathering consortium in Europe, companies share ENG equipment, digital satellite channels, twenty-four-hour transponder access, and coverage.

ABC

Recently, ABC was purchased by Walt Disney. ABC's global interests include majority holdings in the ESPN sports channel, part ownership of the A&E and Lifetime cable channels, and 80% ownership of WTN, the news agency discussed in Chapter 3. It also has an exchange agreement with NHK, the state broadcaster in Japan, and with the BBC.

Richard Wald, senior vice president of ABC News, comments,

ABC is the 80% owner of WTN—one of the two major international news picture syndication systems. It's in business with roughly 1,000 foreign broadcasters. As we watch it, what works and what doesn't work, and what is valuable and what isn't, we understand how news broadcasters see the world. Everybody makes fun of the tabloidization of television network prime time news magazines. But those TV news magazines, in addition to what people point their fingers at and giggle, contain a fairly large amount of quite serious, relatively detailed, high quality news reporting that any serious journal of any kind in the United States would be happy to have. The reason for that is not because people got better, the reason for it is that that's what attracts an audience.

But you get down to the fact that there is an audience that is seriously interested in news—roughly 25% of the viewers. Over the last five years certainly, and ten years possibly, the content of news has increased. It used to be a simpler system of reporting on events. If you took a picture of the thing happening, that was a news story—not exactly as simple as taking a picture of a burning building, but quite like that. Here comes the president into the Rose Garden. There goes the president back into the White House. That was a news story. Now, you have to know something about it. You have to tell the audience something about it.

It would be totally unthinkable ten years ago to suggest that a serious news program at 11:30 at night, like ABC's *Nightline*, would challenge Johnny Carson's "The Tonight Show." But it has lasted. And Leno and Letterman are also in competition with *Nightline*. What does that mean? It means that there is an audience that is interested in serious news content.[16]

FOX

The fourth and newest major television network in the United States, Fox is only a few years old. Their twenty-four-hour news started in 1997. See Chapter 3. While a new network, Fox has done very well in the ratings, sometimes surpassing the other three major networks.

CNN

This premier cable news network is based in Atlanta. It's discussed in some detail in Chapter 3. The only note of significance at this point is that the international coverage on CNNI tends to differ from the domestic version, which has a less adequate selection of global news. It's a pity. One would think the citizenry of a superpower should be well versed on their global neighbors.

C-Span and Public Television

These are two of the best outlets for news and information in that their coverage is usually thorough. As public television's financing is limited, much of its news is really intelligent commentary. The programming quality is excellent, but they have some distance to travel before one can say that the commentary represents a real cross-section of the American public and its views. More often than not, the problem is one of elitism and "speaking for" people rather than inviting persons with diverse views to speak for themselves. Consequently the viewership is quite low.

C-Span, the American cable industry's channel providing unedited gavel-to-gavel coverage of government decision-making, was discussed in Chapter 2. C-Span's contribution to democratization is excellent and a model for the world.

Computers and News

Chapter 3 discusses the many kinds of news and information one can get on the Internet, all of which is available to Americans in their homes and to many Canadians. If there is not equipment at home, in the United States, President Clinton's program to wire every school by the turn of the century should provide access in schools and libraries. Time will still be required to conquer the learning curve.

News and information via computer have more implications than those already mentioned. For example, computers are changing political campaigns as well as campaign coverage. In 1992, millionaire independent candidate Ross Perot matched names and addresses with a demographically detailed database to identify voter interests. In addition, he used conference calls, by which as many as 30,000 voters could listen, ask questions, and use Touch-Tone pads as voting devices. The Perot events were listed on computer billboards and messages posted that bypass the national headquarters of the campaign. In 1992, the GOP began to use databases for opposition research. Then, every Friday the Bush campaign would send a video news release to over 600 locations. Candidate Clinton did an "onLine forum," answering questions on a keyboard. Experiments in using computers still leave many wondering if the new electronic order will create only the appearance of enhanced democracy, remaining as easily manipulated as traditional media.

How democratic is electronic campaigning? Teledemocracy certainly improves vertical communication, but lateral communication between voters is more difficult. Yet, that's what is crucial to the consensus building a democracy requires, by definition.

Case Studies in Democratizing Media

Boston Market

Public and Polls versus Broadcasters and Ratings

Fifteen years ago, over 41% of all American homes watched the evening news programs on the three major television networks. Today, only 26%

watch.[17] Why? The shift to cable news programs doesn't account for that large a shift. Has TV news gotten worse? Can TV news do better?

The polls do show that more people still get more of their news from TV than from other media: as reported in a recent Time/CNN poll, 59% from TV and 23% from newspapers.[18] Other studies show that people are more likely to believe TV news as the principal source of true information than to believe the church.

Viewers seem to be sending mixed signals. In a 1995 *Los Angeles Times* poll, only 17% of the public thought the media was doing good job, down from 30% a decade earlier. A principal complaint is that people think reporters "ignore common concerns and kowtow to the powerful."[19]

One reason for the problem may be that the electronic Fourth Estate has become imprisoned by the Nielsen ratings. Programs and their content—including the news—are dependent on the number of viewers Nielsen says are watching. Station operations and journalists are held hostage by these ratings reports, which determine how much stations can charge for commercial ads, the principal revenue source. At present it seems that the public and its views, as determined by the pollsters, are in one universe, while television news and its ratings determined by Nielsen are in another.

There is, nevertheless, a solution to making television news serve the "public interest, convenience, and necessity," as required by the Federal Communications Act of 1934. University students who study public and community services examined the correlation between community concerns and the topics brought by television to those same communities as news. Are broadcasters indeed isolated from those they intend to reach? What kind of TV news do people really want?

From a broadcaster's perspective, the 6:00 P.M. evening TV news is broadcast to a designated market area (DMA). This DMA includes, principally, metropolitan Boston, with some overlap into Springfield, Providence, Hartford, and Burlington. In mid 1996 this DMA included 2,171,300 households (HH). The number of households that owned TV sets numbered 2,141,400, almost 99% of the total.

Metropolitan Boston (CMSA) consists of 1,547,004 households, according to the 1990 U.S. Census. That's 71% of the households in the designated market area. The demographic characteristics of the metropolitan area provide insight into what information those of us who live here would find relevant. Most people are interested in information touching their own experience and affecting their self-interest.

Demographics and News Interests

The Boston metropolitan region grew from 1980 to 1990 to a total of 4,171,747 persons. It's a fairly well educated population. In metropolitan Boston, 82.9% of the population over twenty-five has a high school education or more. That's about 7% more of the population than a decade earlier. And 30.7% of the population has at least a bachelor's degree. That's nearly an 8% increase over the previous census. The "lowest common denominator" isn't as low as it was formerly. More people might be interested in learning all sides of a story and drawing their own conclusions, rather than being told by commentators what to think.

By and large, while the number of households in the metropolitan area is increasing, household size is shrinking, down to 2.61 persons per household. This suggests a growing interest in the availability of smaller housing units and the full range of economic, planning, development, revitalization, and regulatory dimensions associated with finding and affording appropriate housing—in the suburbs as well as the city.

The region is becoming more diverse. The most recent census indicates that the Boston metropolitan area is 89% white and 11% other racial characteristics. A decade ago we were 92% white and 8% other racial backgrounds. What's most significant here is the trends. Bear in mind that while the overall population has grown 20.9% in a decade, the number of African Americans is up 38% and the Latino/a population is up 113%. We don't have adequate 1980 figures for the Asian population to make a comparison, but in the 1990 census Asians constituted 2.8% of the region. Many of the newcomers of all racial backgrounds are from other countries. This suggests a block of viewers interested in news from abroad and, perhaps, an increased curiosity on the part of the majority population regarding why people left their native countries.

Although the percentage of individuals living below the poverty line has dropped 1.3% over a decade, the actual number of poor people has increased by 4.2%. First, the children. In metropolitan Boston, 11.2% of kids under eighteen grow up in families living below the official poverty threshold. Couple this demographic group with the significant block of middle-income households who have experienced employment downsizing. What use is it to the self-interest of persons in this situation to continually hear about the 1% of the federal budget allocated to welfare? Other things matter more. People need steady work. Often they also need child care. The result is a significant block of viewers interested in the aspects of day-care policy and community economic development that will affect their lives. And these viewers are interested in knowing the priority skills needed in today's market, in having access to potential employers, and in getting better-paying jobs. They're interested in news about higher education and financial aid. How can people create opportunities for themselves? They're interested in job market forecasts and in employer incentives to create jobs. They care about access to jobs—a topic of interest for the mass transit rider as well as for the auto commuter. Many lower- and middle-income households either don't have health care or are at risk of losing it. News about government and private-sector developments regarding access to health insurance is self-interest. News about how to voice their opinion before policy decisions are made enables people to become part of a democratic process and less bitter.

The senior citizen population in the region is growing, especially as the baby-boomers age. At present some 15.7%, over 655,000 people in the metropolitan region, are over 65. Of these, 9.4% live below the poverty line. This block of viewers cares about appropriate housing, health developments, and consumer news pertaining to living on a fixed income. They have something at stake when officials meet to set utility rates. If people knew all sides of these debates—hearing from educated consumer groups, as well as from the industry and the commentators—they might call, write, or even go to hearings about the upcoming choices in utility companies and future rate hikes. Seniors also care about accessible stores and services; they care about transportation, even pedestrian rights-of-way and time to cross streets. Knowing what Walk Boston, the advocacy organization for pedestrians, is doing could affect the day-to-day lives of lots of senior citizens.

While the median income for metropolitan Boston is somewhat higher than in the country as a whole, the gender gap remains noticeable. The median female income is only 70% of the median male income. News of importance might include examples of equity employers, court case settlements, and model solutions. For example, microbusiness opportunities can bring economic opportunity. Microbusiness involves giving small startup loans to would-be entrepreneurs. Interest rates are low and often the people who borrow also sit on the board of the trust fund that raises the money and administers the program. It's been enormously successful in ending poverty by making entrepreneurs out of people. Yet only C-Span, on January 30, 1997, covered a White House Micro-Enterprise national award program that introduced the concept by recognizing success.

There are a wide range of TV news topics that aren't offered because examining the possibilities from within the Nielsen prison doesn't provide station managers, news directors, and reporters the freedom to use statistics in a way that might increase the numbers of viewers—and station profits. Nielsen only tells who hasn't yet turned the "off" switch.

Reactions to the 6:00 P.M. News

Twenty adult university students at the University of Massachusetts College of Public and Community Service examined the news received in the Boston designated media market. They interviewed two hundred people. Most of the students have had at least a decade of experience in the workplace. Some of them hold civil servant jobs. Some have been in the military. Some have kids. A couple were grandparents returning to get college degrees. The group was mixed racially. Some lived in the city, others in suburbs. First, they watched the news every night for a week and reacted to what they saw. Then they went into selected communities to interview local people, partly residents and partly professionals.

Here are the results of the students' watching of the 6:00 P.M. news every night for a week. Observations from the group watching PBS included comments like, "I think we need more middle-class and lower-class people to voice their opinions; it's biased to hear just news reporters. There should be more diversity of races also." "There's never any humor. Life does have some humor. Also, it's mostly white men, nobody from cities, no working people, just wealthy people telling their news to each other." "It was the longest five hours in my life." The week they watched, Channel 2 (PBS) registered, according to Nielsen, 25,697 viewing households. That is 5.6% of those who watched the commercial station's national news during this time period. The PBS format allows much more in-depth reporting than the other networks. PBS could present its news in ways that close the gap between the elite and the democratic majority, thereby increasing the relevance of its news without jeopardizing the quality. Certainly, important topics like the annual review and congressional vote on the president's proposed federal budget can and should be examined from the perspective of people in different sectors of the American population. The result might be a more relevant budget for the American public on both sides of the political aisle—and an increased viewership for PBS. And sometimes humor is a marvelous tool for bringing to public awareness a problem that needs addressing. Laughing about some of the absurdities of corporate welfare and of financing American elections might at least get the topics on the table for a serious discussion. A few years ago, using humor was a technique successfully employed to overcome the taboo associated with suggesting that there was wasteful Department of Defense purchasing.

Those watching the three major networks, on channels 4, 5, and 7, had similar comments. (FOX did not have news at the time of the study.) They watched the week of the 1996 Republican National Convention and had this to say about political coverage. "The information wasn't covered objectively, as straight news. It was interpreted." "There was too much commentary and too much effort to stir up controversy over possible negative aspects of political issues." "Sometimes the TV news person failed to explain political terminology that the public has no reason to know." "They insulted working-class individuals by not covering the issues important to us. These issues include jobs, taxes, health care, education costs." "No female views were offered on the political convention."

The students looked at the time allocated to news in the news "hour." About Channel 4: "Of a sixty-minute 'news' program, only twenty-three minutes was actual news and less than that was really useful. Some of the fillers are just silly—infotainment." About Channel 5: "Ads made up 22.4% of the news hour. Weather and sports made up 7%. Any [of] the stories that got covered had only an average length of one and a half minutes each. Thirty-three percent of the news was political."

Students' thoughts on program content:

"Sometimes Channel 4 does profiles on different communities. That's good, but it needs to be done so you can see the relevance to your situation if you live in a different community. It's not easy, but it is possible." Of those viewing local news, 23%, or 96,363 households, watched Channel 4 at 6 P.M. Of those viewing national news, 21%, or 98,504 households, watched on this CBS affiliate at 7:00 P.M.

"Why did the Channel 5 news on a double murder spend so much coverage on the ramshackle house people lived in? And the local boy who won the bronze medal at the Olympics hardly got any coverage." "Channel 5 did a men's health series that was very good." Of those viewing, 44% or 179,877 households, watched local news on Channel 5. Of those viewing national news, 36%, or 167,029 households, watched this ABC affiliate at 6:30 P.M.

"The newscasters on Channel 7 talk too fast." "There's too much coverage of crime and negative things." "There should be less gruesome pictures." "Channel 7 did a good series recognizing outstanding women." "Channel 7's 'Healthcast' is great." Of those viewing local news, 32%, or 132,767 households, watched Channel 7 at 6:00 P.M. Of those viewing national news, 36%, or 164,888 households, watched this NBC affiliate at 6:30 P.M.

The group that watched CNN noted: "There was some very useful health information that we probably wouldn't get locally." "I wish the global coverage wasn't often either fast or short because I needed to know a bit more to grasp an issue and form an opinion." "I never watched world news before and I learned a lot. I thought it helped me understand people who live around me and come from other places like China or Haiti or Guatemala. I know more about them when I know this news."

During the week the students monitored the news, August 5–11, 1996, the Nielsen Trend Report showed that the total 6:00 P.M. news audience in the metropolitan Boston media market represented only about 21% of the total TV households in the designated media market (DMA). The number is somewhat lower than during the winter, and a lower number of viewers than a decade earlier. But Nielsen doesn't tell the TV broadcasters why more people don't tune in. The numbers tell only who watches and what they watch. It's not about assessing a market for the broadcasters, it's about how to sell products to the existing market. The census demographics of the region, coupled with the anecdotal comments from this class, offer a starting point for examining what it would take for more people in the region to turn on their sets for the evening news.

The students' second assignment, interviewing people in their communities validates earlier-mentioned polling data and offers more insight into the problems and opportunities facing the TV media.

Profiles of Selected Communities

Malden. Some 54,000 people live in this suburb six miles north of Boston. Elton J. Jenkins, one of the students, found that Malden is similar demographically to the metropolitan area. The metropolitan area is 89% white, and Malden is 87.9% white. Minorities, 11% of the regional population, are now 12% of Malden's population. They consist of the following demographic groups: 3,000 (5.5%) are Asian, 2,225 (4.1%) are Black, and 1,500 (2.7%) are Hispanic. Of Malden's population, 15.3% is over 65, and 15.7% of the metropolitan area is over 65. The twenty people interviewed identified their priority issues. The list included safety, health, transportation, schools, race relations, unemployment, and jobs for young people.

Each of those interviewed was asked to comment on TV news. Answers included the following: A local bank executive said, "The media only makes the news instead of reporting the news. We don't get enough information." Others indicated, "There's too much violence." "Much of the violent news we see on major news channels does not reflect my community." "Too much political back stabbing." "There's not enough follow-up in order to learn what actually happened in a story." Several noted, "TV news talks more about the bigger cities than it does the smaller communities." Another person commented about local news, "A lot of reporting is not accurate—at least about my town—maybe it's deadline rush." Elton Jenkins observed, "All the bad news is directed away from the majority population and their communities to focus on the poor or the minority population and their communities."

Interviewees in Malden were asked what they would like to see on TV news. Replies include the following: "Occasionally, tell us what is right with the world." "The real question is, would more people watch the news if it wasn't full of the violence and excitement?" "Get rid of the tabloid news." Commonly mentioned topics for more news included the environment, health coverage, solutions to pollution problems, and material useful for new immigrants needing to learn American customs.

Stoughton. A suburban town with 26,777 people, Stoughton has grown only slightly (1.2%) in the past decade, while the metropolitan area's population increased 20.9%. Stoughton has mostly a white population, but it has seen a growth in the Latino population. Michelle Grigalunas found that among the ten persons she interviewed the issues of water supply, increased traffic, open space preservation, and increased opportunities for youth were most frequently mentioned.

Comments concerning TV news included the following: "It's boring because it's repetitious." "The media doesn't cover town issues. It just covers crime in big cities." "The media makes citizens feel vulnerable."

The student interviewer asked what people wanted to see on the TV news. People replied, "News about successes and achievements, not just catastrophes." One person said, "I'd like to see crime prevention successes." Another commented, "Tell me what I need to know about politics—important issues being decided. There's too much focus on the unnecessary aspects of politics." Another person said, "World news provides us the opportunity to compare ways in which we do things with how others do things—for example, how do other people handle public safety?"

Roxbury, Dorchester, and the South End. In the 1990 census these three urban Boston neighborhoods counted 173,433 people—58,893 in Roxbury, 85,698 in Dorchester, and 28,842 in the South End. These neighborhoods of Boston house an ethnically diverse and economically diverse population. Habiba Davis comments, "My community profile differs from that of the metropolitan area because of poverty. The Roxbury community was for all intents and purposes economically abandoned." Mary Terrelonge describes it as a place where citizen advocacy has accomplished a lot. "The Roxbury Action Program (RAP) has acquired, rehabilitated and manages 115 low-income apartments where 450 people now live. RAP opened a full-service pharmacy in 1973, and in 1995 that pharmacy had $250,000 sales volume. Now RAP is working on a historical pathway to highlight historical buildings." She also pointed out that the Dudley Street Neighborhood Initiative (DSNI) has been lauded as a national model for involving communities in solving their problems, another positive occurrence in this area. Dorchester profiles describe a vibrant community of working families. The South End has experienced an influx of affluent newcomers in recent years. Mary Terrelonge, Habiba Davis, and John McCarthy interviewed a total of thirty persons. The priority issues concerning these neighborhoods include economic development, jobs, and overcoming deterrents to investment; absentee landlords; displacement caused by gentrification; crime and drugs; transportation planning—transit and highway; land use; health issues—for elders, for those with mental illness, and for those concerned about affordability; affordable housing; and day care.

When asked their opinions of what they see on the news, people had a number of observations. Habiba Davis found that "The views about desegregation have usually been presented from the point of view of the area the children were bused to—not the way desegregation impacts the community from which people come." Several respondents said, "The TV news is just negatives, and our community is not represented in a positive light by the media." "There are not enough African Americans on the TV news shown as positive role models." "The news is just a circus exploiting people." "Because the stations don't employ enough minorities, they inadvertently put forth inaccurate or insensitive coverage of minority issues." "TV news makes us out to be a community where no one would want to live." "Once in a while you get a TV news story like former U.S. Secretary of Commerce and African-American Ron Brown opening up third world business. That was good because he was a great role model."

Maria Gonsalves, an active member of the sizable Cape Verdean community, feels totally eclipsed by the news media. "There's a cruel reality of discrimination and prejudice perpetrated every day by the media, by the wealthy people against minorities, especially against immigrants." Gonsalves says, "You see people preach about human rights in other communities. You see them picket in favor of animal rights, but they forget the most elementary rights of all—respecting their neighbors, accepting cultural and linguistic differences."

A local policeman calls TV news "useless. Drugs, guns and gangs are three key issues and I'd like to know how to stop them, and how to work on ways to have people get along. TV doesn't tell me that. It just portrays the South End as a big battleground. It's not so. Why frighten people?" Another person concerned with the homeless says, "Homelessness exists year round, but it's only covered during severe winter storms. There's too much sensationalism and violence." One respondent who works with parks and recreation said, "The only time a reporter asks me to call him is when there's a murder." One respondent in Dorchester said, "TV news is not reporting the facts, it's reporting its own perceptions of the facts. The media portrays Dorchester negatively, and that's not accurate. I would love to meet someone raised in a suburb who does not have an image of Dorchester as crime ridden—an image gotten from TV news." "TV news does a grave injustice to the neighborhoods and communities of Dorchester by only reporting spectacular news like murders, rapes, drug stories. They never focus on the success stories, the efforts to end problems. They are just too repetitious and too negative."

The view of many of these respondents is best summed up by the person who said, "I just refuse to watch news that only degrades my community."

Some of those interviewed pointed out that what people in other communities see on the news matters a great deal. One respondent said, "I'm a professional who travels throughout the metropolitan area for my work. When I speak in some circles and mention that I live in Roxbury, I get a negative response. I ask people why. Their answers often relate to the negative things they have heard about my community on the news. I do not feel the TV news provides an accurate reflection of my community." Another said, "All the crime emphasis prevents economic investment and prevents local businesses from getting customers. It encourages red-lining by banks and insurers."

Those interviewed were also asked what they would want to see on the TV news. One of John McCarthy's respondents said, "Television news should cover more issues that impact the way people live and their quality of life. For example, how do other countries deal with issues of poverty? Cover volunteerism. Provide information on what people's rights are." One person commented on new immigrants and the communities that receive them: "News from countries people came from is important." Roxbury residents said, "Provide news about what proactive government action is occurring to address civic concerns. And tell what private sector efforts are occurring." "Provide news that fosters a sense of community, that promotes higher learning, that applauds the positive things that happen, that shows men being more responsible." "Tell about positive things kids are doing. Give information on working-class and minority business endeavors." "Legislators should debate controversial issues on TV news so the public can form an opinion." Many respondents shared the thoughts of the person who said, "I'd like to see things that make me proud of people's accomplishments."

Quincy. A city of 89,652 people, Quincy is about the same size as a decade earlier. Seniors are 16.2% of Quincy's population. Unemployment in the metropolitan area in 1990 was 6.4%, in Quincy it was 6.8%. The median household income in Quincy is somewhat above the metropolitan figure. Quincy's Asian population is growing very rapidly; it is 12% at present. Arvella Hagan, Patricia Downing, and Martin F. Blake interviewed a total of thirty people, who identified the following priority issues: quality of life, crime, water rates, housing for those in need, and youth. Quality of life includes livability—caring for others—citizen responsibility, community upkeep, and city beautification. Youth concerns include drugs, graffitti, and drinking.

When asked whether TV news deals with Quincy's concerns, the comments were as follows: "Too many sound-bites without any follow-up can misinform people." "The news doesn't address community interests/needs." "Environmental issues are only touched on when there is a disaster rather than covering what preventative things people are doing." "Too negative. Too repetitive." "If a family member shoots another, it's a tragedy—not a community issue. TV coverage is just sensationalism." "The news beats a story to death. Take TWA flight 800. The reporters are like vultures. They don't leave the families of the victims alone." "I particularly dislike the news because I feels it distorts." "I'd like more factual news and less commentary." A number of people shared the view of the woman who said, "We can do without scandals about political figures. I don't need to know about political figures' personal lives, and frankly I don't want to."

When people in Quincy were asked what they wanted from the TV news, they replied, "Global news is important because it can affect the local economy." "As a father I am concerned of the world news because of my children. The nuclear age, terrorism, and the unrest in different parts of the world concern me. I just don't know what's in store for my family." "I would like to see the accomplishments of people presented to everyone."

"Tensions in the Middle East affect the Jewish and the Arabic members of the community here. We all need to know what's happening."

The Merger of Global News and Local News

One unexpected finding was that Boston-area viewers want more international as well as local news. TV network managers believe that Americans aren't interested in global news. Only two of our nearly two hundred respondents commented negatively about global news. The world is more and more a global village for Boston-area Americans. The federal census tells us that our metropolitan area is increasingly diverse. We hear more foreign languages spoken. We have more work colleagues or schoolmates from other countries. Our relatives in the military are stationed in more diverse places. Our employers are engaged in more global business. We travel more to other countries. As a state representative who was interviewed said, "World news is important because it reflects the views, backgrounds, and beliefs of our diverse local population. You must know what's going on nationally and internationally because it might affect you. Boys from Squantum saw action in the Gulf War." A viewer in Lynn said, "Veterans and those in the military always want world news. It can affect their lives and that of their families." A Roslindale respondent said, "CNN had a story on welfare reform in Britain, and how the social security program is based on need and everyone who needs it gets it. We could learn from other parts of the world." It would appear that, if it wished to do so, TV news could give us global news that is useful local news.

Polling Data

"The People, The Press and Their Leaders," a 1995 survey, shows that 71% of America's opinion leaders say that the media is too focused on misdeeds and that 66% of the general public agree; 52% of views expressed on talk radio agree. However, those working in the media see it differently. Only 29% of the national press and just 18% of the local press think their coverage is too focused on misdeed negatives.[20] Another study, *Broadcasting and Cable*'s 1996 survey of TV news directors, seems to support that TV broadcasters' view of themselves differs from the public's view: 74.3% of TV news directors said they didn't think TV news was overly violent.[21]

The TV industry, in response to the rating system entrapment, focuses largely on competition among themselves. Broadcasters, isolated from their viewers and relying on a Nielsen system that doesn't ask the right questions, give their attention primarily to issues of equipment, new technologies, budgets, and hiring behind-the-camera producers. The questions aren't even asked about what new program topics for news might cause more viewers to turn on. That's ironic, considering that 73% of the TV news directors interviewed said their budgets had increased in 1996 and they expect another increase in 1997. More than one-third of the news directors have budget growth in excess of 10%. About half of the budget increases will go into facilities upgrades. There's no argument about the opportunities opening up with new technologies. But, to get a payoff on the increased budgets, TV news must get an increased portion of the potential market once the hardware is in place. The TV news directors might find themselves better positioned to compete with each other, better able to justify the benefit of expenditures on new equipment, and better staffed with behind-the-camera producers if program content were reexamined and restructured as well. If the industry weren't totally beholden to Nielsen, there might be more breathing room for the creative managers of TV news to attract some of the 74% of TV households who don't even bother to turn on TV news.

This study, involving two hundred people from parts of metropolitan Boston's designated market area, seems to indicate that national and local TV news broadcasters are out of touch with the market—sheltered by their Nielsen gatekeepers. Most of the respondents shared the view of one of Zandarina Scott's interviewees from Hyde Park. "After a long day's work, people don't want to hear just negative news. They are interested in what's going to help their community." Add to this view the sentiment of the growing senior citizen population in the region. In Lynn, Virginia Soucy was told by a professional who works with seniors, "Most elders are afraid to watch the news." In Roslindale, Eulah Rodgers was told, "I'm retired. I need to hear crime is under control and my grandchild is OK."

What can the 74% "turn-off" viewers do? As a person interviewed in Roslindale said, "We as a society should be writing station managers and demanding worthy reporting."

Some say that part of the problem is that those engaged in community activity don't know how to work with the media—how to make news gathering more manageable for people working on deadlines. The news-making community needs a better understanding of the need to tell their story within the paradigm of the classic journalistic style—who did what, when, where, and why. TV journalists frequently do not understand the relevance to the community of an issue on which they are reporting. Clearly, this gap between newsmaker and news-gatherer is exacerbated when stations and networks assign fewer people to news-gathering, because of the recently increasing media mergers and shifts in resource allocation.

In order for the TV news to be really *our* news, the industry must find a way to value public opinion as much as it does the Nielsen ratings. News about consumer issues, housing, transportation, the environment, health care, taxes, education, open space, and jobs may well be more within viewer experience, and hence of more interest to the viewer, than news about violence and political scandal. There are many untold TV news stories that affect substantial numbers of viewers, stories of importance to policy, stories with suspense, and stories with action. One can even personalize stories on these topics and can report on them in sound bites if necessary. The clock ticking down to the moment of making a critical policy decision not only brings excitement and intrigue, it also encourages involvement healthy to the preservation of a democratic society. New news, news relevant to the demographics, news that responds to the subtleties of broad-based polling, can attract some of those 74% of potential news viewers that Nielsen just crosses off.

TV news matters. It sets the tone and agenda for the metropolitan community. The perceptions broadcast on TV news become reality for many viewers. Fortunately, our society is not yet so fragmented that everyone tunes in only their niche news on the Internet. It's crucial to a healthy and democratic environment that we share, through all our news sources, some common interests and aspirations.

Minority Coverage

Principal Minority Groups

The United States, this ultimate nation built by immigrants, continues to struggle with fair representation for all its population. Perhaps the turmoil is greater because the expectations are greater. In any event, it's become part of business, political, and community affairs to be aware of "minorities." Before looking at how that affects the news and information industry, let's consider who the minorities are. What percentage of the country's total population are in this cohort? Using 1990 census data, count the 12% of the population who are African American, 9% from Latino/a heritage, 3% who are Asian, 51% who are women, and you have two-thirds of the overall population, allowing for the double counting of minorities who are also women or Latino/a counted as white. The figure would be larger if it included gays and Native Americans.

Below are a few examples of how these minority groupings and the news and information media interact, if at all.

Latino/as. Recognizing the impact this population group is beginning to have on U.S. culture, Nielsen, the television broadcaster's god, decided to pay closer attention. In 1996, Nielsen boosted the Hispanic Universe representation in its data-gathering to determine ratings. Nielsen said there was a universe of 7,510,000 Hispanic TV households in the 1996–1997 season, an increase of 300,000 over the 1995–1996 season.[22]

The 1990 U.S. Census Bureau figures show ten principal concentrations of Latino/a population in the United States. They include New York City, the second largest concentration of Latino/as, with 2.8 million Spanish-speaking residents; Chicago, with .9 million; Los Angeles, with the largest population—4.8 million Latino/a people. The third largest grouping in the country is in Miami, where 1.1 million Latino/as live. The numbers are sizeable and growing rapidly, and the population is concentrated in major media markets.

At present, major Spanish language networks reach 85–90% of these households. They brought in 750 million dollars in advertising revenues in 1993. This was a 90% increase over seven years earlier, in 1986. Imagine the growth in the next seven years.

As the dominant media realign, there's a skepticism about Spanish-language programming. Richard Wald, senior vice president of CC/ABC News, says,

> In the United States, I'm not sure there's a market for Spanish pro-gramming. Take Miami, which has a very large Cuban immigrant population, and now a lot of what you would call the hyphenates, Cuban-Americans. The Cuban émigrés come here and are interested in the good and welfare of Cuba, of the Caribbean, of the United States, of a lot of other things, and they speak Spanish. Their children are bilingual. Their grandchildren are American. Our culture is such a powerful and pervasive influence that the assimilation process works on almost everybody. It may not work on everybody, and it may be changing for all I know. Spanish-language broadcasting in this country is undoubtedly of value. The Hispanic audience is un-doubtedly a good one—economically, socially, and in every other way, but whether there is a future in Spanish-language broadcasting, I don't know.[23]

Until the civil rights movement of the 1960s, it was rare to see a black face on TV, and when one appeared it was certainly not in a position of stature. In the last twenty years, African Americans are appearing more in news programs, not only as news anchors, but as elected and appointed public officials. Still, U.S. media needs to work on overcoming the implicit "we-they" paradigm in which "we," the whites, tell the story about "them," the blacks. Such stories are usually laden with descriptions of vi-olence, drugs, and poverty. "They" are merged with a stereotype of the place called "cities." The result is the perception that cities are dangerous. Dangerous becomes synonymous with poor, which becomes synonymous with black.

The constructive contributions of African Americans are rarely paraded before the viewers—the inventors or scientists or authors or business lead-ers or astronauts or teachers. While the affirmative action efforts of the last three decades have resulted in progress, more needs to be done. Progress occurs only when people have no choice but to make a conscious effort to think differently.

The Asian community in the United States remains small but is growing very rapidly. Until quite recently, Asian Americans have been nearly invis-ible in the media. When one was seen, it was generally as a martial arts expert, a gang member, a houseboy, a greedy businessman, or an exotic and passive sex symbol. Several Asians have begun to appear as news anchors. Some news of the two-thirds of the world's population that is Asian is beginning to appear in U.S. news, but the inclusion and coverage of this segment of the population, by and large, happen without a conscious review of what reflects contemporary global society and what reflects the actual Asian population in the United States.

For some minority groups, the issue is merely an issue. But for most, the unequal treatment has a cultural base. This certainly is true when it comes to discrimination based on gender and skin color. It's so amazing that contemporary society continues practices that an anthropologist studying some ancient tribal society would clearly label as primitive. While each minority group is in a unique situation, together they represent a significant market share. Could the television market bring even more success to the industry if Nielsen gave some thought to this population diversity? Could it benefit the industry to broaden its base of market analysis beyond the retroactive approach taken by Nielsen? Could the country as a whole overcome some of its internal strife if it were mirrored by the media as a mosaic rich because of its diversity?

Alaskan Natives

The United States is more diverse than many realize. Some cultural groups are virtually invisible. Native Americans and especially Alaskan natives often fit that category. There are nearly a million residents on tribal and trust lands within the United States and more Native Americans who live outside those lands. They all have a cultural heritage different from the dominant one. Can people within the dominant culture better see their own culture when it's possible to compare it to another? Is there anything one can learn from other cultures? Should each culture be able to share its own story with others?

Look, for example, at the Alaskan natives. Alaska is an enormous state. It spreads across four time zones. Superimposed on the lower forty-eight states, it would touch South Carolina, Mexico, and Canada. When Alaska became part of the United States in 1959, the land area of the continental United States expanded by 20%—all of it in one new state. Alaska has over half of the country's coal and gold. It has the continent's largest oil field, sending 1.5 million barrels a day through 800 miles of pipe to the port at Valdez. Only 406,000 people live in Alaska. There are 33,904 miles of shore, more than in all the rest of the United States. By the middle 1700s, Russia had established regular bases for hunting in Alaska, but by the mid 1800s, Russia was having trouble in Europe and looked to sell Alaska. In 1867, Secretary of State Seward arranged for the United States to purchase this vast land for $7.2 million. It was called "Seward's Ice Box" and "Seward's Folly." After 1880, gold was discovered, and the people in the lower forty-eight states reevaluated Alaska. The state's value increased again in the eyes of the country during World War II. The United States had 140,000 troops in the Aleutian Islands to guard against any Japanese activity in the Alaskan region. To provide supplies during the war, a highway was built through Canada in 1942. In 1959, Alaska became the forty-ninth state. In 1974, the state got its first live television. Prior to that, cassettes were flown in from the lower forty-eight. Now Alaska has its own satellite, "Aurora," and every village of over 25 people has an earth station.

There are several Native American groups in Alaska. Inuits are Eskimos from the northern and western regions around Nome. Aleuts are a maritime people, largely from the Aleutians. Athabascans are the nomads in interior south-central Alaska. Yupik Eskimos populate the southwestern coastal area; in that same region, one finds Siberian Yupiks whose relatives, not so long ago, came across the Bering Sea from Russia. In addition, three Indian groupings, the Tlingit, the Haida, and the Tsimshian Indians, populate southern Alaska near Ketchikan and Juneau. This state has more Native Americans than any other, although other states, like Arizona and New Mexico, have a larger percentage of their land areas allocated as tribal lands.

Siberian Yupiks. Most Americans don't have any idea about the population of this country's northwestern-most community. Gambell, a village of 494 Siberian Yupik Eskimos, is on St. Lawrence Island just 43 miles from the coast of Siberia and one hundred fifty miles from Nome, the closest town on the American mainland. The older folks remember the shorter trip to town, a two-hour boat ride back and forth to visit relatives in Siberia, before the Cold War closed the border.

A local fisherman described life in Gambell. He said, "People start fishing in late spring. The snow begins to go in early June. They bring the fish, seals and walrus back to dry them. In winter the walrus go farther south. We also hunt reindeer. This island is 100 miles long. There's no tundra here. Just gravel. And, people shoot birds."

He points to a huge whale jawbone on the shore.

That's the mouth of a whale with the baleen sticking out. This is third one we've caught this year. The government allows us eight per year. Just one harpoon gets the whale. It goes in right place right behind the head. The men go out in walrus covered canoes. There are twenty-five boats with a long line attached to the whale and everybody pulls it in.

By October, winter comes. All winter we watch TV. In winter sunset is early. There are may be two hours of daylight. Now, in June, there's way over twenty hours of daylight. In fact, there's no sunset.

The major concerns here are that the U.S. government doesn't cut off our access to subsistence food gathering. That's how we live—not with paychecks and stores. We do carving and some of this is called endangered now. You must have a paper showing you're villager and have permission to sell the carvings. It's the only way to get cash.

We're modernized, and we all have TVs to see other cultures. Two documentaries were made on our community. They are called "At the Time of Whaling" and "Spring Ice."

Inuit Eskimos are found in Nome and Kotsebue, neighboring towns in western Alaska, but not connected by road. Diane Strickland, an Inuit resident of Nome, describes how the Eskimo community gets news and information: "We put on the Eskimo program on radio on Sunday. They do a lot of news from here, then stuff from rest of the world." Commenting on the lifestyle, she said, "There's a lot of suicides and a lot of drinking in the winter when it's dark nearly around the clock. It's good to make friends so you don't get depressed because you have someone to talk to. People here have food that they let sit for months and then they eat it. In the spring, people hunt seagull eggs. They have a tart taste. I was born here, but I lived in Pennsylvania for a few years before we came back. I do a lot of beading and my daughter is really into it too."[24]

June Wardle, a gold-miner's daughter and a member of the Nome City Council, commented on the impact that outside television has on the Alaskan villagers. "TV teaches kids violence and it scares them. Kids raised in small villages are scared of outside world."[25]

Professor Lynn Johnson, an anthropologist and the director of Chukchi College in Kotsebue, offers another view of Native American life and the media.[26] Kotsebue, where he works, is Alaska's largest Eskimo community. An ancient Eskimo trading center, it's twenty-six miles north of the Arctic Circle on Alaska's northwest coast. In 1996, the unpaved main street boasted racks with air-drying seal and salmon catches. The rooftops stored caribou antlers from past hunting expeditions. The largest business in town is the Northwest Alaska Native Association Regional Corporation (NANA). It is one of the thirteen native corporations formed in 1971 when Congress settled land claims with the Alaskan Native Americans. Kotsebue is a town is surrounded by wild-flowered tundra on spongy soil above permafrost. The seasons are June, July, August, and winter. Kotsebue is the transportation and communication hub for the region. Its land area is about the size of the state of Indiana, with a population of 6,000. None of its eleven communities are connected by a road. Everything is transmitted by boat in summer and in the rest of the year by aircraft or snow machine.

Chukchi College is one of six rural campuses attached to the University of Alaska in Fairbanks. It has three full-time faculty members plus a director and two part-timers. They offer a two-year junior college program. Lynn Johnson, the director says,

The students are 75% Alaskan natives who have little or no exposure elsewhere. They are Athabaskan, Aleut, Inuit. The thing that surprises me is how little they know about each other and virtually nothing about Native Americans in the lower forty-eight. Everything is primarily delivered through audio conferences. We also use computer light-pen set up for math—one phone line for the computer, and one for the phone. When oil was $50 a barrel, the state paid a lot of attention to these individual campuses. Now that oil profits are gone, what's left is an audio conference classroom where student scattered everywhere can be on "party-line" together.

Once the university provided a satellite feed beaming up courses from Anchorage. But, it didn't go over well because the course in English, for example, was developed for black urban students. It didn't fit. They were providing courses that didn't fit rural Alaskan Native populations. Also, they didn't provide any support for the students who had signed up for TV course. Liaison with a human is needed.

We used to have RATNET, the Rural Alaskan Television Network through the public broadcasting system. It's been defunded. A station out of Anchorage does a noon-time rural Alaska news program with a bent on rural issues. It uses tapes people send in. Occasionally Native American programming is broadcast on public television or cable in the lower forty-eight, not on the major broadcast networks. The national news is the same as it is in New Jersey. If you have cable here, as most villages do, they get 40-some stations. How relevant that is to people here depends on the individual.

If you're dealing with the main national networks their news is for them. If it's about the Exxon Valdez oil spill, it's on. In actual fact, the larger public has no idea about the cleanup because the national broadcasters are bored with it. It's only on if it will help on ratings. There's not much you can do about that. On state news, all we can get is an Anchorage station that gives mostly Anchorage city news. I find statewide news pretty poor. I'd like to see more of it and more professional coverage. For example, this year Channel 20 provided gavel-to-gavel coverage of the state legislature, but to know what was really going on was almost impossible to find out. So much is not on the floor in formal meetings. So to find out anything, you need to read the newspapers. I don't especially like the newspapers because they have political bents. But, I have to admit that their coverage is more extensive than the thirty words on TV—"The legislature met and had a wrangle about the university." So what do I know from that?

Here there's lots of use of computers. We have a new server here. Everything has to come on a satellite bounce to us. For years we only had one phone company. Internet use was impossible. Now we're getting upgraded service that should eliminate the delays.

The "have–have not" schism will grow when it comes to the new technologies. The legislature and others in universities would just as soon see these rural campuses close down. Because we have a cross-regional mission as well as our region, it's hard to count students. For example, history is taught by someone at another campus. It's taught by radio. There are seven faculty in Nome, etcetera. This is harder teaching because you don't get the body language and eye contact. You can't lecture without constant feedback on the phone. You need to know whether or not you're still "on air." The phones go out with the sun spots. For us, 95% of our courses are not here. They're on radio. Now you can get turn around on student assignments with fax machines. You can't lose two weeks of a fifteen week semester because of postal delivery. We've provided calculators which we sell to students, and if they return them they can get some money back. Most keep them. We're getting ten computers with CD-ROMS and power strips. We'll take them to the villages to teach computer skills. The biggest problem comes with teaching about the Internet when villages don't have phones. All this is hard to explain to legislators who count dollars spent per student and visualize a typical classroom. This is not your typical volume business. But, how else are people going to get the skills for future jobs and for economic growth?

People everywhere need to learn how they are linked to larger picture. We need better news for that. Anybody who doesn't think about that just has to look at the oil prices and what's happened here. People realize that the geese and ducks either go or come from somewhere. They know that the animals need a habitat down there so they can return to wherever it is one sees them. But to protect those habitats, people need to connect. It's the only way to preserve what people value.

Suzie Sun, the bilingual coordinator for KOTZ Radio, and Suzy Erlich, the general manager of the station, discussed their efforts to provide their Inuit community with news and information.[27] Suzie Sun is from a little village about 160 miles north of Kotzebue:

I do my own local news when they call it in. I do it in my language
for the elders. I translate news from across the state and from the
lower forty-eight when it's important for them to hear it. We broadcast for the City of Kotzebue's three thousand residents and for the
twelve villages of the NANA region.

People want to hear about subsistence. We live on whaling and
fishing and hunting caribou. We rely on wild berries. Land use and
water access matter. And people want to hear what's going on with
city people. Probably most interesting is what's happening with the
president, and news from Juneau. There's big interest in international
news with young people—like war, and what other people do. We
don't get news from Russia. But people come now because we're so
close. I think they'll come again for the Fourth of July festivities.

Suzy Erlich continues,

News from outside is fairly new to this part of the United States.
When President Nixon resigned in 1972, we didn't know it until two
weeks later. We don't identify with many of the issues in the national
news. We get excited when it will have a direct impact on us. For
example, we care a lot about the court cases on fishing—commerce
and subsistence. That's a high priority here. The U.S. government
assumes the responsibility for subsistence, having taken that away
from the state, and that's real important. We care about the Anchorage forest fires because we get many tundra fires in the summertime.
We want to know how dry it is and whether the villages are in danger.
The presidential race has little impact except that we turn out to vote.

As far as I can determine, the international news that's of interest
is when it's about circumpolar areas, environmental concerns. When
things happen in Russia—an oil spill, or an accident like the Cher-
nobyl nuclear reactor accident, it sparks an interest here. When the
Canadians and Greenlandics have a spat over whaling, people get
really interested here. A change in who's the president of France is of
no interest up here.

We are close neighbors to Russia. We've had cultural exchanges.
But in terms of news, it's a vacuum unless someone comes over and
decides to tell us what's happening. I've talked with someone over
there about formalizing something—not news so much as more cultural programming. He's working out of Magadan in Siberia, and he
gets frustrated because the system there is very cumbersome. He keeps
calling me to ask if someone has contacted me. No one ever does. He
never gives me any resources. So it's slow.

Regarding getting news from here out to the rest of the world, the
fax is great. I get things from elsewhere, and I spend lots of money

on fax paper to get things no one pays attention to. The news has to be about what people care about. We get our Inuit news out through the Native American Network. There's something called Native America call-in and National Native News on the AP wire. Whoever wants it can pick it up.

Until we join the mainstream, news will always play second fiddle unless we want to join the United States, as you say. That may never happen, because by choice, I think, we want to remain different. Our values are so very different than the western culture. These attitudes aren't just held by the older generation. They're held by the young too. Of course, there are larger world news issues that affect us. For example, will the Native American communities have access to their air space?

In 1996, in Anchorage a third public radio station was launched—the first native-run station based in an urban area. KNBA is operated by the Koahnic Broadcasting Corporation. That's Athabascan for "live air." There are 20,000 natives of many tribes in the city of Anchorage. The station carries music, youth talking-circles, words from various villages, and Native American news from across the United States. The station also trains native journalists. Alaska natives are 17% of the state population but only 8% of the state's journalists, says a spokeperson for KBNA.

Summary

In some respects, we are together as one country, indivisible, because the national news and information broadcasters have provided homogeneous news and information, broadcast to everyone, with a selected standard acceptable to the people making the broadcasting decisions—their racial and ethnic views, their economic and political views, and their social and ethical standards. Mostly, the news has been about the economic and political decisions that might advance or destabilize the powerful. A lot is omitted. Within those constraints, Americans have gotten more objective, less biased, less censored news than have people in many parts of the world.

At the same time, the dynamic in the United States is to constantly question. Except when this questioning turns to outright cynicism, the practice makes it possible for the nation's institutions to continuously seek to improve themselves—or to be improved by others. Nancy Woodhull, executive director of the Media Studies Center, articulates a current criticism. "We don't have an information explosion because people want more information. We have an information explosion because of the invention of technology that can bring everything to us in a second."[28] Are we becoming better informed for some useful purpose, or are we just overwhelmed? It is said that we overdo the trivial, which may cause a shrinking interest in news among young people—the ones who may need news and information to hold the social and economic fabric together.

Lots of people get left out of American news. Their voice is heard only in the alternative stations. Their contributions to and benefits from the larger economic and social community are forgotten, too. This omission creates anger and cynicism. It gives birth to militia movements and other extremist activity. That's the profile of the two media worlds on a national scale.

What happens as we move into an international arena and some are included and others are excluded? The stakes will escalate with the power of those excluded. For example, with the coming of global superstations like Murdoch's A-Sky-B, will those in the United States who formerly found themselves representing the dominant media—those bothered by the outcries for inclusion—now find themselves singing the song of the marginalized? The question here is not only how democratization can occur for people in the many regions of the United States, but how a news and information delivery of the future can protect those free exchanges of information, the liberties and rights that people in the United States tout and enjoy so much more than the rest of the world.

The technologies that make superstations possible also make it possible to rationalize exclusion by lauding the opportunities for "narrowcasting." Perhaps the words of President Clinton in his 1997 inaugural speech summarize not only the fabric of American society at this point in history but also the problem that narrowcasting can create. "We must find ways to come together or we will surely come apart."

This holds true for access to TV news and information as well as for the Internet. TV provides universal service, although there is still work to be done on content. For the Internet, the challenge is, will there be universal service? At present, those involved are haggling over the costs of "wiring" the nation. Some think the cost will be offset by future business markets. Others think that if schools, libraries, rural health clinics, and the like are wired, then they, the haves, will simply end up paying for someone else, the have-nots.

Vice President Al Gore set the tone for the debate in a 1993 National Press Club speech. "If we allow the information superhighway to bypass the less fortunate sections of our society, we will find the information rich getting richer while the information poor get poorer."

LATIN AMERICA

Overview

Central and South America have a different culture from Canada and the United States only because in the colonial era the Spanish and the Portuguese invaders arrived rather than the English and French. However, the media, especially television, has conquered and promises a more lasting impact than anything the Spanish or Portuguese did.

Latin America is home to more than 400 million people. Two-thirds speak Spanish, but one-third—over 120 million Brazilians—speak Portuguese. In Mexico, Guatemala, Ecuador, Peru, Bolivia, and Paraguay, there are fifteen million Indians who speak their native languages. In Brazil there are more television sets than refrigerators. In Argentina more people subscribe to cable than have telephones. Never underestimate the power of the little box in the living room.

The television industry is growing at an amazing pace, both in terms of consumer use and in terms of the local industry. In Mexico, Argentina, and Brazil, especially, the communications industry's offerings can match the best anywhere in the world. They use the full range of technologies available, are sophisticated, well-financed operations. As things evolve, many local stations find themselves competing with cable and satellite superchannels. Other local communication groups like Televisa in Mexico, Clarin in Argentina, and Globo of Brazil have expanded themselves and signed onto joint ventures. No doubt, the benefits for the affluent and the growing middle class are increasing in many ways. Yet, many poorer people don't feel the benefits; even those more affluent, with media access, find that their news and information don't reach the global mainstream, defined by the Europeans and North Americans. In the words of Enrique Diaz Arboleya, an Argentine traveling in the United States, "At home we get CNN, a Mexican channel, Globo from Brazil, other news and information from the United States and Spain, Italy, Germany, and Israel. But here, in the United States, it is impossible to get news about Argentina. We must telephone home to learn what's happening. I think people in the United States should see more about Argentina."[29]

Perceptions of Latin America, from a U.S. perspective, tend to evolve around images of drug lords, corruption, poverty, and crime. Unfortunately, perception becomes confused with reality. From the dominant media, it would be difficult to tell that, in most respects, Latin America is very much like any other place in the world. It has creative people working in a full range of professions, lovely places to visit—in cities and in the countryside. It also has a serious rich-poor gap that threatens to destabilize the economic prosperity of those who do well, a rich-poor gap considerably more severe than that found in the United States or much of Europe.

Jeff Herman Gutierez from Costa Rica had two radio programs in his home country before he went to the United States.[30] He commented on how news and information dissemination works in his country. He says that those in power don't stop the rain forest clearing partly because they don't bother to find out how bad it is. The president's data on the rain forest is out of date. The parking-lot attendant next to the rain forest access road knows far better just by counting the trucks that go by. He refers to the prominent South American educator Paulo Freire, who blamed the problems of society on the lethargy of the general population. Herman comments about the media. "Ninety-nine percent of the potential journalists aren't allowed to write because they can't get a license without a college degree in journalism—an unrealistic criterion." Even those with a license must watch what they do. He cites a case of a reporter questioning the president who got fired because of his questions. He expresses further outrage that free speech is blocked if it doesn't fit establishment interests. He cites as an example that, in 1997, when the Nobel Prize winner and former president of Costa Rica Oscar Arias tried to organize a demonstration against visiting U.S. President Clinton, who planned to lift the embargo on weapon sales to Latin America, the current government of Costa Rica made it illegal to demonstrate. Consequently, he says, the press and the public don't know about this decision made on behalf of the international weapon dealers.

In the 1990s many countries of Latin America have emerged from their period of dictatorship and are living in a fragile state of democratic development. The transition is not easy, especially in the area of free speech. In many ways, from many parts of Latin America, the matter of free press and safety for journalists continues to be a top agenda item. For example, the *Bolivian Times* in June 1997 reported that 392 journalists had been killed in Latin America since 1970.[31] Another 150 had disappeared. Mexico and Colombia had the highest number of deaths in 1990 and 1991 respectively. "If you want to stay on the air, you had better be prepared to censor yourself," commented a spokesman for the Inter-American Press Association (IAPA). The IAPA had recently concluded its conference to lobby for Latin American press freedoms, for journalist security, and for abandoning the laws of former dictators that remain in effect.

Nonetheless, it's a promising era in Latin America. The movements toward democratization are stronger than in the past—even though there's a long way to go. Economic opportunity is improving. But the rich-poor gap remains enormous.

For example, there's a much touted economic recovery and job creation. At the same time, one in five families have incomes too low to feed themselves adequately.[32]

Communications Technology

Fiber Optics

Some 7,300 kilometers of fiber optic cable, buried in the ocean floor, link South America and the Caribbean with the rest of the world. It is to be operational by the Fall of 1998. This Pan-American cable system runs down the Pacific coast, connecting Chile, Peru, Ecuador, Colombia, and Panama. Then it cuts across the Caribbean past Venezuela and Aruba to the United States. Argentina and Bolivia will connect over land. Telefonica Peru will manage the system. Once in service the quality of phone service will improve immediately. Many more radio and TV stations will become available. The time required for Internet connection will be cut dramatically. At present, poor phone connections leave many either without phones or with very poor connections. Where possible, those who can afford it resort to cell phones to bypass poor-quality phone lines. Of course, this situation makes it extremely difficult to get reliable Internet services in many locations.

Global TV

Latin American media companies are exporting their product across the Spanish-speaking world. Profits have been significant in recent years. The five major television producers grossed revenues of more than six billion dollars in 1996, an impressive sum for a new market!

"Latin America is getting more attention from foreign global marketers. Economic stability, fewer trade barriers and growing consumer markets are the main lures."[33] While there are several participants in this media market, the most aggressive is Rupert Murdoch.

Murdoch

News Corp., with help from its U.S. network, Fox TV, opened a Spanish version of Fox. In addition, in November 1995 Murdoch announced a joint venture between News Corp, Televisa of Mexico, Organizacoes Globo of Brazil, and Tele-Communications International, Inc., a U.S. company that builds cable service systems. The service began with one million cable subscribers. By 1999, they expect to serve three million, and in the future, they expect to serve 10% of Latin America. The deal is that Globo will get a larger percentage of the profits from Brazil and that Murdoch will take his profits from the rest of Latin America. The bottom line is that while the local companies benefit from the mergers, local markets lose control over their product, thereby making broadcaster and consumer alike increasingly dependent upon Murdoch.

CBS

In June 1996 Westinghouse, the owner of the U.S.-based CBS network, bought TeleNoticias, the cable channel previously owned by Telemundo, Reuters, and two Latin partners—Artear in Argentina and a Mexican consortium.[34] This twenty-four-hour Spanish-language news service is available for cable systems reaching over 20 million homes in the United States, Spain, and Latin America. Telenoticias has been based in Miami—as much a Latin city as a North American city. Expansion in the U.S. Latino/a market was one reason for the purchase.

DirecTV

Other kinds of companies are entering the Latin market. For example, DirecTV, the provider of satellite Direct to Home TV or DTH TV, entered Latin America in 1997. The company is betting on being in the right place at the right time. Their product is home satellite systems through which other companies' programming is offered. It's an alternative to cable.

NBC

In March 1993, the U.S. network NBC launched a Latin American satellite service, Canal de Noticias, which broadcasts for twenty-four hours a day in Spanish and in some countries has local news.[35] The service is seen in a number of countries in Latin America with news from throughout the world. The special emphasis is the Americas. It's prepared by NBC, New York.

CNN, Reuters, and Others

Scores of other corporate transactions are occurring regularly in this volatile period, all intended to capitalize on the emerging Latin American television market. The flagship of global news and information, CNN, began its regular Spanish-language service in January 1997. It has been in Latin America for some years, but in English. Reuters, as a print news agency, has been in Latin America for decades. The company promoted Enrique Jara, a South American, to be its first director of television at its London headquarters. Reuters has played an important role in the development of TeleNotecias and continues to be an important player in South American news-gathering. In 1996 CBS purchased TeleNoticias. The Hughes Company, a U.S. communications corporation, TVA in Brazil, Cisneros Venevision from Argentina, and Vargas MVS Multivision are just a few of the others to watch.

The Internet

The Internet began mainstream use in Latin America in 1994. In the first two years, use in Argentina grew 419%, in Peru 171%, in Venezuela 65%, and in Mexico 48%.[36] It's growing very rapidly, but the overall number of users remains small. A major impetus for this sudden growth was the 1994 Summit of the Americas, focusing on telecommunications and information infrastructure.[37]

A huge number of Internet sites are available for access to information on various aspects of Latin America. This certainly increases the opportunity for people from across the world to gain information. For ongoing updates on this topic and how it's affecting Latin America, there are a number of Web sites available. For example, <www.dbsdish.com> and <www.panamsat> provide satellite information. For material on how indigenous peoples are surviving the cultural, economic, and environmental impacts of the late twentieth century, try <www.halcyon.com/FWDP/ fwdp.html>. Examine the World Bank site for information on the wealth-poverty gap in Latin America, at <www.worldbank.org>.

Regional Giants

Mexico

Within Mexico, 85.4% of the households have television. That's 14,738,000 households; 13.3% have pay TV. Mexico has two government television stations and two private ones—Grupo Televisa and TV Azteca. The trend is to encourage private stations.

Grupo Televisa, the largest communications company in Latin America, serves Mexico, and it exports throughout the Spanish world. Televisa, at <www.televisa.com>, is the world's most prolific producer of Spanish programs and the region's largest entertainment conglomerate. Televisa's four networks have 80% of Mexican business. In 1995, they joined forces with Murdoch's consortium, mentioned above, to launch and operate the direct-to-home (DTH) service for Latin America, the Caribbean, and Spanish-speaking audiences in the United States and southern Canada. Murdoch's involvement provided an opportunity to expand that wouldn't have been possible without his investment. In addition, through Televisa's majority-owned subsidiary, Cablevision, S.A., Televisa operates the largest and most important cable system in Mexico. In 1997, it had approximately 200,000 subscriber households. It carries CNN and a range of other global offerings.[38] They also produce their own news programming.

As Jim Williams, vice president of APTV, states, " 'Televisa' in Mexico City spends more money covering international news than anybody in the world. They're a major player."[39]

Grupo Televisa has interests in television production, broadcasting and international program distribution, direct to home satellite services, publishing, music recording, radio production and broadcasting, cable television, professional sports and show business promotion, paging services, outdoor advertising, and feature film production and distribution and dubbing. It has substantial equity in Univision in the United States and in PANAMSAT, the first private sector company providing satellite services. It distributes programming in Mexico and to 58 million Spanish-speaking households in ninety-eight countries. It operates a school for acting, technical training, writing, directing, and related skills needed in the profession.

Televisa's news comes through ECO, the twenty-four-hour news and entertainment service of the conglomerate. It offers programs by satellite to audiences in over eighty countries on four continents, employing over 200 correspondents across the globe. ECO is a pioneer in global Spanish-language news distribution. The U.K./U.S. global broadcasters tend to compliment ECO for fine programming, but they caution that the Mexican government is sometimes heavy-handed, giving too much of a Mexican establishment slant. They give as an example an incident that occurred during the 1993 debate about the North American Free Trade Agreement (NAFTA). Before the NAFTA vote, a live production on ECO featured four panelists answering questions from U.S. senators. All four were against NAFTA; they were cut off the air—poof! The Mexican government didn't want problems for NAFTA. ECO's bias isn't unique. One must bear in mind that, although more debate is allowed in the U.S. media, there are also times in the states when value judgments are made regarding how many opinions will be heard.

On its own merit, ECO has recently launched several news innovations. Among them, *Detras de la Noticia* is a program providing in-depth investigation into national, cultural, and political issues of the day. *Punto por Punto* is a new program targeting young entrepreneurs, professionals, and students. It includes news forecasts and segments on computer technology, economics, marketing, politics, and environmental and social coverage.

With a decade of experience by 1996, Televisa is more established than many and certainly a power in the region. It invests heavily in its news programming.

Cable is the fastest growing segment of Mexican telecommunications. With nine out of every ten Mexican households having TV sets, even though less than 20% of them subscribe to cable, there's a significant number of potential subscribers—one and one-half million. Two private subscription services lead the Mexican cable industry—Televisa's Cablevision and MVS Multivision. MVS Multivision is the wireless pay-TV leader with twenty-three channels. Competition is fierce, and marketing is clever. To appeal to audiences, Televisa has its own version of MTV called "Telehit," a twenty-four-hour music channel that sends out two trucks called "Rolling TV." They promote the cable service and enable the public to see entertainers live. Televisa also produced a 1996 "Chiapas Fair" with conferences on medicine and journalism and a "Festival Indigena" as part of this fair, an opportunity for local leaders in Chiapas to participate.

As indicated, Mexico actively exports its television products. The largest export company in Latin America, Protele, is here. In 1996, Protele indicated sales of over 95 million dollars. The company distributes over two new satellites, SOLIDARIDAD I and II. These birds have three times the capacity previously available. They cover the southern United States, the Caribbean, and South America.

Brazil

In this country of 155 million people, 120 million live within reach of television. To understand the power of the picture, consider that 21% of the population is illiterate and has moved from an oral culture to a visual one without ever having passed through the stage of a written culture. The question is, does this make people unduly susceptible to what they see, without any interpretation and analysis of the material presented?

Government in the past protected-subsidized-controlled—pick your word—the media. "Brazilian businesses have long enjoyed official aid and comfort in making everything from canned goods to computers. Television was equally coddled. Backed by constitutional bans against outsiders, the central government controlled the domestic broadcast market and restricted the number of TV concessions."[40] Brazil is Latin America's largest country. Its media industry has made impressive accomplishments. For over a decade, it has had its own satellite, BRAZILSAT, launched in 1986 to supplement the services available through PANAMSAT and INTELSAT.

Organizacoes Globo is the fourth largest privately owned television network in the world. It dominates the Brazilian market. Television in Brazil is owned by fewer than ten families. Globo's prosperity is due, in large part, to its close relationship to government. Globo exports 80% of its product throughout Latin America and Portugal. The rest is sent worldwide. In November 1995, Globo signed the above-mentioned agreement with Rupert Murdoch, TCI, and Televisa of Mexico to develop and operate a direct-to-home satellite service for entire Latin American region. Pay TV is growing fast. Already there are more television sets than telephones. There is one TV set for every four people, and one phone for every eleven people. There's every reason to believe that enough people can and will buy pay TV to make big profits.

The news and information produced in Brazil tend to have a flamboyant style, frequently showing pictures that wouldn't be on screen in the United States.[41] One show, *Aqui Agora*, Portuguese for "Here and Now," provides one example of aggressive journalism in Latin America. The show started in 1991. Boris Casoy, the anchor, listens to local residents complain about the police, the government, politicians, and businessmen. Then, he takes these citizens to an offender's office or home for an on-camera confrontation. The show is seen on the STB Network. This style of news and information provides a kind of "anecdotal democratization." It's effective in drawing viewers and, no doubt, brings action to redress some grievances. It's not clear that it has any major effect on lasting democratization.

Argentina

Things changed very rapidly in Argentina after the country lost the Falkland Islands War in 1982. This war between Britain and Argentina over a few small islands in the Atlantic Ocean had a disproportionate impact on global affairs. For the telecommunications industry, it was Ted Turner's opportunity to showcase live TV—a new and relatively unheard-of possibility. For the industrialized nations, it was a chance to showcase "smart" weapons with guidance systems that demonstrated that wars of the future will never be the way we think of war. For Argentina, it marked the end of an era of dictatorship.

U.S. Foreign Service Information Officer Melissa Ford, who was stationed with the embassy in Buenos Aires, observed,

> After the Falkland debacle, Argentina elected a democratic government and the military faded into the background. The system change meant that there were no laws on broadcasting and licensing so all over the country little tiny broadcasting and cable stations popped up. There were over 1,000 by the time I was there in the early 1990s. Little stations—40 people maybe. When I left, one person who had the second largest cable company in Argentina had sold 80% of it to TCI in the United States for a half billion dollars and still retained 20% ownership. You could tell that once the telephone hook-ups were in place, Argentina would move quickly to get on the information highway—just based on what was happening with cable. Regulation wasn't hampering private investment growth.
>
> Also there were eight to ten daily papers in Buenos Aires alone. They really had a spectrum and really revelled in their new "press freedom." We'd keep asking if they checked their sources. But, it was a time for having lots of fun. The government was still trying to put libel laws in place. Also there were many radio stations offering a very dynamic way to get information out.[42]

With the exception of the poorly programmed government station holdover from the pre-1982 dictatorship era, all television stations have private ownership. In this period, cable television growth went from 3% subscribership in 1987 to 51% in 1995. There were eight large cable companies, but after the 1995 consolidation and sales, TCI International, the U.S. company, became a 51% partner controlling Cablevision. University of Buenos Aires Professor Nora Mazziotti notes, "In 1996, 50% of homes here have phones and 52% have cable subscriptions. We're one of the most cabled countries in the world. In relation to the size of our population, we're first in the world."[43] Cable is, at present, far more important than direct-to-home satellite.

Grupo Clarin began with the founding of a daily newspaper in 1945.[44] After democratic institutions reappeared and legal obstacles lessened in the 1980s, Clarin grew into Argentina's largest communications group. This highly respected enterprise owns the principal newspaper with six million readers on Sundays, and it publishes a number of other publications and has expanded into radio and television. It has rapidly incorporated the new technologies into its offerings. In 1995 Clarin celebrated its fiftieth anniversary by publishing a special edition on CD-ROM, accessible through the Internet at <http://www.intr.net/clarin/>. In 1996, it published, in conjunction with Radio Mitre and Channel 13, a CD-ROM called "Digital Memory," updating outstanding current events. The user can interact to compare, replay, or add one's own ideas. The Clarin Web page is at <http://www.clarin.com.ar>.

Artear S.A., or Arte Radiotelevision Argentino S.A., began in 1989 as the entity coordinating Clarin's television and audiovisual productions. It operates Channel 13. Contact <http://www.webtv.artear.com>. Since 1993, Todo Noticias, an information signal for cable channels, began operating twenty-four hours a day. That year, Artear also launched a cable signal offering classic films.

In 1992, Clarin created Multicanal, a cable television venture that by 1995 was the leader in Argentine cable with over 800,000 subscribers (see Table 4.2). Clarin purchased production studios for cable and Channel 13 use in 1994 and equipped them with the latest in high-tech equipment. Clarin operates a number of other communications enterprises plus a foundation supporting a range of educational, cultural, and information services.

Beginning in 1994, Telefe began exporting Argentine television. In just three short years, Telefe developed a market of over 50 countries—not for news export, but for novels, comedies, and documentaries. Knowledge of Spanish wasn't essential to purchase these entertainment programs. News is another matter.

A hot issue in Argentina is telephony. Fiber optic is being installed with expectations for expanding the use of telephones. In October 1996, "Infovia" came to Argentina, making it technically possible for one to access the Internet without a subscription. There remain a number of problems in practical use of the Internet. In some places, the phone system requires operator callback for long distance. It's not uncommon for there to be many phone failures in bad weather. Even in Buenos Aires, where the access is best, the view of young computer professional, Daniel Blumenfeld, is shared by many. "If I subscribe at home to the Internet, my telephone bill will increase considerably since I'm charged by time on the line. Plus, subscribing to an Internet service provider will be expensive. It's just not practical to do yet."[45]

Change is happening rapidly in Argentina's young democracy. While Clarin has definitely emerged as the industry giant, even advocates for the disenfranchised think that Clarin's agenda-setting editorial policies are fairer than those of its competition. For example, Richard Freeman, a researcher from the University of Chicago who lived for a year in Buenos

Table 4.2
Multicanal Cable TV Programming in Argentina

1 - America	36 - CNN International
2 - Tele Musica	37 - MTV
3 - Much Music	38- The Box
4 - Nickelodeon	39 - Solo Tango
5 - Magazine 24	6 AM to Midnight
6 - ATC	39 - Venus
7 - Manchete (Desde Brasil)	Midnight to 6 AM
Midnight to 6 PM	40 - GEMS
7- Rai (Desde Italia)	41 - 26 TV
6 PM to Midnight	42 - Utilisima
8 - Canal 9 Libertad	43 - TVE (Desde Espana)
9 - Metro	44 - Discovery
10 -Telefe	45 - Infinito
11 - Multicanal A	46 - El Canal de la Mujer
12 - Canal 13	47 - Cable Salud
14 - Todo Noticias	48 - Big Channel
15 - TYC Sports	11 AM to 8 PM
16 - Multideporte	49 - Canal Rural
17 - ESPN	50 - O'Globo (Desde Brasil)
18 - Magic Kids	51 - TVS (Desde Montreal)
19 - Space	52 - TV Chile (Desde Chile)
20 - Cinemax	53 - El Canal de la Estrellas
21 - Cinecanal	54 - Deutsche Welle (Germany)
22 - I-SAT	55 - Siempre Mujer
23 - HBO Ole	56 - Travel Channel
24 - Volver (Nostalgico)	57 - Eco Noticias
25 - USA Network	58 - CVN
26 - Fox	58 - La Bolsa en Directo
27 - Uniseries	12 noon to 5 PM
28 - Tele Uno	59 - Alef Network (Jewish Culture)
29 - TNT	60 - TV Quality
30 - Sony	61 - 365 Cine
31 - Telenoticias	62 - TV Universidad Catolica
32 - Antena 3 (Desde Espana)	63 - CV-SAT
33 - Cablin (Program Infantil)	64 - CNN en Espanol
34 - Cartoon Network	65 - TVA
35 - The Warner Channel (Infantil)	

Source: The Clarin Publishing Group, Buenos Aires. <*http://www.multicanal.com.ar/*>

Aires, noted, "Last week there was a big march in front of Parliament. It consisted of 15,000 students and members of the teachers' unions demanding that there be a higher budget for education. It's related to the hunger strike you see in the large tent by the Parliament Building. The entire event was peaceful except that at the end a handful of kids started throwing rocks at the police. The same thing happens at a football game. In the media coverage, Clarin showed pictures of everyone gathered peacefully, and on later pages showed the kids disturbing the event. The other media capitalized on the sensational, at the expense of the truth. They showed only the kids throwing rocks."[46]

The fragility and vitality of a young democracy are evident in the demonstrations and the ever present handbills, and also in the outrage over the killing of a journalist who was pulled from his car in early June 1997. The industry's growth benefits more in this country, with its larger middle class, than in countries of South America where a larger segment of the population are "indigenous" and discriminated against. However, union-management disputes serve as a reminder that stability has not yet been realized.

The prognosis remains optimistic, however. As retired civil engineer Jose Blumenfeld said, "The loss of the 1982 Falkland Islands war caused a lasting shift in things in Argentina. People went from 'the government must' to 'we are the government.' They began to take responsibility. The problem still is institutions. Courts work very poorly. So, the people look to the media, not the courts."[47]

Selected National Developments

Venezuela

Of all households in Venezuela, 89% have television sets. Of these 3.9 million TV households, slightly over 10% had cable in 1994. Until the 1980s, Venezuela was economically better off than most of the rest of Latin America and consequently had a viable economic base for industry growth. Supercable in Venezuela was the first company in Latin America to install fiber optic. The difficulties of installing fiber optic in a country with rugged terrain was expected to pay off with enormous growth in pay TV. Projections expect a doubling of subscriptions in just three years, resulting in a half million subscribing households by 1998. While direct-to-home satellite has not been as common, this part of the industry is expected to grow. Since 1994, when 3.6% of households had direct-to-home satellite, changes have occurred in building practices. Now, most new buildings are built with dishes. The big parabolic dishes of a few years ago can now be replaced with the smaller ones offered by the DBS companies.

The two national channels are Omnivision (NCTV) and Venevision

(RCTV), at <*www.venevision.com*>. Venevision is a well-established television company with a good reputation. Long before the current global broadcasting era, Venevision had an exchange agreement with ABC in the United States.

For the Internet to flourish in Venezuela, telephone service will have to improve. Not only are there problems with the lines, but it takes several months of waiting to get a line—and that's for an executive in the telephone company.

Colombia

There are three government-owned and -operated television channels in Colombia. In addition, there are eight companies providing cable. Most programming is of Colombian origin. Programmers bid for time slots. A lot is imported, much from the United States. Within Colombia, there's an active telenovela production business. A considerable amount of programming space is allocated to education.

This country has a literacy rate of 88%; it has 7,029,000 TV households, 99% of all households. Only 4% of households have pay TV via cable, all of which is in major cities; but 16% have direct-to-home satellite television, an appealing alternative because it has more programming options.

Chile

Some 72% of Chile's households have television sets. There are eleven channels in Chile, but only three have a national market. Some forty cable companies have established themselves in the early 1990s, but this mountainous country is difficult to wire. In 1997, direct-to-home satellite television arrived via PANAMSAT (PAS-3), Hughes Communication (HIC), and INTELSAT serving the Southern Cone Region.

Chile remains a country with serious human rights violations, a place where telephones are scarce.

Other Countries

In Paraguay, Uruguay, Ecuador, Bolivia, Costa Rica, Cuba, and Puerto Rico, television is very popular. In the more affluent areas of these countries, cable or satellite TV exists. In Cuba, so far, politics have prevented such foreign intrusion. In all of these countries, telephone lines tend to be more scarce than television sets. For example, in Paraguay, there are 16 lines per 1,000 people. Each country varies economically and politically, but by and large, democratization is beginning and the market for transnational television is growing. With this will come more transnational news and information to supplement the local offerings. All these countries still face enormous poverty problems.

Case Studies in Democratizing Media

As indicated earlier in this chapter, democratizing government and inaugurating free speech are inevitably complicated—both in lawmaking and in practice. Many of Latin America's terrestrial broadcasters live with some level of political censorship. There are twenty-three major countries in the region. Of these, only five are said to enjoy relatively full press freedom—Costa Rica, Colombia, Venezuela, Jamaica, and Trinidad.[48] Twelve have had serious censorship—Cuba, Haiti, Guatemala, El Salvador, Honduras, Nicaragua, Guyana, Bolivia, Chile, Argentina, Uruguay, and Paraguay. Others have considerable press freedom—Mexico, Peru, Brazil, Ecuador, and the Dominican Republic. But nothing is ever constant. For example, in the late 1990s, Guatemala's government has become more tolerant, as has Paraguay's government. On the other hand, Bolivia, where for a short time things improved, may now be regressing. In the region, there has been an international news tradition even in places with censorship, enabling reporters to get political and economic stories for global consumption. Look at the following two case studies highlighting the impact of the media on democratization.

Bolivia

In Bolivia, 1997 was a watershed year. President Gonzalo Sanchez de Lozada ran against former president Jaime Paz Zamora and former dictator General Hugo Banzar Suarez in the national election. Also running was Remedios Loza, an Aymara Indian woman talk-show host. She broke new ground in many ways. Nonetheless, Banzar, the seventy-one-year-old head of the Conservative Nationalist Democratic Action Party, won.

Bolivia has just elected the former dictator, who had previously been thrown out of office. They elected a so-called democrat, under whose previous tenure those who disputed his views just "disappeared," never to be seen again.

This spectacular country in the Andes Alta Plano is a study in extremes. The institutions of power and affluence use multipoint, multichannel microwave distribution system (MMDS) technology to bring pay television to 18,000 households. This MMDS can transmit a satellite feed as "wireless cable." This luxury is for only a small portion of the two-tiered economy, where the minimum wage is 205 Bolivianos, or $39 U.S. per month. The more fortunate Aymaras live in modest communities like Ciudad Satellite, where homes are comfortable, kids are loved, and the necessities of life are provided. To be sure, almost everyone has a TV, maybe a VCR, and the kids can even find video games. Even in places like Ciudad Satellite, not to mention the really poor communities and the rural areas, the country's 60% indigenous Indian population has limited opportunity in contrast to the lives of those supporting the transnational economy found in Santa Cruz and in La Paz high-rises.

In this climate, one man took it upon himself to meet the needs of the poor. His actions, using the media, not only brought resources to those in need but also contributed to the public's learning a bit about the meaning of democratization. Carlos Palenque Avilez, the son of a teacher, started his career working in a beverage factory. He began to sing folk music, which was very popular but not heard frequently in the mid 1970s. He was invited to give concerts in the United States, won prizes, made a film, and appeared on a Bolivian radio program and also on a television program on Channel 7.

Eventually, he bought a radio station. He financed it with money from his concerts, loans from a bank, and the help of friends. He decided to provide a program on which poor people had a chance to tell their problems. The idea was that help would come if people were able to hear about the problems. The format was such that the poor people paid some money in order to tell their problems on the air. Palenque then used their own money to help them.

According to Marcela Llanos Vidaurre, a translator representing community people who support Palenque's effort, the radio program *La Tribuna Libre* accomplishes a lot.[49] For example, a sick person who couldn't walk and who didn't have a wheelchair would go on the program, and Palenque would call rich people to ask for money to buy the person a wheelchair. Someone burned in an accident called, and Palenque helped to get the person medicines. He also helped find lost children who couldn't find the way home. He got gifts for families to give the kids at Christmas. If a person had difficulty with land or with housing, Palenque used to supply a lawyer free of charge.

The radio station, 930 AM, began to grow, as did his popularity. However, according to Marcela, middle-class and rich people didn't like him because they said he earned the money from poor people who paid to be heard. He did not call the rich people during the broadcast. During a broadcast, he'd just announce an address where people who wanted to collaborate could send money. By 1997, he'd owned Metropolitan Radio for some twenty-five years.

Eighteen years ago, around 1980, Palenque bought a television station, Canal 4. Now, he can do more for the poor. On TV, there's a talent show, *Sabados Populares*, where talent from the whole community can go to act and to sing. The actors don't pay to be on air, but those who go to the auditorium to be part of the "live" audience do pay. At night on the TV, they run the radio program based on a filming of the morning program.

Palenque continued to use his microphone to find ways to benefit the community. He wanted to build a house for children without parents, but he never got enough money. He collected beverage caps to pay for this house, when the beverage factory agreed to take the caps back and give him some money. He wanted the government to buy the land, and he would pay for building construction. The government never answered his request, so he bought the land but didn't have the money for construction.

These programs on Metropolitan Radio and Canal 4, Palenque's TV station, do exceptionally well in the ratings. Consequently, they attract advertising dollars, making possible even more investment. Marcela noted, "The poor people love him and he is like a god for them. He is not even Aymara, but people believe they can trust him. His mother was from a small town and a teacher. His father was a military man."

Eventually, Palenque became involved in politics by starting a political party, "Condepa." In 1992, when it was time to elect the mayor of La Paz, he said that his wife, Monica Palenque, would represent his political party. She was elected and served as mayor from 1992 to 1996. She knows how to talk with the people, and she worked with her husband at Metropolitan Radio. She began to be popular on her own and formed her own party, called "Insurgentes."

In 1997, Palenque ran for president because he knew that the Aymara, the majority of the Bolivian population, would vote for him. However, he had a heart attack in March 1997 and died. Since his death, the oldest child, Veronica Palenque, manages the radio station, whose name is now "Carlos Palenque Radio." She continues with the program *La Tribuna Libre*. The radio still helps individuals through this program. The rest of its programs are news and music, as on all other stations.

Poor people think that Palenque provided the opportunity that they need. Before Palenque, poor people didn't have opportunity to express themselves. Now more poor people speak up. Now, another radio station is trying to copy his approach. Now, for the first time, an Aymara woman is a cabinet member in the new president's administration, beginning in late 1997. Had it not been for the media, used as a tool to deliver news that meant something to local people, this increase in stature and self-actualization would not have been likely to happen. In a country with censorship, it is, to be sure, indirect democratization. But it provided a route for a real change in the quality of life for the indigenous population, and it's a step toward democratization.

While this case study doesn't describe "global" news and information, it does describe an approach to programming that built some bridges between the two tiers of contemporary society. It highlights a story that might have been told to TV viewers in news and information programming.

Palenque never really directly addressed the issues of economic opportunity or free speech; he worked around them by providing help rather than empowerment. He let his actions speak louder than his words. Perhaps the situation in Bolivia was too volatile to approach any other way. While scores of individuals found life better because of Palenque and the spirit of the community of the poor was clearly bolstered, lasting improvement is yet to come to Bolivia's Indian population. And it's not clear whether the former dictator elected president in 1997 can really transform himself into a democrat. There's much more to learn about democratization. Palenque's approach may have been only a first step, but it was more than anyone else had done. It wasn't charity; it served Palenque's stations very well in the competitive market arena. There's a message in this case study for industry professionals as well as for those concerned about the problems of two-tier societies.

Peru

Twenty-four million people live in Peru, and 82% of them are literate. An estimated one in fifty have telephones. Nearly all of them have television sets. This land of the Inca Trail uses satellites for domestic transmission. Centuries, as well as mountains, divide populations in various parts of this country. Pockets of population live every bit as comfortably as those in a U.S. suburb, maybe more comfortably. At the other extreme, communities of Indian families live in adobe houses, farming and herding animals much as their ancestors did, except that they have television sets. Those working for the multinational corporations, the national government, and in professional capacities exist nearby, but in another world. Unless they travel into the countryside, they don't physically see the poverty there. However, it is impossible not to see the poverty of the cities—perhaps a worse kind, because people in the countryside at least have homes and some food. How common it is everywhere for people to see only that which is part of their world. All else is invisible—someone else's problem—until there's disease or crime or civil unrest, of course.

This case study focuses on the communities at the northern edge of Lake Titicaca—Puno and the surrounding rural communities. It's a part of Peru where city folk can earn hardship pay. Some of the population live in Puno, a small city servicing the area. Others live on the Uros, or islands made of reeds, floating in Lake Titicaca. Some live in a campos, where everyone in the community is related and it's been that way for 1,000 years. The rest live in small pueblos or villages, like Chiquito, housing a mixed population. Most are Indian, either Aymara or Quechua. In 1996, some of the pueblos and campos got electricity for the first time. Others chose not to because they couldn't pay. For the campesinos who live by subsistence agriculture, there's not much cash economy in 1996. At issue is the exchange of news and information and democratization.

Lack of electricity was no deterrent to watching television. Sister Blanche LaMarre, CSC, lives on a small plot of land in a campo.

They use a 9-volt battery to operate their TV. Occasionally, you see them taking their battery into Puno to be recharged.

What TV has done is bring to the campesino parts of society that they never saw before. As it is, we get one channel. We don't have a dish and transmission is poor on a pampa (flat area) between two mountain ranges. The news is on TV at 6 A.M. and at 10 P.M. People aren't up at 10 P.M., so they watch in the morning. This one channel is biased, but also gives controversial topics. Aside from TV, the news comes in both Aymara and Spanish on the radio. As far as newspapers go, where I live in the campo, not in Puno, people don't know what a newspaper looks like. It's not a literacy question. People are taught to read. It's a problem of accessibility. They'd have to take a half hour minibus ride into Puno to get it. And then, it would be a waste of money given the other priorities for what little cash there is. In the campo, people aren't aware of books and magazines. Here the children go daily with a copy (a notebook) to write inside. It's rare for a teacher to have a textbook. Material is simply written on the blackboard and the children copy it and memorize it.

On the one hand, for the campesinos, news from elsewhere doesn't matter much. They'll do tomorrow what they did today. Their lives are centered on the animals and the farming. Everything revolves around the seasons. On the other hand, I think modern communication will change them much more than the Spanish invasions did. The Aymara didn't let themselves be conquered by the Spanish or the Incas. Even though the Spanish expected them to learn the Spanish language, they maintained the identity of their native language. But the lifestyles and cultures seen on television are very seductive. I asked our young Aymara postulants what effect television would have. They said that it will affect the young. They're the ones who question tradition. They will see what's happening in other parts of the world. They'll realize that something other exists. They'll want something other. Whether good or bad, and I think there's lots of good in this new revelation, they'll realize the world and realize that the rest of it is not like this.

A big part of the problem is that people just absorb what they see. Spontaneity and creativity in thinking has never been encouraged, so the very idea that you don't have to think what I think is a foreign concept. They have no experience in critical thinking regarding media literacy, no experience learning to look critically at the truth or the value or the bias in what's shown.[50]

Bessie Teran Pineda, a correspondent for Pan Americana TV, does the newsgathering in this part of rural Peru.

I see a big difference between Lima and Puno. The people here are so poor. The primary interest is in "getting by" tomorrow and it's hard to understand the value of getting their news out to parts of the world where things are better. Conversely, the people in authority aren't concerned about these little people; their primary concern is how can I become richer by holding this position of authority.

The campesinos very rarely question authority. Those who have, sometimes have been killed. So most people just accept things as they are.

Let me tell you a story that illustrates my point. The story is about Lake Titicaca, a site very important to Peruvian tourism and to the well-being of Peru. It's a story that could be told in Lima about this region. But there are many problems in telling the story. I want to bring out a point about the fear that campesinos have. In one of the bays of Lake Titicaca, by Puno, all the sewage is dumped. There are fourteen points where sewage flows into the lake. The military commander in charge in this area notified all the people who work and live in this area—the islanders on the Uros, the food sellers, etcetera. He told them to come and clean out the lake. The people have such respect and such fear of authority that they gathered together, pulled up trousers, and waded in to get the garbage and the sewage out. I went there to get the story. I asked, what do you think? People generally said, we have to help clear this out. Then I interviewed an older lady dressed in a traditional Aymara skirt. She must have felt that she had nothing to lose. She said, "I think that commander is a jackass. Look at what he's doing. Doesn't he know that tomorrow morning it will be the same because the same pollution still comes down from those same fourteen points."

This is just part of the story. We have so many problems in the ecosystem and we're not addressing them. The fish are dying in the area. It may well have to do with wells drilled in the lake floor by industry fifty years ago. Reportedly, they capped the wells and left; but the caps may not fit correctly or pressure may have caused them to leak. The sulfur, or whatever, is seeping into Lake Titicaca. But no one will check into it or discuss it because the powers in the area are frightened that it might hurt their businesses and that they might have to pay to correct the problem.

I have [the] impression that people here still live under a feudal system. The land passes down from one generation to the next. Those in charge still manage the same way their ancestors did. Each "feudal group" in power has their own (reporter) spokesmen, and you get different versions of news depending on where the power is. Those with power get richer. By their silence, all others—including the media—do nothing to improve life for the population, rather the silence just helps the rich get richer. Challenging this system is dangerous. The danger isn't necessarily from the government; it often comes from self-appointed "bosses." People may not be killed, but there are re-percussions.

When I go to a campo, I see that campesino people are intelligent. They know what's happening. But they're controlled and repressed. They can't say what [they] want because they don't know who to trust. I don't know what will happen—rebellion or what. But for severely repressed people, there is a breaking point.[51]

The question is, can the news and information available through the new technologies affect this situation in ways that bring democratization and lessen the wealth-poverty gap? Clearly part of the solution rests in bringing news from this area to the rest of the world, so there's less excuse for inaction. Sr. Blanche LaMarre notes that when she returns to the United States, she finds that people know nothing about the real Peru.

They see lots of documentaries on Machu Picchu and ancient arti-facts. That's very interesting, but not relevant to today. Then they hear sensationalized political news—that the country is quite unstable and it's a scary place to live—with the Ecuador-Peru border, with the Shining Path, with the MRTA. The ordinary running of a day, no-body hears about. My family doesn't think that an ordinary day is possible. Based on the news and information they have, they say, "Blanche, you're crazy. Stay off the cover of *Newsweek*."

If I could change things, I would make it the job of the embassies and consulates to be sure that the media get information about the real Peru.

Then there's the new technologies. When will a computer ever ar-rive in the schools in the campo? They only just got electricity in three classrooms and that's because we paid for it. Will a TV or computer *ever* get into these classrooms? Then, on the other hand, the highly competitive places with industry and money use computers and get sophisticated news and information. But they idolize the Aymara cul-ture because so many other cultures have died out. They envy the strong family and community values that we've lost a long time ago.

Ecuador

Ecuador has 10.8 million people. The literacy rate is counted at 87%. About one person in 300 has a phone. The country overall is not rich. The elite have all the amenities of global television channels. Most people do not.

The country is in a state of transition after its experience deposing a president in early 1997. All sectors of the population in Quito and Gua-yaquil are concerned about how to enhance stable democratic society and minimize corruption. People like Dra. Jessica Ehlers de Gallegos are working to strengthen the civic sector through programs like her group, Coriem. She knows that's an uphill battle and illustrated the problem by describing an assignment she gave her university students.[52] They were sent to the national legislature to learn what the legislature is and does, just to bring back some material. Most returned with nothing. One student returned with the nameplate torn off a legislator's door. When the student had asked for information, the legislator furiously replied that there wasn't any and handed the student his nameplate. There's lots of opportunity for the media to provide news and information that illustrates, by example, how democratic systems might work in terms of public access. There's also room for the local legislature to rise to the occasion and prove their skills in democratic governing to the television cameras and those across the world who heard about the deposition of the president. In the short run, the media industry may, wrongly, decide it's not worth the bother to foster democratization. But, in the long run, stability and democratic operations in Ecuador are important to multinational business operations and to the safety of those in the media.

The deposition of the president triggered a unique discussion of social responsibility in Ecuador. One illustration of this is the entire page that *El Financiero*, the local *Wall Street Journal*, devoted on July 7, 1997, to the relationship between the state, nongovernmental organizations, and civil society in a socially responsible democracy.

Parts of Ecuador are, however, far removed from the debate among the power brokers of the big cities. The following in a case study on how television is affecting one such community, the Galapagos Islands.

Ivonne Torres, a local resident who once was an exchange student to the United States with the American Field Service, describes the changes in the community since television has been available.

> Ten years ago, in 1987, I came to live in the Galapagos. These islands are 600 miles from Guayaquil, on the Ecuador coast where I had lived before. I came knowing that I wouldn't have electricity twenty-four hours a day. Even now, we don't have electricity between midnight and 6 A.M. because we're saving fuel. We have only running water for about six hours of the day. So you need a big cistern. Ten years ago, there wasn't even piping for a municipal water system. Then, people didn't have television. They only had one radio station. Nowadays we only have two radio stations on the island.
>
> What most drew my attention was seeing people working together. For example, somebody said you know we need to work for this little school. People got together and made the school a reality. I liked it because everybody lived in a colony where they wanted to help each other. Nowadays it's different. People don't get together to do things. Why? Maybe it's because we have television now. Television began maybe just five years ago, in 1992. Now, if you walk the back parts

of town where lots of kids used to play and people sat outside their houses to talk with their neighbors, it's empty. All you hear is television. People don't talk. They sit in front of TV and think "I need that new refrigerator." Before they didn't even have a fridge. I wonder if people have the needs and the industry offers the solutions? Or, is it the industry that creates the needs and the people think they need them? It's a "created necessity," so people believe they need it. In the past, you'd be pleased if a neighbor got something new. That's all. Now, people think, because they are exposed to television and other cultures, if someone else has a better fridge, I should have an even better one.

We're getting more news and information now. In addition to our one local channel, we have satellite now. It carries South American channels—one from Peru, one from Bolivia, and one from Ecudaor. The local channel carries *Power Rangers* and *I Love Lucy*. We hear more news from Peru or Bolivia than from Ecuador. A most useful news service is provided to the National Park Service. Because all these islands are part of the National Park, occasionally they need to say something to the entire community. They'll announce it on TV. 'We're doing this with the giant tortoises this week, so please———. . . ." Or, "The iguanas are suffering from———, so please don't let your dogs run free." It's good. It's somewhat effective.

If I could change news and information on TV, I'd run more about the environment—especially during prime hours. I'd also run some good news so people can see that not everything is bad. Such news might encourage other people to do the best they can instead of encouraging people to behave worse than the person they saw last on TV.

Also, I'd try to get more news from Ecuador out to the rest of the world. Very little news from Ecuador goes out unless it is either very bad or very trivial. Why is it news that the former president cut a CD? Everyone in the world knows about the Galapagos, and cares about it. People should know about efforts to conserve the animals on the Galapagos. Maybe people across the globe should know that there's no genetic labs at the Darwin Research Station on the Galapagos. Genetic labs are critical to preserving the many unique animals here.[53]

Summary

WTN president Robert Burke describes the industry view of the continent.

South America has been emerging into a period of relative political and economic stability in the last five years. There's a great deal of local wealth. It looks like television, especially cable TV is beginning to grow. WTN is working slowly in Southern Hemisphere. There's still a bit of a payments problem in some places, so we insist that you advance pay. Piracy is a small problem in some cultures. South America is really doing extremely well. There's obviously some gaps—but Chile, Argentina, large parts of Brazil, Venezuela, and Colombia are going to be a very robust—no question. You have people with some money. You certainly have a very capitalist culture. They have a high level of consumption of major consumer products—Coca-Cola, Nike sneakers—the usual stuff that drives television advertising. So I think there'll be a very quick growth in Latin America. News is an exception. You'll get more of it, but it's still politically touchy.[54]

From the content perspective, the global exchange of news and information is not very global when it comes to South America. Professor Anibal Ford from the University of Buenos Aires describes the problem as follows.

CNN has a vision of the world, but not the only one. It's not CNN's fault that our vision isn't seen globally. We don't have programs with our view and our vision of the world. I don't think there's a difference in the Argentine view and that of the rest of South America. People in the United States especially don't have much knowledge about our countries. They are very poorly informed. This is a problem of the cultural policies in our countries. To advance interculturalism, people in the United States and Europe need to understand the Latin American point of view and the extent of Latin American competence. To whom is it helpful for the intelligence gap to increase?[55]

From the point of view of narrowing the rich-poor gap and the potential unrest manifest in that problem, those who receive global news and information—inside and outside Latin America—it may be possible to do better. For a very large percentage of South American viewers, TV is their school. For people to see only how much more opportunity others have, when they seem to have very limited opportunity, can certainly produce impatience, if not anger. Carlos Palenque in Bolivia showed how the media could both expand opportunity for the marginalized and expand opportunity for a business. Are there ways that new technologies can facilitate global broadcasters in engaging in projects built on this model?

Is it in industry's self-interest to dispel the cynicism of those who look at the dominant influences in southern Peru and say, "All the talk about addressing real problems is poetry, not reality? Very little trickles down." Does that matter?

NOTES

1. "That Eye-Popping Executive Pay," *Business Week*, April 25, 1994; "Pay at the Top Mirrors Inflation," *Business Week*, May 11, 1981; "Most Incomes crept up in '96: Poorest fell farther behind, Census Bureau Says." *Boston Globe*, September 30, 1997, p. A.3.

2. See *The U.S. Statistical Abstracts—1994*, U.S. Government Printing Office; Paul P. Krusman, "Disparity and despair." *U.S. News and World Report*, March 23, 1992; U.S. Census, 1990, U.S. Government Printing Office.

3. *Fortune*, September 4, 1995, p. 73.

4. Richard Zoglin, "The News Wars," *Time*, October 21, 1996, p. 58f.

5. Raymond Akwule, *Global Telecommunications* (Boston and London: Butterworth Heinemann/Focal Press, 1992), p. 21.

6. Aaron Zitner, "With TV Satellite Plan, Murdoch Launches Own Version of Air War," *Boston Globe*, March 23, 1997, p. 1f.

7. Also see <*http://www.mediacentral.com*> regarding major U.S. media issues.

8. Katharine Q. Seelye, "The New U.S.: Grayer and More Hispanic." *The New York Times*, March 27, 1997, p. A18.

9. The sum of all incomes divided by number of families.

10. The U.S. Department of Health and Human Services official poverty threshold numbers for 1995.

11. Martha T. Moore, "Women, Minorities Fading Out of News Picture." *USA Today*, March 17, 1997, p. 11a.

12. Note, in 1990, that about 12% of the population was of African descent, 9% Latino/a, and 3% Asian. However, it's difficult to count, because some minority groups, Native Americans and Latino/as, can appear in more than one category or can disappear into the white majority.

13. Michael C. Keith, *Voices in the Purple Haze: Underground Radio and the Sixties* (Westport, CT, and London: Praeger, 1997), p. 2, quote from Carla Brooks Johnston.

14. Bill Wheatley, Vice President of International Development, NBC News, 30 Rockefeller Plaza, New York, NY 10112. Telephone interview with the author on July 11, 1994.

15. Ranier Siek, Senior Vice President, CBS International, 51 W. 52nd Street, New York, NY 10019. Telephone interview with the author on June 8, 1994.

16. Richard Wald, Senior Vice President, ABC News, 77 W. 66th St., New York, NY 10023. Interview with the author in New York on May 20, 1994.

17. Richard Zoglin, "The News Wars," *Time*, October 21, 1996, p. 58.

18. Zoglin, "News Wars," p. 58.

19. Associated Press, "Ratings of Media Fall, Poll Says," *Boston Globe*, April 2, 1993.

20. "Newsletter," Fall 1995, Wadsworth Publishing Co., 10 Davis Dr., Belmont, CA 94002–3098.

21. Harry A. Jessell, "TV Raising Its News Budgets," *Broadcasting and Cable*, October 7, 1996, p. 42.

22. "Nielsen Boosts Hispanic Universe," *Broadcasting and Cable*, October 21, 1996, p. 33.

23. Wald interview.

24. Diane Strickland, Inuit Eskimo, Nome, Alaska. Interview with the author in Nome on June 16, 1996.

25. June Wardle, Nome City Council Member. Interview with author in Nome on June 17, 1996.

26. Lynn Johnson, Director, Chukchi College, Kotsebue, AK. Interview with author in Kotsebue on June 14, 1996.

27. Suzie Sun, Bilingual Coordinator, and Suzy Erlich, General Manager, KOTZ Radio, Kotsebue, AK. Interview with author in Kotsebue on June 14, 1996.

28. Zoglin, "News Wars," p. 58.

29. Enrique Diaz Arboleya, Banfield, Argentina. Interview with author in Nome, Alaska, on June 16, 1996.

30. Jeff Herman Gutierez. Telephone interview with author in Boston on May 15, 1997.

31. Jeremy Leonard, "Latin American Journalists Work in the Shadow of a Gun." *Bolivian Times*, June 15, 1997, p. 17.

32. Anthony DePalma, "Mexico's Recovery Just Bypasses the Poor." *New York Times*, August 12, 1997, p. A3.

33. *Advertising Age*, 68, no. 2 (January 13, 1997): 128–30.

34. Michael Burgi, "Telenoticias Joins El CBS," *Mediaweek* (Latin American Edition), July 1996. Also see Latin World <*www.latinworld.com*>

35. Bill Wheatley, Vice President for International Development, NBC News, 30 Rockefeller Plaza, New York, NY 10112. Telephone interview with the author on July 11, 1994.

36. Molloy y Molloy, "Internet Resources for Latin America," <*http://lib.nmsu.edu/subject/bord/laguia/lagl.html*>.

37. Patricia Rodriguez, researcher, Emerson Program in Mass Communications, Fall 1996. Also see <*www.isoc.org/infosvc/international/summit94-plan-eng.html*>.

38. *Annual Report 1996*, Grupo Televisa, S.A., Av. Chapultepec 2B, C.P. 06724, Mexico, D.F.; Tel: 525–709–3333.

39. Jim Williams, Vice President, Director of Broadcast Division, Associated Press TV, Washington, DC. Telephone interview with the author on June 22, 1994.

40. "In the Company of Giants," *The Economist*, 6, (June 10, 1995): 150f.

41. Jack Epstein, "News Aggressivo: Aqui Agora (South America's Passionate Controversial News Journals)," a Globo-Brazilian TV program, November–December 1993.

42. Melissa Ford, Information Officer, U.S. Information Service, U.S. Embassy, Harare, Zimbabwe. Interview with author in Harare on June 20, 1995.

43. Nora Mazziotti, Professora, University of Buenos Aires. Interview with the author in Buenos Aires on June 5, 1997.

44. *Grupo Clarin*, industry publication, Clarin, Piedras 1743 (1140), Capital Federal, Buenos Aires, Argentina. Tel: 307–0330. Fax: 307–0311. Also, author meeting with management on June 3, 1997.

45. Daniel Blumenfeld, young man working with computers. Interview with author in Buenos Aires on June 6, 1997.

46. Richard Freeman, researcher from University of Chicago, attending the weekly demonstration by the Madres de Cinco de Mayo (the mothers who stand

vigil weekly to remind the nation of their relatives who disappeared during the years of dictatorship). In front of Casa Rosada, also called "the Pink House" (the presidential palace), Thursday, June 5, 1997.

47. Jose Blumenfeld, retired civil engineer. Interview with the author in Buenos Aires, June 5, 1997.

48. John C. Merrill, ed., *Global Journalism* (N.Y: Longman, 1983), pp. 290, 295.

49. Marcela Llanos Vidaurre translated for Norah Alvarez de Carrasco, Fernando Carrasco Vidaurre, and Omar Flores Alvarez in the Aymara community of Ciudad Satellite, above La Paz, Bolivia. Interview with author on June 12, 1997 in Ciudad Satellite, Bolivia.

50. Sr. Blanche LaMarre, CSC, Apartado 295, Puno, Peru. FAX: 51–54–35–1574. Interview with author in Chiquito, Peru, on June 17, 1997.

51. Bessie Teran Pineda, Corresponsal, Pan Americana TV, Puno, Peru. Interview with author in Puno on June 16, 1997.

52. Dra. Jessica Ehlers de Gallegos, Ph.D., Presidenta Ejecutiva, Coriem, Ecuador. Interview with author in Quito on July 2, 1997.

53. Ivonne Torres, Ecuador. Interview with the author in the Galapagos on May 27, 1997.

54. Robert E. Burke, President, WTN, The Interchange, Oval Road, Camden Lock, London, NW1, U.K. Interview with the author in London on January 26, 1994.

55. Prof. Anibal Ford, University of Buenos Aires, Teodoro Garcia 2989 (1426), Buenos Aires, Argentina. Interview with the author in Buenos Aires on June 5, 1997.

THE ENTIRE WORLD CAN RECEIVE NEW INFORMATION,
THANKS TO THE 1990s TECHNOLOGIES.

Lack of transportation in the Middle East can't prevent people from trying to bring a TV home. This pilgrim arrives from Saudi Arabia to the port of Suez returning from the annual Moslem pilgrimage to Mecca. *Credit: AFP. Egypt, 1992.*

Miles away from roads and towns, on the Mekong Delta in Vietnam, people can find a neighborhood video rental store providing access to the window on the world. *Credit: Mark V. Hilliard. Southeast Asia, 1993.*

While not affordable for most local people, satellite dishes can be found on upscale homes like this one in Mwanza, a city in northern Tanzania. *Credit: Michael C. Keith. East Africa, 1997.*

High in the Bolivian Andes, video club rentals thrive in worker neighborhoods. *Credit: Author photo. South America, 1997.*

WILL GLOBAL MEDIA EXPAND DEMOCRATIC LIFESTYLES OR EXPAND REPRESSION AND UNREST, CREATING MORE VICTIMS?

This photographer's backdrop featuring a painted television set adds status to the typical Chinese family portrait. In some countries, despite the status of TV, the government tries to limit what is seen. *Credit: Qin Baolian. Harbin, China, 1991.*

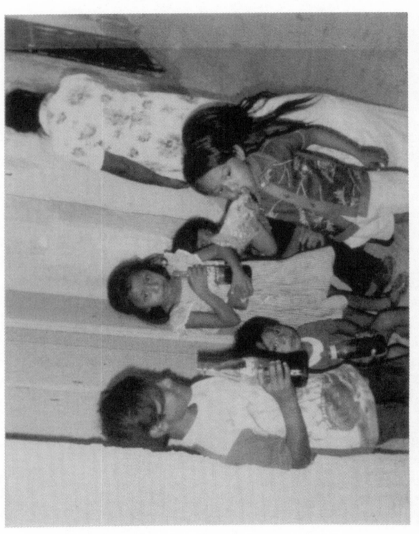

Persuasive Coca-Cola advertising convinces parents to get the best for these Mayan children, even in the baby's nippled bottle. With no exposure to media critique, it's easy to believe everything one sees. And who would pay to provide the other side of the nutrition story? *Credit: Author photo. Village in Yucatan Peninsula, Mexico, 1986.*

Aymara Indian children play video games. It's "cool" to play the violent games and have the Rambo posters. What's the message here about acceptable democratic behavior? Will the next generation of global villagers learn collaboration or control? *Credit: Author photo. Ciudad Satellite, La Paz, Bolivia, 1997.*

WILL THE "HAVE"–"HAVE-NOT" GAP WIDEN OR SHRINK?

Credit: Author photos. Jordan, 1994.

Within a span of a very few miles in the Middle East, some live in Bedouin tents nearly as their ancestors did a thousand years ago, while others live the modern life—working in the offices of global aid organizations or at transnational businesses.

Credit: Robert L. Hilliard. Bombay, India, 1995.

Credit: Author photo. Kuala Lumpur, Malaysia, 1995.

On the Asian subcontinent, some are born into the hardship of the virtually cashless lifestyle of India's poor, who live in tents not far from the high-style economic prosperity of Bollywood—Bombay, India's new media market. Similarly, in Malaysia, some plan the growth of the Pacific Basin from Kuala Lumpur's high-rises, not far from others who live a subsistence lifestyle.

Credit: Author photo. Inuit Eskimo village near the Arctic Circle in Alaska, 1996.

Credit: Adam Auel. U.S. kids learn to use the Internet in school.

Even in the United States, visible symbols of the rich-poor gap exist.

THE NEW MEDIA CAN ENABLE VIEWERS TO BECOME VICTORS.

The new technologies make education possible for children who are geographically isolated from traditional schools. *Credit: Author photo. School of the Air, Alice Springs, Australia, 1987.*

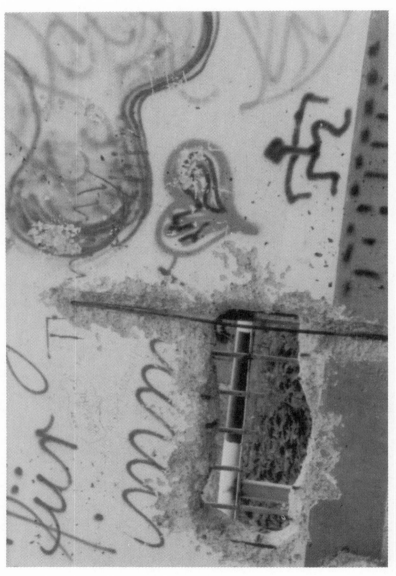

Global news brought social and political change to Berlin and to much of Europe. Because the East Germans saw West German TV, they felt empowered to tear down the Berlin Wall, which had divided a city, a country, and a political world for nearly a half century. *Credit: Author photo. Berlin, Germany, 1991.*

Credit: Author photo. Moscow, June 1991.

Credit: Robert L. Hilliard. Moscow, June 1991.

In over 1,000 years of history, Russia had never elected its political leadership. In 1991, it did. Some folks read about the election outcome over the week or more afterward—from newspapers posted on walls. Others were able to watch the news immediately, as it was broadcast on TV across eleven time zones.

Women, who raise humanity's next generation, constitute half the globe's population but over two-thirds of the globe's poor. New media greatly increase opportunity for them to obtain information needed to improve their health, education, and economic opportunity. *Credit: Michael C. Keith. Women radio producers, Moshi, Tanzania, 1997.*

Safeguarding the environment from hazardous substances and protecting the wonders of nature is becoming, by necessity, a top priority. New technologies make it possible for Greenpeace and similar advocacy organizations to inform the public and its leaders about the state of the world. *Credit: Author photo. Rainbow Warrior ship in Auckland, New Zealand, 1987.*

WILL WE MOVE PAST OUR FASCINATION WITH HOW THESE NEW TECHNOLOGIES WORK AND HOW MUCH MONEY CAN BE MADE BY SELLING THEIR PRODUCTS? CAN WE USE THEM AS TOOLS TO BRING PEACE AND AN IMPROVED QUALITY OF LIFE FOR ALL MEMBERS OF OUR GLOBAL VILLAGE?

Looking from Jewish West Jerusalem into Moslem East Jerusalem at the Dome of the Rock, through the symbols householders have erected to pay tribute to the power of the media. *Credit: Author photo. 1993.*

5

Europe

OVERVIEW

Europe is in many respects the model for global village development—and perhaps for global democratization. This is because of increased efforts, primarily through the European Union, at forging collaboration among diverse countries with different cultures, different languages, different laws, different forms of government, and different states of economic well-being. Different religions are also represented but, with a few exceptions, in most of Europe, as in North America, religious tolerance is greater than in the past.

Parts of the European continent have standards of living higher than that in the United States, although, in respect to mass communications, their infrastructure had not been as open for flexible development as that in the United States until the 1980s, when two things happened. Deregulation permitted commercial television station development and telecom competition. And, the new technologies brought satellite, cable, fiber optics, cell phones, digital systems, and the Internet—all within a decade.

By 2005, 60% of European households are expected to have cable. Direct satellite broadcast (DBS) has grown rapidly in Europe since 1990. It's estimated that two million households will receive DBS TV by end of 1990s and that by 2005, 15.5% of European households will have satellite dishes.

Several digital TV packages were launched in 1996. Already the continent has moved in less than a decade from no cable to the point where 34.5% of households in western Europe had multichannel cable. Now, with digital TV, it's possible to have access to more in pay per view (PPV) and near video on demand (NVOD). Digital TV is more likely to target homes with satellite reception and not much cable—initially, households in France, Italy, Spain, and the U.K.

DEVELOPMENTS IN COMMUNICATIONS TECHNOLOGY

Satellites

INTELSAT was the first system to service western Europe, and it was the model for the 1977 creation of the western European satellite EUTEL-SAT. In the late 1990s EUTELSAT is a major influence on telecommunication opportunities in Europe. Between 1995 and 1998 alone, EUTELSAT launched five digital satellites with ninety-eight transponders. The first of these was Hot Bird 1. It reaches 55.4 million homes, who need only a 45 cm dish for good reception. About 75% of the Hot Bird subscribers were in western Europe, but already 20% are in the emerging democracies of eastern Europe. The remaining 5% are in the Middle East and North Africa. Within these numbers, the majority of subscribers access the satellite programming through cable rather than direct-to-home (DTH) satellite or Satellite Master Antenna Television (SMATV, ie. one antenna for all households in a building).

In 1971, the former Soviet Union created INTERSPUTNIK to facilitate communications across its vast geographic area, which covers eleven time zones in just one country. INTERSPUTNIK membership is open to any country. Its members have a historical base in the old alliance of Soviet states. For example, the following countries have held membership: Afghanistan, Belarus, Bulgaria, Cuba, Czech Republic, Georgia, Germany, Hungary, Kazakhstan, Turkmenistan, Romania, Russia, Syria, Yemen, and Vietnam.

The ASTRA satellite system is operated by Societe Europeenne des Satellites (SES), a Luxembourg company that's been in business since 1989. SES leases channels on ASTRA to various broadcasters. At present it dominates the European digital satellite market, having launched five digital satellites between 1995 and 1998 and made ninety-eight transponders available. In mid 1994, ASTRA was servicing 52,145,000 households, mostly in western Europe plus Hungary, Poland, Czech Republic, Slovakia, Slovenia, and Croatia. It launched five digital satellites between 1995 and 1998, with ninety-eight transponders.

In addition, other satellites service Europe. They include TURKSAT, GORIZONT, KOPERNIKUS, TELE X, TELECOM, THOR/TV, EXPRESS 2, TDF, HISPASAT, ORION, and PANAM SAT.[1]

Global TV

Global TV availability increased dramatically with the arrival of the several digital TV packages launched in 1996. European multichannel cable TV with PPV and NVOD became attractive options. With the increase in channels comes an increase in access to global TV news and information.[2]

The global news and information giants—CNN, BBC's WSTV, and Rupert Murdoch's B-Sky-B are all present for the European cable or satellite TV viewer, as is NBC's Superchannel.

In 1991, CNN opened a London production center in order for several of its programs to originate out of London for prime-time Europe: *World Business Today,* and two *News Hour* programs. In addition, in the mid 1990s, CNN bought a partial interest in a German model of CNN called NTV. It's the CNN of Germany. It focuses on the subjects of news, the business news, the political situation, the weather, and the sports of Germany for its German viewers, all in German. CNN does some subtitling in Scandinavian languages, including Finnish, for distribution on a separate satellite to Scandinavia.[3]

BBC's World Service Television (WSTV) could be seen on 1.8 million homes in Europe by January 1994. This was an increase from 700,000 in 1992. This news and information channel is widely distributed by cable and also by direct-to-home satellite transmission via INTELSAT VI. In some cases, people receive it through terrestrial rebroadcast. In eastern Europe, rebroadcast is the most common form of distribution. For example, Czech TV rebroadcasts daily the WSTV bulletins of international news. This arrangement, which began in January 1994, put WSTV's half-hour program into 2.5 million of Hungary's 3.7 million households. Lithuania and Latvia bought rebroadcast rights for WSTV news in 1993. Similar arrangements exist with stations in Moscow, in St. Petersburg, and in seventy-three other CIS cities.[4]

B-Sky-B was launched in 1991; and by 1992, it had 2.3 million subscribers in Europe. As expected, it was an expensive start-up operation, but subscriptions have grown rapidly over the decade. This Murdoch effort is, of course, strengthened by other ventures such as by the upgrading of the global news offerings via Fox News out of the United States, by the Asian link with Star TV, and by numerous other ventures for incorporating advanced technology into Murdoch's global offerings.

One U.S. network in addition to CNN, NBC, has established a growing presence in Europe. NBC Europe (NBC Superchannel) is available on cable in the UK and in continental Europe with news, sports, and entertainment. NBC is transmitted via cable and satellite to 70 million homes in forty-four European countries as of the mid 1990s. It's on digital packages such as Nethold's DSTV for Benelux and Scandinavian countries and on Kirch's

DFI package for Germany and Austria. Both are on ASTRA satellite and are subscription. The partner channel is CNBC, which is the first twenty-four-hour financial and business TV broadcasting throughout Europe, with live reports from the global financial markets in Europe, the United States, and Asia.[5]

A nongovernmental organization, the European Broadcasting Union (EBU) began in 1950 as an independent, nonprofit, noncommercial organization with the objective of circulating news and information among its member organizations in an open and objective manner.[6] To provide further news exchanges, the EBU works with other regional broadcasting unions to provide such as the Arab States Broadcasting Union (ASBU), the Asia-Pacific Broadcasting Union, the Caribbean Broadcasting Union (CBU), and, during the communist period in eastern Europe, the former Organization Internationale de Radiodiffusion et Television (OIRT). It also works with UNESCO, the World Intellectual Property Organization (WIPO), the International Telecommunications Union (ITU), and other international bodies. EBU TV provides "Euronews." In 1993, this channel began as the first multinational, Europe-based, twenty-four-hour channel. It's available to over 35 million viewers in thirty-nine European countries. The initial collaboration included the EBU, Antenne 2 and 3 of France, RAI of Italy, ARD and ZDF of Germany, and RTVE of Spain. Euronews builds on the EBU's fine track record of providing news exchanges for this region of the world.[7]

The Internet

While the revolution in access to global television news is occurring, another revolution is also changing the way business is done in Europe. Use of the Internet expands daily in Europe. By the turn of the century, fewer and fewer parts of Europe will find themselves restricted by the old problems of poor-quality phone lines. Major European cities have Internet cafes, popular especially among younger people. Many "pan" pages link people between countries.

The Internet is available in all former eastern European countries, although access is sometimes limited and always expensive. In Estonia, there are more online users than in Japan and France, in part because since 1988 they've gotten lots of aid from neighboring Finland. Consequently, over 50% of the secondary schools are now connected. It's estimated that all secondary schools will be connected by 2000. In 1996 this was expanded to libraries, medical facilities, and cultural institutions. The Estonian Information Technology Fund and the Nordic Council of Ministers are making it happen. (See Table 5.1 for popular European Web sites for those interested in news and information.)

Table 5.1
European Internet Sites for News and Information

<www.pit.edu/~wesnews> Western Europe Resources

<www.citeresearch.com/studies/esat.htm> Satellite Communications in Europe

<www2.echo.lu/parliament/en/resoluti.html> European Community multimedia

<www2.echo.lu/echo/en/manuecho/html> EUROLIB library periodicals

<www2.echo.lu/tentelecom96/en/tthome/html>

Trans-European Telecommunications Network

<europa.eu.int> European Community

<www.bid24.com/esat/satpages.html> European Satellite Information Services

<www.astra.lu/home> ASTRA home page

<www.op.dlr.de/wit-m/eutelsat.htm> EUTELSAT

<www.hri.org/nodes/grprov.html> Internet Providers and Telecommunications in
Greece

<www.service.uit.no/norge/geographical.html> Norway information

<www.apu.fi/tv> Scandanavian TV schedules

<www.sunet.se/sweden/servers.html> Sweden general/ Computers/ Internet Cafes

<www.funet.fi/resources/map> Finland general

<www.best.com.tr/email> Registered e-mail addresses in Turkey

<www.mfa.gov.tr/grupdArt.htm> Turkish Radio and TV Corporation

<www.worldbank.org/> individual country and regional information

<www.afp.com> Agence France Presse

<www.nic.nl> Netherlands general

<www.efe.es> EFE, Spain's News Agency

<www.cafeinternet.es> El Cafe Internet, Barcelona

<www.agenziaitalia.it> Italian News Agency

<//chw3.span.ch/> Swiss Web Servers

Source: Guney Keser, Emerson researcher.

EUROPEAN MEDIA POLICY HIGHLIGHTS

While not all the countries in Europe are official members of the European Union, the EU is setting the tone for business on the continent in the century ahead. With member countries stretching from Reykjavik to Lisbon to Dublin to the Danube, the union includes some 500 million TV viewers. The EU brings about major changes for its member countries and for those across the globe who deal with the EU. In addition, a wide range of collaborative agreements influence the business practices of all the countries across Europe. Two documents deserve mention in this discussion of the exchange of global news and information.

"The European Broadcasting Directive" was adopted on October 3, 1989, by the European Community Council of Ministers. It obligates member states "where practicable and by appropriate means" to allot the majority of broadcast transmission time (except for news and sports and ads) for European works. While designed to protect Europe from U.S. cultural imperialism, the directive has resulted in two distinct actions. Many more international coproductions are occurring, a move that saves money for the Europeans, develops skills in new European industries, and insures a role for U.S. experts in the field. In addition, the policy streamlined the bureaucracy meaning that non-Europeans need to deal with only one regulatory agency rather than a dozen. Consequently, the number of exports from the United States to Europe have doubled.[8]

In August 1990, the "European Convention on Transfrontier Television" was produced by the Council of Europe. The convention focuses on program services embodied in the transmission of television by terrestrial, cable, satellite, or rebroadcast technology. It reaffirms the freedom of reception and retransmission in accord with Article 10 of the Convention for the Protection of Human Rights and Fundamental Freedoms. Included in the provisions are the following: People are entitled to information about the broadcaster. Programs shall respect the dignity of the human bring and the fundamental rights of others—no pornography, no violence to incite racial hatred, fair presentation of news to encourage free formation of opinion, and respect for children's programming hours. The public should have access to major events without undue broadcaster "exclusive rights" provisions. Wherever practicable, broadcasters should reserve for European works the majority portion of their transmission time. No misleading advertising or editorial influence should influence program content. No more than 20% of the program time should be devoted to spot advertising during any hour of programming. Ads should be clearly identified as ads. Tobacco ads should not be permitted. Alcohol ads should be restricted. This convention is open for the signature of members of the Council of Europe, the European Cultural Convention, and the European Economic Community. However, it's considered valid after just seven countries sign.

On May 26, 1994, the Bangemann Group Report set forth proposed rules and regulations for Europe's telecommunications industry.[9] The main message has been to loosen regulation, to let the new technologies have freedom to develop. They also cautioned that this stance might exacerbate the problems caused by having a two-tier society of haves and have-nots. The rationale for moving ahead was that Europe couldn't afford to be late to meet the world market on the cyberspace ride. It might not be able to catch up to a competitive place in the market.

SELECTED COUNTRIES AND MEDIA ACCESS

British Isles and Western Europe

United Kingdom and Ireland

Many of the 58 million people in the United Kingdom have access to the best of the new communications technologies. This is also true for the population of Ireland. Updates on communication technologies can be found by looking at the Commonwealth Telecommunications Organization Web site. They work with all commonwealth countries on quality, consumer issues, commerce, and social and economic development support. See <http://www.cto.int>; email: info@cto.int.

It should be noted, however, that as in so much of the world, tensions between the U.K. and Northern Ireland existed for decades. Whenever violence breaks out, the media is there to report it. Might the content of news and information contribute to the cross-cultural understanding needed to forge peace? Might it make possible an exchange of information, thereby reducing the resentment felt by people who feel their views are not placed before the decision makers? The Brits, of all people on the globe, should understand that two-tier societies can't last today any more than they did when the Empire crumbled a few decades ago.

The 1997 tragic death of Diana, Princess of Wales, killed when her car was trying to lose the pursuing press, highlights another aspect of media coverage of so-called news. In the U.K. and the United States in the last two decades the media competition has been so great that reporters have had an increasingly difficult time differentiating between real news and the personal lives of prominent people. The U.K. coverage has often provided constant soap-opera headlines, calling it news. Where is the line between free information exchange about those in leadership positions and an invasion of privacy? The majority of the globe, with a censored press, has no difficulty drawing that line. The question is, can Britain now help the global democracies to clarify the issue?

The Benelux Countries

Belgium, Luxembourg, and the Netherlands are affluent countries. In the Netherlands, for example, 98% of the households have TV and 88% have cable. In the mid 1990s, one-quarter of the households had satellite. Belgium began cable TV in the mid 1980s, earlier than most of Europe. Luxembourg came early to global TV by providing the home base for the SES corporation, which launched the ASTRA satellites and played a major role in bringing global TV to Europe.

France, Germany, Italy, Spain, Switzerland, and Austria

The French entered the computer age early. In 1980 Teletel, the videotext network, was launched for 20 million telephone customers to access online services. The system has 6.5 million terminals plus 600,000 microcomputers with emulation software. The only problem in making this a model globally is that it's mostly in French. English has become the second language in most of the world, a sad fact for the French, who look longingly at international postal and visa forms and remember the time, not too many decades ago, when French was the language of diplomacy and certainly the language used for international transactions. This reality stands as proof of the enormous influence of global TV, the world's English teacher.

Nonetheless, France's Telecom is the world's fourth largest telecommunication company. It provides voice, data, video, and multimedia. In addition, France has become a battleground for satellite-delivered digital packages. Satellite has been more popular than cable in France. Canalsatellite Numerique launched a twenty-four-hour channel service in April 96 via EUTELSAT Hot Bird 2. Later in 1996, TPS, a company consisting of five terrestrial channels, launched a service to provide satellite delivered digital TV.

Germany has had, since the end of World War II, a strong public television presence modeled after the BBC. Its first competition came with the arrival of cable in the mid 1980s, and now Germany is Europe's largest cable market. By 2005, it's expected that cable will be accessible for three-quarters of the country's homes. Satellite has developed more rapidly in the former East Germany simply because the infrastructure wasn't in place for cable. At present over 15% of East German homes have satellite TV. It's anticipated that shortly after the turn of the century there will be 10.3 million satellite subscribers in Germany overall.

Germany is the seventh wealthiest nation in the world, with a GNP per capita of $23,560 in 1993.[10] This is after Germany absorbed the former East Germany into itself. Despite the many difficulties of that transition, Germany is well situated to make maximum use of the new communications technologies.

Widespread Internet development will dramatically change the way business is done. For example, the Saxony Telecommunications Development Corporation was founded in the mid 1990s to ensure that the state of Saxony in former eastern Europe has a systematic Internet system for use by schools, hospitals, business, government, and residents of the area. It's a highly focused, well-funded effort. The information superhighway has provided a roller-coaster ride for the media industry since the 1989 end of the national broadcaster monopoly.

Cable and satellite are a bit newer in Italy even though UNESCO estimates that 99% of Italian households have TV. For over two decades Italy has had private television and television advertising, making it unique in the region. However, private channels are owned by media magnate Silvio Berlusconi. Cable became a significant force only in 1995. Satellite is growing. Berlusconi's appointment as prime minister in 1994 serves as a reminder to the world of the power of the media to influence public opinion.

Spain shares the same rapid growth in channel availability that exists in other European countries. For example, Cablevision Barcelona has forty channels. Spain has about 11.7 million TV households. In 1995, about 6% of them had satellite dishes. It's estimated that by 2005, 30% of the TV households will have either cable or satellite access.[11] Spain has one added advantage—access to the global television developed for the Spanish market in the United States and the Spanish population of Central and South America. Spain provided a good example of a country where a minority population, the Basques, has its own media access. It's required a strengthened commitment to democratization to have the majority and the minority Spain coexist peacefully.

Switzerland and Austria rely more on cable than on direct-to-home satellite, even though that's difficult in parts of these mountainous countries. By 2005, it's expected that 95% of the households in Switzerland will have multichannel subscriptions. The public broadcasting system has emphasized high-quality programming and news, and there's been a genuine skepticism about privatized commercial media. These two countries also have very high standards of living and therefore should have no trouble taking rapid advantage of the latest new communications technologies. Switzerland is the globe's wealthiest country, with a 1993 GNP per capita of $36,410. Austria ranks ninth in the list, with a 1993 GNP per capita of $23,120.

Scandinavia

This part of Europe is generally affluent, with very high living standards. In fact, the third, fourth, and fifth wealthiest nations of the world are Denmark, Norway, and Sweden, with 1993 GNP per capita figures of $26,510, $26,340, and $24,830 respectively.[12] Many Scandinavians began early to take advantage of both commercial television and the Internet. As early as 1988, Finnish broadcast officials were heavily involved in a reexamination of their public broadcasting, with justified concerns for preserving the rich cultural heritage that they saw eroding as the younger generation turned to commercial programming. The task for national broadcasters is not easy because they don't have the budgets, the skills, or the desire to imitate Hollywood-style programming. The question is whether, in a quarter century, the enticing style offered by the new, the global broadcasters, will preserve and enhance the content integrity of the old, at least the old as presented in free societies like Scandinavia.

One little-noticed commercial venture to take root early in Europe is the Scandinavian Broadcasting System. It's wholly owned subsidiary of the U.S. network ABC. This advertising-driven system began in Scandinavia in 1990 and is expanding into the Netherlands and Belgium. It's not a global news broadcaster, and not necessarily a news provider, but it has the ability to offer an interesting blend of the kind of news Scandinavians are accustomed to from their skilled professional public systems, coupled with a contribution from ABC's American view of news and with the help of ABC-owned WTN, the London-based Worldwide Television News agency. That, of course, depends on how much thought is given to program content. Where will news program content rank on the hierarchy of priorities, competing with the heady issues of profits and market share?

Other important developments in Scandinavia include the development of cable and the Internet. Direct satellite TV arrived in Scandinavia before cable, so those who could afford to enter the market in its early, and expensive, years have dishes. In some parts of this mountainous terrain, DTH satellite is more realistic. It's estimated that 22.3% of Norwegian households will have dishes by 2005. Denmark, on the other hand, has a flatter terrain and is rapidly being wired for cable.

Internet use is spreading rapidly in professional and academic circles. In Sweden, just ask the patrons at Stockholm's Internet cafe. NORDUnet, just one of the ISPs, reaches research and educational institutions in all Scandinavian countries. Anders Burholm, an executive for SAS, comments on the arrival of the Internet:

> It's amazing how quickly the Internet has become a household name here in Sweden during the past year. No advertising is complete without the company, at least the major companies, making a reference to its Web site. My daily newspaper has a weekly IT section. And in many of the articles in all sections of the paper there are mentioned Web sites where you can read more about the subject.

> On a personal level, I'm just beginning to explore this new world of the Internet. But already I can see that now I can get quick access to information that was not within my reach before. For example, I love the musical theater, and now I almost daily check the Internet news on Playbill online and I feel that this deepens my interest and

makes it more fun. I have also gotten in touch with people all over the world who share my interests and I have already met some of them and count them as friends. The Internet is really remarkable in that respect.[13]

For the latest information on Internet use in Scandinavia, contact the Norway Statistical Center at <*www.sds.no*>

The Baltics

The Baltic bloc of countries found its independence not even a decade ago, after the collapse of the Soviet bloc. Until the 1990s, there hadn't been the resources to provide state-of-the-art telephone lines. However, television was common in households across the Soviet bloc. The government encouraged it as a way to provide some cohesion among the population. Since independence, cable and satellite are beginning to expand. One of the most interesting areas of new technology is, however, the rapid acceptance of the Internet wherever phone lines and economics allow it.

No doubt, the most fortunate of the Baltic countries is Estonia. Because it is geographically very near to affluent Finland, with which it shares common linguistic and cultural roots, the Finns have been most helpful. Internet use is extremely popular, and youngsters are learning in secondary school how to use it. In addition, libraries, medical facilities, and cultural institutions are active Net users. The Estonian Information Technology Fund and the Nordic Council of Ministers are making it happen.

In Latvia, the largest Internet server is LATNET, which focuses on creating an internal network as much as on access to the Internet. It connects academics and commercial users. There are an estimated 4,000 users. LATNET is funded by educational institutions and the Ministry of Education and Science. There is also a private server called Bilteks, Ltd.

Taide UAB is a Lithuanian ISP, as is LITNET. The latter is a project of the Nordic countries and UNESCO, with some Lithuanian government money contributed as a matching share.

Balkans

The Balkans, a group of countries in southern Europe near the Mediterranean, represent diverse cultural, linguistic, and religious groupings. Some were part of the Soviet bloc, and others were not. In this region, one can find areas, like the former Yugoslavia, where the thinking remains as it was well over a half century ago.[14] Ethnic hatreds and divisiveness are deeply rooted and result in a failure to understand that pluralism is a common self-interest in a global village era. Stability and, consequently, economic vitality are difficult to maintain in some sectors. Nonetheless, the global television era and the Internet have arrived. Cost and quality telephone lines are the primary obstacles, aside from political and ethnic hatreds. By the end of the 1990s, it's estimated that 2 million people in the Balkans will have DBS. Material on Bulgaria and Albania can be found in the case studies at the end of this chapter.

Romania

This country of 23 million people has thirteen broadcast stations. Since 1995, the new PRO TV offers Western shows like *NYPD Blue, X-Files, ER,* and *MASH,* some live sports, films, and news. Usually the films are subtitled in Romanian. The news offered is not unique. However, one should note that films like *Broadcast News* are shown dubbed in Romanian. While the film is not news, it does use the entertainment genre to provide an education on how free speech and an independent media do work.

Romania has been favorable to news programming, allocating about 20% of its time to news, more than most Western countries. Perhaps their most interesting experiment was a 1991 innovation, Free Romanian Television. This is a channel on which citizens can present their views.[15]

Another service comes from Romania. Programming is made available to U.S. cable for Romanians and others in the United States to get Romanian TV via Romanian Voice Television (RVTV), on Channel 25 (WNYE) in New York City. This service may expand to Atlanta, Cleveland, and Chicago. The program includes business news and other materials.[16]

Phone service has been very poor. It's improving. Romtelecom, the government telecom operator, gave a $60 million fiber optics contract to Siemens and Ericsson to install 5,000 km of fiber by 1997.[17] In 1996, about one in every hundred people had a phone. Automatic service, without operator assistance, reached only 89% of the customers.

Large universities have Internet access through EuropaNet. In some cases, secondary schools are also connected. Access is, of course, available to government and commercial users.

Greece

This country, while part of the NATO block of countries and part of the Western alliance during the Cold War era, is also a Mediterranean, almost Middle Eastern, nation. The nationally controlled media system has, until recently, mirrored the Middle East more than western Europe. It changed leadership every time the government did until recent years, when more private stations have begun operation. Some 99% of the households have television. Aside from the standard Western fare, available to those with satellite or cable, they contribute to and receive from the European Broadcasting Union, including the EBU's Euronews. Greece's geography also places it on the western end of the Asian media services, meaning that

STAR TV is available. For updates on Greece, contact the American Hellenic Media Project at *<http://www.hri.org/ahmp>* or on email at *<ahmp hri.org>*.

Macedonia

Macedonia has three state-owned channels plus a few private channels with coverage of part of the country. There's no cable, but there is satellite. In addition, two commercial companies provide Internet connections, according to Ognen Firov, Internet systems engineer for PTT Macedonia.[18] The two companies are PTT Macedonia and Ultra-Net. In addition, the university has a server called MarNet. There were about 2,000 users on the Net in late 1996.

Central Europe

The central European countries are having the easiest time converting from the planned economy of the Soviet bloc to their new situation as market economies. This is because they abut affluent western European countries, which find it in their self-interest to be helpful in that transition. It's also because the mode of doing business is not so foreign to them, partly because many people have seen cross-border television from West Germany and Austria.

Czech Republic

Czech Republic, the country that had the "velvet revolution" at the beginning of the 1990s and elected playwright Vaclav Havel as its president has moved relatively easily into a market economy.

On the media front, Czech Republic has public television on CT 1 and CT 2, descendants of the old state-operated systems, and private television on stations such as Nova TV and Premiere TV. Cable is growing rapidly and provides access to a wide range of programming such as pay TV Film Net Eastern Europe, multichoice pay TV coming in on the ASTRA satellite. On EUTELSAT one can get the BBC's WSTV, among other programming.

Internet use is also growing rapidly. Internet server CESNet provides government-paid access to electronic communications. The users are scientific and R&D organizations, libraries, government, schools, and health care organizations. One can learn current monthly Internet rates at *<altavista.monthlyrates>*.[19]

Hungary

Here, as in the rest of Central Europe, Telecom changes are rapidly upgrading telephone service. For example, Motorola's Cellular Infrastructure Group (CIG) is completing in 1998 a $100 million contract to supply the "Wireless Local Loop" telephone system for 200,000 subscribers. Other companies work on similar ventures. The Westel 900GSM Telecommunications Company is also developing a network to upgrade technology infrastructure in Hungary.[20]

The national TV networks are Duna Televizio, Magyar Televizio, and Top TV. Duna has a satellite-distributed channel for expatriates living elsewhere in Europe, and it distributes on cable in the United States. Magyar, also state owned, reaches 4 million households via TV1 and TV2. Top TV is the Hungarian music channel. Private commercial channels are accessible via cable TV.[21]

One interesting venture is the Hungarian American Coalition (HAC) collaborating with Duna TV, Hungary's satellite television station. The HAC secures airtime on U.S. public access channels to provide Duna programs to cable subscribers in the United States. The idea is that it will help Duna raise money in Hungary and expand U.S. exposure to Hungary. It also is an opportunity for local public access channels to make some money and for people of Hungarian heritage in the United States to keep contact with their culture. See <http://www.hungary.com/hac/press/94/html>.

A similar Hungarian example is the two language service started by Maras TV, a commercial station in Hungary. They started broadcasting in Romanian in Hungary and in Hungarian in Tirgu Mures, a Romanian city where ethnic violence has occurred.[22] The project, undertaken with very little money and no government help, was launched as an effort to improve relations between Hungarians and Romanians, who were frequently clashing in this geographic area. It's not clear what the program content is. That can be the deciding factor in whether this helps or exacerbates relations between the two cultural groups.

HUNGARNET is the Hungarian Academic and Research Network, which serves principally the academic and research community. Home phone links are expensive. One program called NIIF provides free Net access to Hungary's Ph.D.s through Eunet, but modems and phone expenses aren't free.

Poland

Poland has its own satellite service, called POLSAT. In addition it uses EUTELSAT and ASTRA satellites. On satellite TV from ASTRA, Polish subscribers can get CNBC, RTL, RTL2, CNN, ZDF, WDR, SAT1, VH-1 Germany, ORF, and Sky One. A subscriber needs only a 1.1 meter motorized dish, and the ability to pay. On Hot Bird/EUTELSAT II-F3, Polish subscribers get Deutsche Welle TV, NBC Superchannel, and TV 5.

Modernizing Polish Telecom is difficult, but it is happening. See <http://gurukul.ucc.american.edu> for updates. Polish Telecom as privatized in 1992 (TPSA) remains a monopoly that makes it a challenging environment either for updating service or for offering competitive service. Sprint has a contract to construct a digital telecom network in Pila and Selisia. In this region about 125,000 lines were scheduled for service beginning in 1997. This new system will also provide cable television, available online.[23]

Internet use is expensive and limited mostly to academic and business institutions. In some parts of Warsaw, secondary schools have access. See <Altavista.poland.online> for updated information on costs.[24]

Turkey

TV was available only through the government until 1986. At that point, one private company that made its programs in Germany sent them to Turkey by INTELSAT. The government couldn't stop the transmission. That year there were three new private stations. In a matter of only a couple of years, lots of people got satellite dishes. In fact, in 1990, a Turkish government channel began broadcasts in Turkish to its expatriates living in other European countries. Programs were carried on TRT-INT (TV V), transmitted mostly to Germany, where a sizable number of Turkish people live as guest workers. In 1992, TRT AVRASYA started beaming programs to the Turkic republics in central Asia. Also in 1992, the government authorized cable TV, which is, however, fairly expensive. Only thirty-five channels were selected for broadcast by the government, including NBC Superchannel, CNN, five German channels, and three sports channels.

In 1994, Turkey launched its own satellite, TURKSAT 1B. That year the government ended its monopoly of radio and TV with a new broadcast act. This act has a provision requiring foreign programmers to deal with the PTT in order to get permission to rebroadcast in Turkey. That provision hasn't had much influence on the satellite programmers with direct-to-home connections. By late 1995, laws began to appear on how to program and when ads could be inserted.

It is said by the Publishers Association of Turkey that more than a hundred journalists are currently in prison. The government has very strict laws that punish criticism of the government, and it employs a government prosecutor whose job it is to monitor the media for any such stories. The government considers such journalism a form of terrorism. One such prosecutor, Mr. Canozkan, reported "I get a very good feeling doing this work. I'm defending the Turkish nation and its unity."[25]

The major "have–have-not" issue in Turkey is ethnic hostility toward those of Kurdish background. The Kurds have a private channel, which they put on INTELSAT and broadcast in Turkey. The Turks want it banned. They say that it violates the broadcast law because it is not in the Turkish language. So, CAN TV plans round-the-clock broadcasts to the Kurds in the Kurdish language. While in Instanbul the Kurds and Turks get along fine, that's definitely not the case in other circles. TV no doubt has the power to win over the hearts and minds of people—the power of a weapon, some might say.

The Commonwealth of Independent States (CIS)

This region has undergone enormous change over the past decade. The Soviet Union dissolved in 1991, and the CIS replaced it as a loose federation of twelve independent states: Ukraine, Belarus, Armenia, Azerbaijan, Georgia, Moldavia, Kazakhstan, Kyrgyzstan, Russia, Tajikistan, Turkmenistan, and Uzbekistan.[26] While far from the usual destinations for travel, regardless of where in the world, some of these republics were home to Soviet nuclear weapons. The danger to the planet of those weapons, if detonated, requires that the world not ignore this region.

The entire region has had functioning state television for a couple of decades, in accord with the Soviet conviction that TV was a way to communicate common information to the population.

The very existence of the CIS owes a debt to the new global information technologies. In 1991, there was a coup attempt by old-line communists seeking to curb Premier Gorbachev's power. The principal reason that the coup did not succeed was that the organizers were so "old school" that it never occurred to them to block the media from collecting and communicating information. As they never cut the communication lines, CNN and others gathered and distributed news. People with satellite dishes inside the Soviet Union saw what was happening. Russian national TV and Ostanko were getting the feeds by dish and just rebroadcast it. The task of cutting off the TV channels was exceedingly complex, and even the authoritarian regime orchestrating the coup could not succeed, because it's a complex web with many branches. There were too many leaks. They did try to turn off Russian national TV, but the technicians figured out how to bypass their blockage and uplink the signal. The KGB general wasn't clever enough to block it. Had the whole world not been watching—outside as well as inside the Soviet Union—the government might have been overthrown. Instead, Boris Yeltsin became the hero in seeking an end to the coup. Gorbachev returned. Yeltsin was elected president of Russia in the Russian republic's first election. In a few short months, the Soviet Union ceased to exist, and Russia was a country. This is probably the ultimate test of democratized media. However, the reason for examining the full range of ways in which ongoing media can encourage democratization is to ensure that one can avoid reaching such destabilizing circumstances for individuals and for the economy alike.

Developing the market for satellite or cable TV is another matter. Russia became a member of EUTELSAT in 1994, and in 1998 Russia will supply a new communications satellite for EUTELSAT, thereby helping EUTELSAT and keeping the Russian space scientists employed at home.[27] In 1996, the Russian INTERSPUTNIK offered southern India satellite TV channels, declaring itself one of the important participants in regional global TV in Asia. Within Russia, and more so within the other republics, satellite TV is expensive. Purchasing the dish is an initial obstacle. The once-free service is becoming increasingly limited as people are expected to pay subscription fees. But cable TV has proved a problem, too. The economy has been so bad that in many places that people steal the cable as soon as it is laid down in order to sell the wire.

A major step to bring the CIS region into the twenty-first century has been the Kiev Ku-band satellite earth station. This installation in late 1994 is part of a $7.7 million "International Media Center" located in Kiev. It was funded by a three-year USAID grant. It's the first and only nongovernmental earth station in the Ukraine. It'll be able to send to any satellite in the region. Initially, it used a EUTELSAT bird for distribution of about one hour per day of high-quality educational, humanitarian, and documentary programs. Roughly half of the programming comes from the region, the rest is acquired abroad. This distribution project is called "Open Skies," and it's funded by Soros and USAID (a different grant) with some help from other foundations.[28]

Belcom arrived in 1990 and now has a number of communications projects, one of which is providing Cyberia Internet Services, an ISP Internet service provider. Belcom also has TVRO locations where viewers can get up to thirty Western TV stations via satellite.[29]

Telephones are coming to the CIS republics. For example, in the Ukraine, in the mid 1990s there were 52 million people, 20 million TV sets—virtually one per household—and 8 million phones, or one for every six persons, roughly. Kazakhstan in the mid 1990s has 17 million people, 5 million TV sets—virtually one per household—and 2.2 million telephones, or about one phone per every eight persons.[30]

Internet servers do exist in all of the former eastern-bloc countries. Access is sparse because of the lack of training in the use of the Internet, the lack of equipment, the lack of adequate phone lines; access is expensive with a restrictive pricing structure.

In the early 1990s, there were fourteen phones per 1,000 people in Russia. Eleven million people were on a waiting list for telephone hookup. Phone line upgrading has seen steady progress over the 1990s.

But, what a job! It's understandable that the fledgling networking efforts have not moved rapidly into easily accessible Internet hookups. In 1989 in Moscow, Demos, the software and networking company, founded the first private Soviet company to link into Western networks. They founded the Relcom network, and they are a major provider in the region. The Internet in Russia is expensive, except that a domain name can be registered for free through the On-line Resource Center ORC in Moscow. Another ISP, in St. Petersburg, is Nevalink. GlasNet is a nonprofit, nongovernmental network that offers email service to those without computers.

Belarus has seven Internet servers, all in Minsk. The largest, Belpak, is state run and is built from Relcom, this now-old Soviet network of businesses. The expansion to the public has occurred since 1992, but by 1996 there were still fewer than 1,100 Net users in the country.

In the Ukraine, all the service is in Kiev. Most of it is built onto the old Soviet Relcom network, with thirty-four phone lines on three nodes. But it is expensive. There are other servers in Kiev. One is the youth-oriented one called LuckyNet. Its Web page says, "You [sic] know, there are different brands of the Internet—academical, educational, governmental, even military. Our Internet is just friendly. We do not wear neckties. We have hundreds or thousands of friends in this city. And we like *beer*."[31] Then there's Kyiv FreeNet in Kiev, a service operated by the UN Internet Project.

In Kazakhstan there's an ISP called Kazinformtelecom, which is a Relcom server. In Tajikistan there's been an email service since July 1995, called Perdca. Kyrgyzstan has three commercial data providers, two of which provide Internet connections. They are AsiaInfo and EIC, the Relcom descendant. A nonprofit email site began in late 1995, but there's no dial-up access yet. It's at the National Library in Bishkek, and over 500 students and professors have accounts.

The U.S. Parliamentary Human Rights Foundation founded a project in the country of Georgia in 1994 called "Supporting the Rule of Law in Georgia through Internet Connectivity." It connects parliament to the Internet and uses an ISP called Sanet in Tiblisi.

Table 5.2 lists useful Internet sites in the CIS countries.

CASE STUDIES IN DEMOCRATIZATION

Russia

Changing the definition of a country is not easy. It's happened in Russia with remarkably little bloodshed despite the political turmoil and economic hardship. Now, at the end of the decade, the jury is still out on the final state of the republic and its economy. The opportunities are enormous for all concerned, as are the problems in this fragile new system. How is success possible when people expect their leaders to transform the nation into a market economy and neither the people nor their leaders have any idea what that means? For three generations, the nation found virtue in behaving exactly opposite to the way that one would behave in a market economy. For scores of generations, people behaved opposite to the way one would expect in a democracy. In fact, never, until 1991, had Russia elected a head of state. What people wanted was the freedom and economic living standards of the West. How would they transform themselves from where they were to what they might become? The West said, "Just do it. We're watching." It's quite remarkable that it hasn't been a total failure.

Here again was an enormous opportunity for global leaders of news and information television programming to provide models. Their lack of ini-

Table 5.2
Internet Sites in CIS and Baltic Countries

Russia
<http://www.demos.su> or <info@demos.su> Demos Co.
<http://april.ibpm.serpukhov.su/friends/telecomm/freenet.russia.html> FREEnet
or <dasha@ncc.free.net>
<avoronov@glas.apc.org> Glasnet in Moscow
<http://www.orc.ru/eng/> or <webmaster@www.orc.ru> Online Resource Center
<http://www.arcom.spb.su/info/english/index.html> NEVAlink
<natasha@ibpm.serpukhov.su> Friends and Partners

Ukraine
<http://www.cs.kiev.ua> or <paul@ua.net> Monolit-Internet in Kiev
<http://www.lucky.net/about.shtml> or <admin@lucky.net> LuckyNet
<http://www.ts.kiev.ua/about/about-e.html> or <web-wizard@ts.kiev.ua> Relcom

Tajikistan
<root@td.silk.glas.apc.org> or <aso@td.silk.glas.apc.org> PERDCA

Kazakhstan
<http://www.kit.kz> KAZINFORMTELECOM
<http://www.relcom.kz> Relcom Kazakhstan

Kyrgyzstan
<http://www.freenet.bishkek.su> or <irex@freenet.info.bishkek.su> Freenet

Belarus
<postmaster@gis.minsk.by> BelPak
<alexeyko@by.glas.apc.org> Glasnet
<admin@unibel.by> Unibel
<minskadm@sovam.com> Sovam Teleport
<minvolk@glas.apc.org> Transinform

Latvia
<http://www.latnet.lv/LATNET> or <webmaster@latnet.lv> LATNET in Riga
<http://www.bitnet.lv/clients/bilteks/english> Bilteks Ltd. in Riga
<lnb@mii.lu.lv> National Library
<http://www.parks.lv/home/LNT> Latvian Independent Television

Lithuania
<http://neris.mii.lt/litnet> or <sulcas@ktl.mii.lt> LITNET information
<root@lnb.mce.lt> National Library

Estonia
<teatsaal@venus.nlib.ee> National Library

Source: Douglas Gray, Emerson researcher.

tiative and lack of comprehension of the opportunity indicate that the global television industry leaders don't know how to serve their own self-interest on a grand scale.

In order to achieve a stability that would result in prosperous markets across Russia, it is imperative that people in all walks of life survive the economic transition successfully. It's in the industry's self-interest to see that happen. It's not charity. Would it have been a problem to explain in news stories about government budgets what a budget is? A lot of folks in the West might benefit from decoding the coverage, too. Would it have been a problem when ending a news broadcast to have a disclaimer that states that the media in a democratic country does not buy information from sources, but is expected to be able to gather news freely? Would it have been a problem to highlight new entrepreneurs occasionally, telling how they succeeded in establishing their business?

It would, in fact, be much more useful to provide this information as news and not just protocol economic news. Protocol economic news is as useless as protocol political news that tells us when the king came and went, but never tells us how or why. Would it have been a problem to elaborate on a news event by showing how an individual's initiative contributed to the result? That might be inspiring to viewers anywhere. Would it have been a problem when reporting on a civic group action to explain the role of groups of citizens when they join into nonprofit organizations, taking the lead to change a policy or provide a service? This civic sector is essential to democracy, yet many new arrivals among the democratized countries may not know that that such activity is legal, let alone desirable. In short, why is it a problem to democratize news reporting?

The lack of such models and explanations has left Russia in the position of "winging it." It has cowboy capitalism. The rule of force wins, because the rule of law hasn't been developed as an alternative to the kind of law known in a dictatorship. The bottom line is only money, because no one knows how to make free speech a bottom line. News-gathering succeeds to the extent that the media can afford to buy information sold to them by the bureaucrats.

The mindset issues are important in Russia, as everywhere. The public doesn't appreciate human rights because they have no appreciation of the fact that such respect is possible. They don't expect press freedom or freedom to travel because they have never known what that is. Journalists are arrested. News is restricted, and equipment is destroyed. Civil society doesn't exist in the form of active nongovernmental organizations (NGOs) advocating for various concerns. The public believes, based on their Soviet experience, that initiative is bad and that if they make no decisions, they will make no mistakes. How can one reach the point of establishing press freedoms and realizing a healthy and stable economy if one is expected to do it by trial and error?

Aside from these basic mindset problems, understanding how to balance the economy remains a problem. For example, press freedoms collided with economic reform from the onset in 1992. The Russian press advocates freedom but wants a government subsidy. Countless independent commercial enterprises in the West succeed only because there is a balance between those extremes and the government laws and regulatory bodies required to ensure the balance. Do any of the news reports on these transactions ever explain what's happening and why it's in everyone's interest not to go to the extremes of total government control of the press or total abandonment of fledgling business?

The print media has been caught in the economic transition. On the one hand, there are many more papers, each often advocating a specific position. But, on the other hand, newspaper circulation declined in the first half of the 1990s from 220 million readers to 20 million readers. There are numerous problems. Newsprint is a problem because the former government industry is now privatized companies who can sell their product abroad for a better price. The newspaper distribution service is still state run, but now it is expensive.[32]

In December 1991, Russia passed a new broadcast law. As the system of law and regulation developed, President Yeltsin needed to satisfy the members of the Russian parliament who came from Russia's member states. He effectively gave the decision making to individual states for those aspects of broadcasting that need national standardization. Each republic within Russia uses a different frequency for cell phones.[33] It's as if the FCC in the United States gave the individual states the right to decide frequency use and to set their own telecommunication standards. It's hard to understand the significance of decisions unless one has the institutional infrastructure and taps the expertise required.

Russian TV was reorganized by presidential decree in October 1994. ORT, the former state-operated TV 1, is now semiprivate, with Yeltsin as chairman of the board of trustees. The former Channel 2 is RTV, part of a state company through which regions produce and air their own programs between 6 and 9 P.M. There is private TV, principally in Moscow. Transmission across the country is difficult for the private companies. TV 6 and NTV are two channels. In the regions, independent TV has had a difficult time starting, primarily because of the costs, coupled with transmission problems. A TV station may spend 15% of its budget on program and up to 80% paying the government for transmission. Then occasionally, as in 1993 and 1994, the communications workers are not paid because of government financial problems. They go on strike, and there are TV blackouts. By 1996, radio and TV had over ninety state companies and 800 private ones, but 95% of all TV and 85% of all radio were state transmitted.[34]

Mikhail Kazachkov, the president of Russia's Freedom Channel, notes,

I am seeing that the economy won't provide the juice for rapid expansion in TV in Russia. But there is one resource, still not used completely. It's the microwave transmission system built originally for the Russian military. NTV uses this relay system. It's pretty cheap to upload your signal. The expensive part is the downloading over eleven time zones. That's where the independent broadcaster has problems. It's almost unthinkable to build substitute transmission facilities. So it remains a monopoly. There's still a lot of transponder space not used because the ground piece is not in place. The Ministry of Communications has the monopoly because they own the ground facilities.[35]

While television domestic structure evolves, knowing how to use TV programming in a civil war is almost instinctual. In the rebellion from Russia occurring in the republic of Chechnya, a Suni Muslim Russian territory, the Chechens are regularly welcoming media coverage while the Russian government issues statements warning journalists to stay away.[36]

Everyone knows that this region has enormous economic potential. The media has enormous potential as an industry, as a vehicle for telling the public about market products and services, and it is hoped as a vehicle for the exchange of information needed to keep increasing the viability of the quality of life. Investors are coming. Advertising is growing fast. In 1991, total advertising sales were $3 million. In 1992, they were $51 million. In 1993, they reached $220 million. In 1994, advertising reached an annual level of investment of $1.2 billion. Some 50% of the advertising is on TV, while the other 35%–40% is in the print media. With these revenues, it is hoped that the proliferation of stations will continue and stations will become stable businesses. Maintaining numerous channels for communication, with numerous owners of differing viewpoints, stabilizes democratic development and makes it ever more difficult to stage military coups.

Certainly the events of the last decade in the CIS provide food for thought in assessing the democratization of the media. How much more rapidly and how much more painlessly might these events have occurred had the media not been indifferent? This is not to suggest that the media should in any way become an advocate. This is simply to suggest that a common ground could be established with a goal of facilitating viewer understanding of the elements necessary for viable democratic governing. It's not unprecedented to expect such high ground. During World War II, news and information media and entertainment media alike set such a common ground, contributing greatly to civilian morale and motivation for adjusting to a wartime economy.

Parliamentary Models

Other examples of democratizing the media are cited in the following. One model is to televise gavel-to-gavel coverage of the lawmaking processes, as does C-Span in the United States. In France, Parisian cable has a channel devoted exclusively to the French parliament. The British have their own parliamentary channel and are considering launching a TV channel of their own.

Albanian Case Study

This country has experienced turbulent times since the communist economy collapsed in 1990. Understanding the concept of a free press was, of course, difficult for the population, who had had no experience understanding what that might mean. Failure to air political issues in open debate before the all-important first election meant that the election results were overturned, putting yet more strain on the fragile young democracy. Failure to utilize the media to explain the advantages and disadvantages of various financial investments in a market economy meant that millions of people invested in a pyramid scheme. When it failed, hope for a viable market economy and confidence in the government were destroyed—as was the economic viability of countless households. Albania is a very poor country. The EU provided a third of its national budget in 1996.[37]

Without examples, it's always hard to understand new concepts. The West hasn't done much to provide examples of market economy and democratic government to the former Soviet bloc countries.

What's a free press? "Just have one" has been much of the message from the West. How do you do something that you have no idea how to do? For example, ART, Albanian Radio-Television's Statute (Article 5) says that Albanian radio and television must be pluralistic, impartial and objective but that it must be directed by the "national ideal" and "defend and develop the national culture and tradition." With this legal directive and with the state-operated media secure in their funding base, the new private stations have a hard time competing. Free speech has been somewhat easier to accomplish in the print media simply because of the proliferation of journals. Since 1994, over 250 journals registered with Ministry of Justice. But because purchasing newsprint, paying for circulation, and hoping readers can afford the luxury of buying a paper are all difficult hurdles, most publications have very short lives.

There's an implicit, not explicit, policy of censorship by the government, suggesting economic censorship of the media, if the media are not cooperative. *Nieman Reports*, commenting on the media coverage of the election to vote on a new constitution in 1994, stated, "Albanian radio and television had given definitive proof that it was just as servile to the ruling Democratic Party as it had once been to the Communist Party of Labor."[38] They're likely right. The question is, is it loyalty or is it ignorance about how a free press works, or is it economic blackmail?

One of the major deterrents to a viable independent media are taxes. Clearly all governments need money to provide services, but the wrong tax policy can hurt the country more than it helps if leaders fail to understand how to establish a viable tax policy. Would it be a problem when talking about taxes to put stories in context and explain when a tax is progressive or regressive? Where else, other than on TV, would a broad cross-section of the populace see such models? How can a new business survive if it's paying a 15% circulation tax, a 15% advertising revenue tax, a 25% tax on imported (all) newsprint, and a 30% tax on all profit?[39]

Some of the new media have been fortunate enough to have Internet access. One of first private companies, the Independent Albanian Economic Tribune Ltd., has an online branch called Albanian Daily News, designed by a French Web company. It provides daily updates in English. It also has a Net subscription service priced at a level suitable for business and institutions, not individuals. To access this publication, see <http://web. albaniannews.com/albaniannews/headline/text3.html>. To subscribe, see <http://ww2.AlbanianNews.com/AlbanianNews/subscribe.html>.[40]

One way around the free press difficulties, for those with access, is the Internet. Newsgroups such as <soc.culture.albania> have an overflow in information exchange.

Bulgarian Case Study

Bulgaria, with a population of nearly 9 million people, is another of the former Soviet bloc countries. The new technologies are moving in quickly, despite the economic hardships faced in this country during its transition to a market economy. The number of phone lines has increased dramatically. In just six years, from 1990 to 1996, they increased from 1.9 million to over 3 million. Now, persons can use coaxial cable to direct-dial thirty-six countries. Some 77% of families have phones at home, but the waiting list is long, and it takes months to get service installed. As of 1996, 96,000 of the new lines are digital.

One can get satellite TV from ASTRA, EUTELSAT 1 and 2, and Hot Bird 1 and 2 and via the Italian Berlusconi service. Nelly Andreeva, a physicist and the recipient of Bulgaria's "Best TV Producer of 1996" award, says,

> People like the film channels from Scandinavia like FilmNet, TV 1000, and they like to watch sports on Eurosport. Satellite dishes cost two to three months' salary plus the monthly charge of $50–$60. Prior to 1989 it was illegal to have a satellite dish without police permission. At that time, the only outside information came from radio—BBC, VOA, Radio Free Europe and Deutsche Welle. There's still only one national TV network, and Bulgaria is slow in launching private TV channels. So more and more people have satellite dishes. Satellite is thought to be better than cable.

In 1989, national censorship was decreased, and as a result there was much experimentation with novel presentations of the news. The journalists prepared and presented the news themselves, as opposed to the past when the so-called speakers just read the news approved by the editors. News documentaries and journalistic editions with different views appeared as well.[41]

There are approximately 10,000 Internet users in Bulgaria, primarily companies, universities, and the media. There were ten providers in 1996.

In 1994, the communists won the national parliamentary elections and reinstated some censorship. Nelly Andreeva's popular Channel 1 show, called "Coo-Coo," with poignant political and satirical materials, was the first show to be taken off the air, temporarily.

Nelly represented a group of young Bulgarians who took control of TV production in the heady days of the new democracy. She said,

Young people should care about news but it's hard to make them. I'm very surprised that six years after democracy came, the major news shows in prime time are still not interesting. They are boring. But older people watch them. They still believe them. It's amazing. In the United States people want to be entertained, but in Bulgaria they want to be aware. Anyway, to interest young people, you need to find new ways. I think we found one with "Coo-Coo." It was very nice to have a lot of young people stop me on the street and talk about the information that they got from a program that was humorous. It's a different point of view. I'm not sure we reached the older people, but we targeted the younger people.

Whatever is on TV, people will believe. That's why we did a program that pointed up the errors so that people would learn to think and to be more skeptical of what's said.

One example is when we got an African student to come with us and speak with some politicians about what Bulgarian's relationship should be with a fictitious country that we said was in Africa. The politicians we interviewed all spoke very convincingly about the importance of one aspect or another of Bulgaria's relationship with this country. None of them realized it was fictitious until we announced it on TV.

Of course, we had some problems. It's possible for people inside the station to view a program a couple of days in advance. Some people contacted the politicians, who demanded that the program not be aired. They spoke to the station boss. It was agreed that if they asked me personally, as producer, I should pull the show off the air. However, if I disappeared and they couldn't find me to ask me, well— the show would go on. It was broadcast and it was a huge success.

The press isn't totally free in Bulgaria, even now after our last election when we outvoted the communists who had won our first election. It's not direct censorship. We call it "cellular pressure." It adds up to censorship. The politicians using their cellular phones call the news editor before a program and make requests about changing the program. A lot of people think that the only difference between now and when the communists were in power is whose hand is on the cellular phone.[42]

SUMMARY

Eastern Europe, in the last decade of this century, serves as a model for the world should anyone question the importance of the media in democratization. Aside from the many examples previously cited, consider the situation in Serbia.

In February 1997, the wire services announced that Belgrade's first non-communist mayor in fifty-two years said that the next battle would be to get media control from Serbian president Slobodan Milosevic.[43] It was announced that people planned to demonstrate daily in front of the state-run TV station. Milosevic said he wouldn't give up without a fight and that he'd take steps against "pirate radio and television stations." The interior minister was named the head of the state TV's managing board. The interior ministry's main responsibility is the police. This story underlines the importance of media news and information.

The vitality of the emerging democracies in Europe provides vivid examples for those of us who have become complacent about free speech, stability, and economic well-being.

Couple the political and economic opportunities emerging in eastern Europe with the dynamism of the new European Union and the opportune timing to utilize the new communications. Europe is affluent enough to make use of them. It's a remarkable period of history in Europe. How will the Europeans build on this moment of opportunity? Will they harness the creativity of their young? Will they bog themselves down in the bureaucratic procedures that have smothered so much creativity? No doubt, the answers will vary from country to country.

Europe will have to deal with more than the East adjusting to market economies. Many countries have had little experience with racial and cultural diversity and a history of intolerance. Now, many of these countries find themselves with nonwhite populations and people whose religions differ from the dominant ones. In parts of eastern Europe, it's as if a heat wave melted the ethnic and religious hostilities that were frozen in ice half a century ago, when the communists refused to tolerate such bigotry. The rivalries began exactly where they left off.

Creating a mosaic, or a melting pot, is harder in Europe than in the United States, because it is not a continent of people "from" somewhere.

The United States, a nation of immigrants from every corner of the globe, has had to realize that diversity exists. On the other hand, the relatively stable economies and social systems in place in Europe make it easier to overcome the gaps that create instability—at least on most of the continent.

As we move into the twenty-first century, the real question is, how much of a model will Europe be for global village life? Will the media within Europe help facilitate understanding between people, or will it incite hostility? Will the rest of the globe be able to learn of Europe's successes as well as its failures? Maybe there will be some models useful to others. Will Europe be able to learn from and about others via the media? Might it be helpful to a global marketplace to broaden the view of the globe's nations and abandon the stereotypes of the colonial era—now a century out of date?

NOTES

1. For information updates, see <hkb@nic.funet.fi> for more information on European satellite channels. Also see Web sites on European satellite TV: <http://www.igd.fhg.de/www/projects . . . d/projects/image_com/anam1003.html>, for EBU Technical Department on the European initiatives for digital image distribution, and <http://www.hf-fak.uib.no/institutter/smi/ksv/SatFaq.html>, "European Satellite TV Frequently Asked Questions," for information on frequently asked questions from a Scandinavian perspective.

2. With appreciation to Guney Keser, researcher, Emerson Graduate Mass Communications program, December 1996.

3. Peter Vesey, Vice President, CNNI, One CNN Center, 4th Floor, North Tower, Atlanta, GA 30303. Telephone interview with the author on October 25, 1994.

4. Carla B. Johnston, *Winning the Global TV News Game* (Boston and London: Butterworth Heinemann/Focal Press, 1995), chapter 3.

5. See NBC Superchannel Web sites for information updates: <www.nbceurope.com>. To send comments, write <stmp:talkback@cnbcsuper.nbc.com>.

6. For history of EBU, see Robert L. Hilliard, and Michael C. Keith, *Global Broadcasting Systems* (Boston and Oxford: Butterworth Heinemann/Focal Press, 1996), p. 192.

7. Johnston, *Winning*, pp. 188–189. Also see *Catalogue of Publications* (Geneva: European Broadcasting Union, Ancienne Route 17a/Casa Postale 67, CH-1218 Grand Saconnex, Geneva, Switzerland, February 1990).

8. See <http://www2.echo.lu/parliament/resoluti.html>. Also see <webmaster@echo.lu>.

9. Bangemann Group Report, "Recommendations to the European Council: Europe and the Global Information Society." For updates see <http:www.ecu.gov>. Also see Media Programme Newsletters on this independent advocate for European production development at the following Web site: <http://europa.eu.int/en/comm/dg10/ . . . ia/news-14/en/nlmulti.html>.

10. *Progress of Nations*, UNICEF, 1995.

11. Contact *<http://fundesco.es>* for information on Spain from Agencie EFE, the Spanish wire service.

12. *Progress of Nations*.

13. Anders Burholm, Stockholm. Email interview with author on August 31, 1997.

14. For information on Slovakia see *<Altavista.Essat>*.

15. Hilliard, *Global Broadcasting*, p. 134.

16. For information on Romania, see *<http://www.romamcc.org>*.

17. See *<Altavista.Business Briefs>*. Also see *<http://ibspur.wawpl/html/esattd3/usergroup>*.

18. Ognen Firov, B.S., E.E., Internet systems engineer for PTT Macedonia, interviewed by Guney Keser, researcher, Emerson Graduate Program in Mass Communications, December 1996. See *<ognen@lotus.mpt.com.mk>*. Also see *<http://www.mpt.com.mk>*, the homepage for Macedonia.

19. For added information on the Czech Republic, try *<http://tvnet.com/tv/czkz.>*

20. Anna Matsuzaka, researcher, Emerson Graduate Program in Mass Communications, Fall 1996. Also see *<Altavista.Business Briefs>*.

21. Several Web sites can provide information updates. See *<http://www.hungary.com/hac/press/94/html>* for information on providing Duna TV in the United States. See *<http://www.intercall.com/hamilton>* on Hungarian media law.

22. Anna Matsuzaka, researcher, "Issues of Global TV and the Internet in Selected East European Countries." Unpublished paper, Emerson Graduate Program in Mass Communications, December 1996. Also see *<Altavista.developments>*.

23. Matsuzaka, "Issues of Global TV and the Internet."

24. See *<http://gurukul.ucc.american.edu>* and *<http://www.org/Publicat/Press/data/1994>* for comments on telecom in Poland.

25. Stephen Kinzer, "A Terror to Journalists, He Sniffs out Terrorists." *New York Times*, September 1, 1997, p. A4.

26. Johnston, *Winning*, p. 198f.

27. See *<http://www.eutelsat.org>*.

28. Eric S. Johnson, Communication Coordinator, Internews, at *<71064.2533@compuserve.com>*. Email interview on November 14, 1994.

29. Douglas Gray, Internet researcher, Emerson Program in Mass Communications, Fall 1996. Also see *<http://www.belcom.com>*.

30. All data is from the CIA Factbook, available online at *<http://www.odci.gov/cia/publications/95fact/index.html>*.

31. Douglas Gray.

32. It's possible to view the St. Petersburg Press online, at *<http://www.spb.su/sppress/>*.

33. Mikhail Kazachkov, President, Freedom Channel, Inc., 30 Stone Ave., Somerville, MA. Telephone interview with author on November 24, 1994.

34. Elena Androunas, Russian media consultant, "Russian Media and the Myth of Freedom." Unpublished paper presented Spring 1996 at Harvard seminar. Interview with author at Harvard on May 20, 1996.

35. Kazachkov, interview.

36. Douglas Gray, Also see information on the Chechen Republic of Ichkeria at <http://www.chechnya.org>.

37. Douglas Gray. Also see *The New York Times*, March 7, 1997, at <http://search.nytimes.com/ . . . />.

38. *Nieman Reports*, 50, no. 2 (Summer 1996): 78, Harvard University.

39. See <http://www.osi.hu/colpi/albania/achp7.htm>.

40. Douglas Gray, "Economic Gatekeeping in the Eastern European Country of Albania." Unpublished paper, Emerson Seminar in Mass Communication, Spring 1997.

41. Nelly Andreeva, recipient of Bulgaria's "Best TV Producer of 1996." Tele-lecture to Emerson International Communications class, November 8, 1996. Also see the financial newspaper's Web site on Bulgaria at <www.pari.bg>. See <www.bulgaria.com/NTV/>, the Web site for "New Television." Related information can be found on <http://www.odci.gov/cia/95fact.> and <http://ibspur.wawpl/html/esattd3/usergroup>.

42. Nelly Andreeva, interview with author in Boston on August 11, 1997.

43. "Belgrade's New Mayor Vows to Fight to Control State Media." *Boston Globe*, February 21, 1997, p. A15.

6

Middle East and Africa

OVERVIEW

Middle East and North Africa

Arabic heritage and the Muslim religion are the unifying characteristics of much of this area. The region is at the junction of three continents—Europe, Asia, and Africa—and it embodies characteristics of all three. An equally compelling characteristic of the region is the fact that three of the world's major religions—Judaism, Christianity, and Islam—consider Jerusalem to be their holy city. Waging peace continues to be a precarious process.

But, rest assured, whatever happens, you'll be able to see it on television, and so will most of the people in the Middle East/North Africa region: the UN estimates that 80% of the people in this region have access to television despite enormous rich-poor gaps.

The Middle East could be called the birth place of "live" global TV news. The hallmark event was CNN's Peter Arnett describing the Persian Gulf War from Baghdad rooftops in 1991, proving that "live" global TV news can be better than a movie rerun. Scores of national broadcasters signed contracts with CNN. In addition, the BBC, Murdoch's News Corp., and others like NBC Superchannel and APTV launched competition for CNN.

There are twenty-one major countries in the Middle East and North Africa, plus the West Bank/Gaza. Included are Algeria, Bahrain, Djibouti, Egypt, Iran, Iraq, Israel, Jordan, Kuwait, Lebanon, Libya, Morocco, Oman,

Qatar, Saudi Arabia, Sudan, Syria, Tunisia, United Arab Emirates, and Yemen. Only Israel and Iran are not Arab. The Israelis and Arabs share a common Semitic racial and cultural heritage, despite their religious differences. The Iranians share the Muslim religion with their Arab neighbors, although they have an Aryan background racially and speak Farsi.

Two of the globe's top ten wealthiest countries are in the Middle East. Kuwait is eighth in wealth with a 1993 GNP per capita of $23,350, and the United Arab Emirates is tenth with a 1993 GNP per capita of $22,470.[1] These countries have funds for infrastructure improvement. Compare their gross national product per capita with the GNP numbers for some other Middle East countries—$660 per capita in Egypt, $420 in Sudan, and $520 in Yemen.

By and large, the media within countries in this region is tightly controlled. For those without satellite or cable television, as the countries are small, cross-border viewing often brings the consumer more than just the few local stations. Nachman Shai, director general of the Second Television and Radio Authority in Israel, commented on the cross-border viewing in Israel, "We watch television from Jordan, Egypt, Syria, and Morocco. They don't watch Israeli TV. Except, in Jordan it's different, because our transmission signals are strong enough to reach there."[2]

Sub-Saharan Africa

According to the UNESCO Statistical Yearbook for 1995, the sub-Saharan region of Africa had a population of 562 million people. This region includes all of the ten poorest countries of the world; they are listed here with their 1993 GNP per capita.

Mozambique	$80
Eritrea	$100
Ethiopia	$100
Somalia	$120
Congo Democratic Republic	$120
Tanzania	$120
Burundi	$160
Malawi	$170
Rwanda	$180
Sierra Leone	$180[3]

Consequently, the challenges are enormous in sub-Saharan Africa. Securing a piece of the twenty-first-century marketplace isn't easy. Nineteenth-century colonialism in this region took the form of exploitation of natural resources and underinvestment in infrastructure. Now, over a century after the heyday of colonialism, Africans are still paying the price for what was done to them. In the early twentieth century the affluent regions of the globe were using the latest technologies and building their resource base for viable economic development. This didn't happen in sub-Saharan Africa, except in those few places with large communities of Europeans. By the time African nations became independent in the mid twentieth century, much of the globe was realizing the damage caused by colonialism and racism. Substantial financial revenue finally flowed in. Often this helped. But brand-new countries did not have established enough judicial systems to restrain corrupt misappropriation of funds when a leader cared more about himself than his nation. This wasn't always the case, but it has undermined progress. The moneys came to these new countries as aid, rather than as a commitment to ongoing investment in jobs with long-term trade options. Consequently, prosperity was short lived. When the grants were gone, things hadn't changed much. Catching up in a marketplace where others have a half-century lead is extremely difficult.

The region still has a 25% literacy rate. In all, 800 languages and dialects are spoken.[4] The best legacy of colonialism, however, is that in eighteen countries English in spoken, in twenty countries French, and in 3 Portuguese—tools for participation in a global marketplace. In addition, there are regional African languages that help facilitate the development of intra-African economic growth. Most East Africans speak Kiswahili. Many in West Africa speak Gausa, and in South Africa many can speak Afrikaans—although it doesn't please them.

Infrastructure to support media advancement is poor in most of sub-Saharan Africa and, for that matter, in North Africa and much of the Middle East. The centers of major cities are the same as those anywhere in the world. But just a short distance away, roads may be nonexistent, sanitation infrastructure is likely a fantasy, and people live in their native tribal lands much as they have for centuries. Except, of course, most of them have access to a communal TV viewing center if they don't have their own TV. The rural poverty is appalling, and 85% of the region is rural. Where would one earn a living to climb out of poverty? The press has generally not been free, resulting in limited exposure to new ideas or to new opportunities. Politics are difficult for several reasons. One is that the national borders were creations of the colonialists and don't necessarily reflect local preferences. Another is that many of the countries told to "be democracies" don't, as in the case of the former Soviet countries, have the slightest idea what that means for the average citizen. Consequently, it's very difficult to have a nation of laws and multiparty elections. Besides, what *do* retired "presidents" do? Why would one step down?

The media has all too often contributed to Africa's problems by focusing

on its famines, revolutions, and scandals. Little or no attention is paid to
the remarkable accomplishments that are made against almost insurmount-
able odds. There are lots of good news stories that can provide models for
people in other developing countries.

For example, how much coverage has been given to the remarkable
strides toward democracy and development that have occurred in South
Africa in the years since F. W. de Klerk made possible a nonviolent end to
apartheid and Nelson Mandela led the African National Congress government to draft a new constitution, create election districts, explain what
elections are, and provide electricity and sewers, housing, and health care?

DEVELOPMENTS IN COMMUNICATIONS TECHNOLOGY

Fiber Optics

On a global scale, Africa isn't forgotten. For example, the Fiberoptic
around the Globe (FLAG) project has a cable along Africa's north coast,
provided as a project of French Telecom. In addition, AT&T plans an
"Africa One" fiber optic network to encircle the continent, and Alcatel has
a proposed fiber link along Africa's west coast. But, the challenge remains
enormous to complete these systems when their use may not be great unless
the continent's economies improve.

In the early 1990s, 5% of Namibians had telephones. That was four
times more than the continental average. Without internal infrastructure,
how can the economies develop? And without economic development, how
can the infrastructure develop?

Given the circumstances, the infrastructure improvements that are happening deserve special appreciation. Look at the Pan-African Telecommunications project as an example. PANAFTEL has been created for the entire
continent—North Africa as well as sub-Saharan Africa. During the colonial
period, intra-African telecommunications was ignored in favor of colony-
to-colonizer communications. With the national independence movements
in the mid twentieth century, momentum for communications development
grew. The Pan-African Telecommunications Network was conceived of in
Dakar, Senegal, in 1962 and developed into plan in 1967 in Addis Ababa,
Ethiopia. In 1968 the International Telecommunications Union asked the
UN Development Program to fund detailed technical studies. By 1990,
39,000 km of microwave relay links, 8,000 km of submarine links, thirty-
nine international switching centers, and forty-two of the forty-five member
countries had at least one earth station and segments in use. Only twenty-
nine links, or 4,000 km, remained to be installed.[5] The Northern Zone was
relatively complete. West Africa had maintenance and operational problems. East Africa had a working system, but politics handicapped its functioning. Central Africa was less developed, mostly because of a lack of

political will. The Southern Africa region was nearly complete. By 1989, analog equipment was being replaced with digital; and as fiber optics technology became available, plans were made for conversion.

Low user demand has slowed the project. As late as 1992, only 14% of the continent's international telecommunications was intraregional. It's remarkable that the legacy of colonialism remains a central force impeding self-development generations after the fact. On the other hand, once the economies within Africa begin to grow, their external contacts should serve them well for expanding into the global marketplace. South Africa, the continent's most affluent country, has a different story. Its apartheid policies caused it to be isolated from the rest of the continent and most of the world until the 1994 elections. The end of apartheid is bringing investment into South Africa and should hasten the availability of the latest technologies to people in the whole southern part of the continent.

Global TV

Satellite dishes are for the wealthy, who seem to find ways around the small matter of local illegality, if they live where such laws exist. But, increasingly, TV is accessible to a majority of people—if not in their own homes, then in some place where they go. This may limit viewers to one or two local channels. But as competition increases in the major cities, the local channels are signing rebroadcast agreements to send to their viewers programs previously available only to those with dishes. Certainly, many people in this region live in virtually cashless societies and don't have the currency needed to own TV sets. They may not have the electricity. Somewhere there is someone who owns a set and has a 9-volt battery. Is the power of the program less, because fewer people are exposed to TV? Or, is the power of the program more, because what one sees is such a novelty in comparison to daily life tending herds and raising kids?

Middle East and North Africa

These countries have a love-hate relationship with the new technology. On the one hand, they want nothing to do with this tool for Western cultural invasion. On the other hand, it's fun to watch—certainly more interesting than the standard fare on local channels—and it's a great idea to be able to transmit one's own programming to others.

Kuwait, Egypt, Dubai, and Jordan transmit satellite programming. Syria plans to. MBC, ART, and Orbit are commercial stations for the region that use satellite transmission. Kuwait's decision to invest in satellite television was based on the belief that the best way to counter foreign satellite TV was to provide a superior alternative.

Other countries ban—or say they ban—satellite TV. For example, satellite dishes are illegal in Saudi Arabia, but in affluent neighborhoods everyone has them. Stores sell them. You can install them. The government imports them. Iran "bans" dishes, as do others. In most of these cases, a double standard thrives.

Those who do receive satellite TV benefit from being included in many European satellite footprints as well as in the footprints for Asian satellites. Consequently, their programming choice is as good as that anywhere in the world.[6]

Aside from the viewpoints of the individual nations in the region, the Arab League of Nations had the foresight to move into the world of satellites in 1974, when the Arab Telecommunications Union began thinking of launching its own satellite. In 1976, the Arab Satellite Communications Organization (ARABSAT) was created, and in 1985 France launched their first satellite for them. See <www.arab.net/arabsat/welcome.html>. For a decade, from 1979 to 1989, Egypt was barred from participating because it had signed the Camp David Accords for peace with Israel. Now Egypt is again a member of ARABSAT. Agreeing to peace with Israel was far from popular in Arab circles in the 1980s. There's still room for growth in Arab TV. ARABSAT has more capacity than is used.

Sub-Saharan Africa

INTELSAT covers all of Africa and carries both African and European services with dozens of channels. Some remain free, but most now require a subscription. Broadcasters in Africa in 1994 were the BBC's WSTV, Deutsche Welle/WorldNet, Canal Horizons (French), Algerian TV, and CNNI. Also, French TV 5 Afrique and Portugal's RTP International broadcast on the former Soviet satellite Ghorizont, the first satellite to serve Europe. INTELSAT 505 carries Worldnet/Deutsche Welle and France's Canal France International. INTELSAT 602 carries South Africa's M-Net and SABC. The two South African services are successful because they have partnerships with internationals to bring in Disney, BBC, HBO, MTV, and CNNI.[7] Satellite upgrades made it possible for CNNI to expand coverage in Africa beginning in April 1992. By April 1993, CNNI distributed to households in Ghana, Kenya, Nigeria, Zambia, and Uganda. In Somalia in June 1993, "The fugitive warlord Muhammad Farah Aidid . . . declared that to keep abreast of events, he had been hiding only in homes that received CNN.[8]

In 1992, BBC's WSTV expanded into South Africa using the M-Net satellite service. This project included a joint venture to sell decoders throughout Africa, thereby enabling WSTV programs to be rebroadcast terrestrially on African national TV services. This service is now available in a number of countries.

Internet

Middle East and North Africa

Use of the Internet depends first on access to telephone hookups, second on access to equipment—a factor dependent on both economics and on political attitude—and third on expertise in using the equipment. Across the region, it is possible to find Internet access, and certainly the expatriate community has encouraged development of such connections as a way to keep in touch. Corporate, government, and academic sectors everywhere have access if their offices are considered a priority by those with the wallets. However, lack of telephones and lack of political interest in providing free exchange of ideas has limited Internet use in many places in the Arab world. Israel accounts for 60% of all regional traffic, and Iran is next in the number of users.

Jordanians have more personal and press freedoms than do their fellow Arabs. Here the Internet has been available to the public since July 1996, but it's expensive. Five or six hours access per month costs about $45 U.S., a lot when one realizes that the average salary is about $150 U.S. per month for a laborer and only $600 U.S. per month for an office worker with a college degree. Still, according to Mary Roodkowsky, regional programme officer for UNICEF's Office for the Middle East and North Africa,

a sizable elite is using the Internet and it's available in some public schools.

There was a local Internet before the global one became available. It has local discussion groups, chat groups, local email, and a service in English only. There is one conference in which people can ask questions of the government and the Ministry of Information will answer them. Generally, they answer pretty rapidly. Typical questions might be about traffic, food cost increases, tourism. There's another conference where the head of Jordanian TV answers questions. These questions are often about programming changes.

Before the Internet, government organizations like the UN, news agencies, and businesses already had built dedicated email lines. This was done through nodes in other countries, usually Egypt or Israel. This was costly because it involved an international phone call. For example to call Israel from Jordan costs about $1.50 per minute. To use a node in Israel would not have been possible before early 1995, when Israel and Jordan established diplomatic relations. Prior to that, there was no telephone or mail contact. Everything had to go via Cyprus.

One problem preventing full use of the Internet in Jordan is the phone lines. Some areas still use pulse dialing and the quality of the lines cannot support modems with speeds faster than 4800 bps. That means it takes a long time to download and to send data. It will improve as installation is completed on the new lines.[9]

Sub-Saharan Africa

In 1995, only about a dozen African countries had Internet access. Regional cooperatives like the East African Internet Association and NGOs like South Africa's African Internet Development Action Team (AIDAT) are working to help expansion. In addition AfricaLink is a USAID project to establish electronic communication between the United States and Africa. Through Africa On-line from Kenya, Zambia's Zamnet, and Uganda's Infomail, Ltd. Internet service is beginning to grow. Table 6.1 lists some African Internet addresses.

REGIONAL MEDIA GIANTS

Middle East and North Africa

Two regional entities provide the major contributions to global television exchange of news and information as a balance to the dominant flow of information from the U.K. and the United States.

Arab States Broadcasting Union (ASBU)

ASBU is a sister organization to the European Broadcasting Union (EBU). It coordinates the exchange of news and information in the Arab states, and it exchanges news feeds and programming with EBU, providing some of the news from the region that is presented by the newsmaker countries.

Middle East Broadcasting Corporation (MBC)

The MBC provides direct-to-home satellite services throughout the Arab world. It's a Western style direct broadcast satellite network to the Arab world. But to protect itself from possible censorship of content, MBC is based in London. It targets 300 million Arabic speakers in the Persian Gulf Region, the Indian subcontinent, and Africa. Its founder is Wald al-Ibrahim, the brother-in-law of King Fahd of Saudi Arabia. It carries movies not available on Arab TV as well as news.

MBC remains controversial. As early as 1992, it angered local Saudi authorities because it was using unveiled news anchorwomen and broadcast uncensored news. Unlike any other Arab broadcaster in the early 1990s, MBC has a Jerusalem bureau. It is the first regional privately operated Arab-language network. It has spread western Arab political views in the Middle East and serves as somewhat of a bridge between the cultures.

Johan Ramsland of BBC's WSTV noted,

Table 6.1
Internet Sites in Africa

<http://www.afrika.com>

<http://www.afnews.org/ans/gateway.html> Internet Gateway: Africa News Online

<http://www.active.co.za/aidat/blurb.html> or
    <http://www.aidat.org> African International Development Action Team

<http://www-sul.stanford.edu/depts/ssrg/africa/elecnet.html> Africa E-Mail Access,
    Electronic Networking

<http://www.ee.ic.ac.uk/misc/bymap/africa.html> International E-Mail Accessibility
    Africa Map

<http://www.africaonline.co.ke> or
    <http://www.africaonline.co.ke/AfricaOnline/welcome.html> or
    <http://www.africaonline.co.ke/AfricaOnline/eastafrican.html> Kenya

<http://www.zamnet.zam/zamnet/zana/zamtoday.html> Zambia

<http://www.mg.co.za/mg/> Mail and Guardian home page--South Africa

<http://www.africaonline.co.ke/AfricaOnline/diary/tvguide/> TV program schedules for
    S.Africa's M-Net satellite programming, KTN, and SUPERSPORT

<http://www.sabc.co.za> South African Broadcasting Corporation (SABC)

<http://www.mnet.co.za> M-Net Front Page

<http://sweb.2.med.iacnet.com/infotrac/session/592> South African daily papers

<http://www.ACTIVE.CO.ZA/> Active Access (ISP)

Source: Donald Coleman, Emerson researcher.

The MBC is getting better and better. It's a general broadcaster. They do a lot of entertainment. They also do a pretty solid international news program. I watched (in London) one day last week to see what the spread of coverage was. I compared their 23:00 bulletin with our 22:00 news. They had all the major stories covered. It's anecdotal, but they do suffer quite a lot of editorial interference from their financial backers. No firsthand evidence, but people who have worked there have said that. I think they are already a Pan-Arab operation. They're throughout the Middle East, and they spin off to distribute programming to expatriate communities as well. I understand they've built up quite an audience. That's because, it's a bit like offering something new in India where everything is so tightly controlled. Something new from the outside is a breath of fresh air.[10]

Sub-Saharan Africa

M-NET is a satellite broadcaster out of South Africa. It started as a cable company owned by the big five newspapers in South Africa. They launched a satellite that has a footprint over all of Africa. WSTV teamed up with them to deliver BBC programming for rebroadcast in Nigeria, Ghana, and eastern and southern African countries. M-NET's independent television news was launched in 1992 at a period of change in South African politics. It looked as if the stranglehold of apartheid might end, but it wasn't clear whether or not that end would come violently.

Other countries, like Kenya, aspire to launching their own satellites, probably as a status symbol as much as anything else. The fact remains that the development priority list is long and resources are short. Plans for a regional satellite system, like ARABSAT, have been discussed, but have not yet reached the stage of implementation. At the local national level, while rigidity prevails in some places, in other countries very exciting things are beginning to happen.

SELECTED COUNTRIES: MEDIA ACCESS

Middle East and North Africa

Algeria, Tunisia, Syria, and Morocco

These countries have a strong tradition of government control of the media. Tunisia and Morocco have, however, legalized the ownership of satellite dishes. Tunis is the location for ASBU's headquarters, Syria's media control, as so much of its government administration, has been heavily influenced by the old Soviet models. Nonetheless, those walking into a major hotel lobby in Damascus can access a Reuters News and Financial Monitor with the latest in business news. In the hotel rooms, one can access CNN, MBC, French and German news, and much of the standard fare available across the globe.

Egypt

Egypt's broadcasting system is among the best in the region, if not the best, because of developments dating back to Nasser's era as leader. In addition to the five national channels, the Egyptian Satellite Channel broadcasts via ARABSAT throughout the Middle East. Nile TV was launched in 1994 to beam broadcasts in English and French to Europe. Part of the reason for Nile TV is to protect the valuable tourism business by providing a broader base of information about Egypt, thereby countering negative publicity about the disruptive activities of the Muslim fundamentalists.

Cairo, as a principal city for regional business, has adequate phone service for those businesses and the wealthier residents. In lower-income areas in the city and in the countryside, work remains to provide adequate phone lines for using the Internet.

Iran

In Iran, there are thirty-five phones per 1,000 persons. The country has twenty-eight television stations. In the mid 1990s, Iran banned possession, use, or distribution of satellite equipment. The objective was to immunize the population against a cultural invasion from the West. It is reported that 90% of dish owners voluntarily dismantled dishes before the April 21, 1995, deadline. Police confiscated seventy-three. The total number of satellite antennas in Iran was estimated to be from as few as 27,000 to a number ten times that great.[11]

Israel

Israel's television structure was established to be like that of the BBC. Israel and Lebanon are the only two countries in the region without government-controlled media. In 1993, there was a TV set for every three people. Cable reaches 70% of the households. Telephones are common except in poorer Palestinian areas. Overall, the standard of living is very high, except for the poverty caused by the religious and political discrimination against the Palestinian population that lives within Israel. In addition, it's been a challenge for the country to absorb the more than 20% increase in the country's population in the early 1990s, caused by the influx of immigrants at last free to emigrate from the Soviet eastern-bloc countries.

Mordechai Kirshenboim, director general of the Israeli Broadcasting Authority, comments on the difficulty of maintaining a balanced independent coverage. He notes that over his tenure, he's been attacked as being too far "right" and other times as being too far "left."

I explain that we operate by the law of broadcasting that forces us to bring all the news views that are being held by the public even if they are not convenient to the government—proportionally, of course. . . . The government forgets sometimes that we are not a government station. We are being sponsored totally by the public. We don't relate to the government budget. The public pays for the broadcasts. We work under a code that things always have to be balanced. Government doesn't have the only say. There is always an opposition. There is always a subject to balance.

Government nominates the IBA Director General in Israel. My board has members of all the political parties, but they reflect when they were nominated. They have three-year terms and a maximum of two terms.[12]

Jordan

As mentioned earlier, Jordan's phone service is adequate for the upper classes to have Internet service. This, obviously, doesn't include the Bedouins living as nomads or those in villages or the lower-income residents of cities. How will cell phones and satellite phones change access to information and services in the years ahead? Read the section in Chapter 7 about Bangladesh.

Television service is nearly everywhere. There are two national television channels, one in Arabic and the other alternating between English and French with Arabic subtitles. In affluent areas, people have satellite dishes. Many dishes are large (two to three meters) and have motors that let them tune to different satellites. By mid 1996 a one-meter dish, not as fancy as the above, cost about $750 U.S., and a 2.5-meter dish cost about $3,000. In less affluent areas, it is common for several families in one apartment block to share a satellite dish. The most popular satellites are ARABSAT with programs from Egypt, Syria, and the Gulf, plus CNN. At one time ARABSAT carried MBC. ASIASAT carries WSTV, Star TV, MTV, and Prime TV. The four EUTELSATs are also popular. One Hot Bird carries the NBC. Superchannel, RAI 1, 2, and 3 from Italy, Deutsche Welle foreign service, Arte and Canal 5 from France, TVE from Spain, Euronews and Eurosport channels, EBN from UK, Dubai TV, and two Polish channels.

At the level of national programming, ideas are hard to change. Radi A. Alkhas, director general of Jordan Radio and Television, explains his problem balancing content news with tradition.

The news in the Arab world used to be all protocol. Pure protocol. No information was given. When I was appointed the director general, four and one-half years ago, the King noted the changes we had to make. For example, in one story with the King of Sweden with the King of Jordan, the TV showed 20 minutes of protocol—kissing each other, the national anthems, the soldiers saluting. When the King of Jordan arrived in Yemen, they showed the same thing. The audience didn't know why he was going to Yemen or what was happening. It's all protocol. We are trying to change this. But it also involves changing the perception of the people who watch it. Some people say, if you don't show the protocol, you don't pay respect to the King. You have this mentality among some people. You have to respect that. We are trying to change things without offending them.[13]

Kuwait

A consortium led by Mohammed al Saqr, editor of Kuwait's only independent newspaper, *Al Qabas*, started a new Arabic language satellite TV station. It began broadcast from Paris in September 1996. The cost for the project is estimated at $75 million. Kuwait and other Arab businessmen own 75% of the station, and the other 25% is owned by international TV stations such as France's TF-1[14] Money is, as was discussed earlier, no problem for Kuwaitis seeking their own place with the new technology giants.

Libya

The tightly controlled government of Libya has no love for Western technologies. However, Muammar Qaddafi is quick to use them when it serves his purpose, and he's quick to understand the power of these technologies across the globe. For example, an example of teleconference foreign policy happened in 1986 when Qaddafi insisted on a CNN reporter's presence at his news conference. He wanted his message to reach U.S. policymakers. And he knew, even in the mid 1980s, that since Turner had given satellite receivers to the Pentagon and to the U.S. Congress, his speech would reach its intended audience if he got it on CNN. At home, he maintains very tight control over the People's Revolutionary Broadcasting Company.

West Bank/Gaza

The challenge of the mid 1990s has been for West Bank/Gaza to create its own communications systems for this emerging Palestinian homeland. The government is brand new, but it isn't a country. It's a nebulous creation of an evolving Middle East peace process. Its very existence is a major accomplishment. Creating the infrastructure and services expected in a cohesive civil society isn't easy. While telephones are available for some, the service in most places is extremely poor or nonexistent. TV sets are much more common, although still a luxury. One of the unique problems faced by Palestinian communication systems experts is broadcasting from 1,300 feet below sea level.

Initially, WAFA, the Palestine news agency, started in temporary headquarters in Gaza. Then, official Palestine TV was launched in 1994. Aside from this, some sixteen pirate TV stations operate in the West Bank. The largest, Nablus TV, has five employees. They are received mostly in cities and with equipment that transmits only a few miles, but they have advertising money. Although the stations are illegal, the government taxes their profits at a 55% rate and sometimes asks for free airtime. As their existence gives a semblance of democracy, they are not usually closed down. One was closed temporarily when it broadcast a program that reportedly "incited violence against Israelis." The deputy Nablus governor Abdel Muiti

Sadek announced that inciting confusion wouldn't be tolerated. None of the pirate stations has even tried to broadcast news. They'll have a doctor giving medical advice, Friday prayers, music and entertainment from Egypt and other Arab TV, or European soccer. The Sanabel station has been recording complaints from the street. For example, a housewife may discuss how there's a need for a youth center for her kids.[15] While information about the Palestinians is frequently seen on global TV news, it's not frequently seen by most Palestinians because of the poor economic conditions and the fragility of their communication systems in these early days of the new era.

Saudi Arabia

Arab Radio and Television (ART) is seen all over the world. A twenty-four-hour variety channel began in October 1993, showing Arab culture. ART is led by Sheik Selah Kamel, owner of the Islamic Banking group Dallah al Barakah. Everything is done, of course, at the pleasure of the royal family. Curbs on satellite viewing are advocated by the Muslim fundamentalists, who are offended by Western customs and especially by the visible face of a woman.

Saudi Arabia is one of the most extreme of the Muslim countries in its controls over women. A woman has no rights as an independent human being. In Saudi Arabia, women must be completely covered. They can't check into hotels by themselves or travel in a group with men. They are expected to stay home. It's quite a contrast to other Arab cultures like Pakistan, where a woman was prime minister, or the UAE, where women jump out of airplanes with their fellow soldiers. The Saudi attitude, however, was a driving force for the MBC to operate out of London.

In 1992 they said, and the government agreed, that the current 200,000 satellite dishes were enough. No more should be put into service. However, time passes and new developments like ART occur. Orbit Satellite TV and Radio Network is another new commercial venture totally approved by the Saudi royal family. In the late 1990s, satellite dishes are illegal, but everyone has one. They provide access to American, European, and Asian TV.

Sub-Saharan Africa

Regional TV Growth

Over half of Africa's political entities had TV access by 1982. Whether and how countries adopted TV varied from place to place. Burundi had outlawed the importation or use of TV. That seemed the safest way to handle this outside influence. However, those in Burundi could see TV from the signals sent out in Zaire (now called Congo). Other countries also had access to TV from their neighbors. Botswana and Lesotho received South African TV. Gambia receives TV from Nigeria and Gabon.

Some had experiences like that of the Ivory Coast. In the 1960s, they received "Tele Pour Tous" program dollars from UNESCO, the World Bank, France, and Canada. They placed TV sets in 70% of the country's schools, but ten years later sets had broken down and weren't repaired, and by 1981 the whole school project had folded. Adults still watched TV some evenings, but the programs were mostly about preventative health care and agricultural techniques. Nigeria, the Ivory Coast, and Niger did increase rural exposure to TV through government-sponsored group viewing. It is still difficult to sustain television in places outside the urban areas. Electricity isn't available everywhere. Programs are limited, and sets are expensive. Finding parts and skilled repair people is very difficult.

All African TV has been state owned, except in Swaziland, where TV was originally started in a partnership with a private company. It has taken several decades for TV to become widely used in much of sub-Saharan Africa. Even in the late 1980s, TV was still seen as a toy for the Europeans and Asians. For example, in the 1980s, in places like Kenya, only 3% of the population had a television set, and only 12% had ever seen TV. However, places with a higher per capita GNP, like Nigeria, had a different story. There, 68% said that they had seen TV in the late 1980s.

Things are changing though, on two fronts. More and more, local entrepreneurs decide to become television broadcasters. One of the earliest, Omar Bongo, the president of Gabon, began his broadcasting on Tele-Africa or Africa Numero 2 in 1988. His family owns the company, and he carries French news and films. In 1993, South Africa's M-Net began its first UHF rebroadcast in Botswana, thereby inaugurating African-owned pay TV. More and more sets find their way into rural areas, where people power them with batteries and find tall trees on which to mount the antennas. In 1995, to cross the street in Dar es Salaam, one had to get past the crowd buying antennas from street-corner vendors.

Kenya

Until 1989, the Kenya Broadcasting Corporation was the only TV available. Then a private station, the Kenya Television Network (KTN), began operation in the Nairobi area providing CNNI, MTV, and, through M-Net, four satellite channels. In the early 1990s, cable television began to grow with the investment coming through Indian and Middle Eastern companies.

While Nairobi is a modern city to rival any, the rural areas are quite different. Take, for example, the Samburu tribal areas and Maralal, the village that functions as their commercial center. The Samburu, relatives of the Masai, are cattle herders. A woman and her children live in a manyatta, which is an oval or round hut made of sticks and mud. The poverty is beyond the comprehension of the average European or American. It's not a cash society. The men traditionally have grown up to be warriors, which means they must spend the day holding a spear. Only there is no occasion to use the spears any more, and no jobs are available, even if one could convince a warrior to put down his spear. The women have been posses- sions. They do the work, nearly all of it. After undergoing the female cir- cumcision rites, which still take place in the late 1990s, they are available to be taken as wives and produce children. In a manyatta, there's likely to be a tape deck and a radio, but there's no electricity. For most people, there's no TV, yet. But in Maralal, there is a community viewing room. In case the reception is poor for broadcast TV, there are videotapes.

While this lifestyle still exists, young men (and a few women) increasingly are finding contacts outside the tribal areas. They have some opportunity for education and they identify increasingly with what they see on televi- sion—a new way of life, maybe a more prosperous way.

Francis Naolo Musili represents one of these young people. He's left his tribal homeland in Machakos to work as a gourmet cook in Nairobi's business and tourist industry, but he goes back frequently to his family. Tribal ties remain very important even to those no longer living a tradi- tional life. Francis's comments about his access to news and information and his attitudes toward television are as follows.

> In Machakos, where I come from, it's hard to see TV. In Machakos we have no satellite. A few people have TV and it works if you put an aerial on a big tree. Sometimes it's hard to find a big tree. But, everybody has a radio. In some places it is hard to get a newspaper. The news is about what's going on in Kenya. We believe it because what they say is true. But, some people—what *they* say is propa- ganda. I especially like sports—football. My secondary school was the best in football. When I was at school we used to watch American sports on TV. I like music too. Some people just buy the tapes to practice their English, but I like watching them on the video and on TV.[16]

Nigeria

Nigeria has nearly 90 million people, and in 1993 there was one TV set for every fourteen people. As mentioned earlier, as early as the 1980s, over two-thirds of the population had seen TV.

The idea was that if everyone had access to TV, it would be possible to provide the education and development material helpful to more rapid na- tional advancement. The results of this experiment were mixed. There was a lack of local journalists and the Eurocentric programming was outside the experience of the viewers. As a local chief said, "If there's no one avail- able to explain what things mean and to answer questions, what good is it?" Sending information through drama and music and sports was much more easily understood than when it came from "talking heads."

In addition, sets break or are broken by rival tribes, and finding new parts or someone who knows how to fix them is nearly impossible.

This early start in TV did, however, put Nigeria in a good position for more rapid advancement in the 1990s. In 1990, this country had over thirty-four stations, about two-thirds of which were government operated. In 1994, Nigeria awarded fourteen licenses for conventional over-air TV and eleven for satellite redistribution through local television broadcast.[17]

Today, Nigeria is Africa's leading producer of local programming. They rely on imports for only about 40% of their programming. In the mid 1990s, M-Net began rebroadcasting BBC TV to a number of countries. All this is fairly remarkable for a country that isn't one of Africa's richest. Nigeria's per capita GNP, at $310, isn't as low as the lowest ten, but it's not among Africa's wealthiest either. There are only five sub-Saharan countries with per capita GNPs over $1,000: Gabon at $4,050, Mauritius at $2,980, South Africa at $2,900, Botswana at $2,590, and Namibia at $1,660.[18]

Tanzania

Tanzania is an excellent example of an emerging democracy, remarkable because of how quickly things are changing in this sixth poorest country in Africa. As a former Soviet ally, the country suffered economically because it was isolated from the wealthy West and at the bottom of the priority list for the less wealthy Soviets.

As of 1997, it still wasn't possible for people in major offices to make long-distance telephone calls. Communication out of the country requires using special satellite phone Internet connections—available to only a select few. Reportedly the telephone improvements are in process.

TV was introduced to Tanzania in 1994. When the government said it was ready to have TV stations operate in the country, three entrepreneurs got together to make it happen. They had the money, and setting up a TV station is an expensive enterprise. Theirs is the first operating TV in the country, CTN. There are two other networks starting now, ITV and DTV.

The story of how one "starts from scratch" is told by Isaack Mwita, news editor, Coastal Television Network (CTN).

We started in September 1993 actually. CTN applied for the license from the Government Broadcasting Council. It took about three months to process. The first six months were a trial. Then the Council decided that they could run effectively and issued them an operating certificate. They started operating commercially in the middle of 1994.

These are not the kind of TV stations that you know. I call them relay stations because they do not produce their own programs. The programs that they run are either copyrighted to them or franchised. For example, CTN holds the franchise to broadcast CNN in Tanzania. CTN pays about $400 U.S. to CNN to do this. We relay CNN news and live broadcasts. For example, we broadcast "live" Nelson Mandela's inauguration in South Africa.

When TV was introduced on the mainland of Tanzania, people already had sets because off-shore, on the island of Zanzibar, TV started in 1972. Also some people here had satellite dishes so they could view programs. I'm not sure if it was legal. When TV was introduced, research showed that there were already 60,000 TV sets in the country. This was in 1992. The population according to the 1987 census was 26 million. Now, in 1995, it is said that there are 200,000 to 300,000 TV sets. It's a fashion now. It caught people out of excitement. Each household thinks they should have a set.

CTN is owned by three entrepreneurs of Indian origin. One is a citizen, but two are not. One of those is a U. S. citizen and one is Canadian. CTN, like the other two stations, is financed by the entrepreneurs themselves. There's advertising to a large extent. There's no government money except that on Zanzibar; it is government-controlled TV.

That is the issue that stuns me. We are being urged by the champions of democracy that in order to develop, people should be educated on what democratization is. But, they are not equipping the private media, whose end user is the common man, to do such broadcasting. The end user doesn't choose whether this bulletin comes from government or private. The private media is not going to hide any truth about what's happening in government. Therefore, in my view, *this* is the media that needs much more finance. Taxpayer money in the form of aid has often gone down the drain wastefully without being accounted for. So long as the Westerners maintain that the private enterprise will bring development, you could find ways and means to obtain taxpayer money channeled through banks, a revolving fund for similar projects, or whatever to equip the private media enterprise. It could be paid back with interest, of course. There's a lot of capital flight from the third world to the first world in terms of interest payments. It surpasses what the first world sends to the third world. I don't see how it's difficult for this investment in media.

Concerning our programming, we've done some audience research. After the CNN programs we have musical programs portraying local personalities. We also have religious programs. We transmit both Muslim and Christian programs. We have interviews—sort of a magazine program interviewing a personality on a particular issue. For example, I do a program called countdown to elections. The first stage was interviews of aspiring candidates from all the parties. (Our first multiparty election ever is this year.) Why did he think of running? What was his manifesto? And what would he stand for if elected? We received a lot of response—letters and calls. The second stage was to see the relevant selection from the different political committees. We are ready for the second stage. We shall have programs of what the public should expect from each party. How will a candidate promote the image of their party? Not only is this our first election, this is the first time TV has ever covered an election.

Largely, all three stations broadcast in English. DTV and ITV have local news bulletins in Kiswahili. They are brought in from the Tanzanian News Agency whom they subscribe to. They have offices in most corners of the country. We plan a news bulletin to begin in a month or so. We've sent some of our staff for training. We are different from the other stations because DTV has SKY news from the U.K. ITV has BBC. Others include sports. We don't have sports yet. I hope our TV has a sports program in Swahili.

Dar es Salaam has a concentration of 3 to 4 million potential viewers. It's the biggest city in the country. In the rural areas, TV is another matter. There are ten or eleven applications before the Broadcasting Commission from entrepreneurs applying from different regions to establish TV stations. They are from regions like Mwanza or Arusha. If they have regional TV, TV will penetrate the rural area. Even though the villages are quite primitive, if signal is there, many people can afford to have TV. There are not community viewings because it's like socialism and Tanzania ended socialism. We are now detracting from the communal-sharing aspect. We now have policies of private enterprise. It's a policy change from before. Maybe a church would devote a space and money to cater to its diocese. I don't think you'll have a citizen who says I'm offering my TV for the village to see.[19]

While TV is becoming established in Tanzania, the Broadcasting Commission is also establishing new media laws for the nation. Dr. Robert L. Hilliard, a former U.S. Federal Communications Commission official, reviewed the draft of the law.

The new media laws include provisions designed to serve and protect the public, such as use of television for the schools, a limit on monopoly ownership and limits on an owner's ability to control media information reaching more than 25% of the population, strengthening the copyright laws, balancing freedom of speech with the protection of children from indecency and violence on the media, and training programs for media personnel. The Broadcast Commission would implement these new laws similar to what the FCC does in the United States.

One clause, however, appears to negate what otherwise might be considered a free-from-censorship media system. This section reads: "The Minister [of Information] may . . . give the Commission directions of a general or specific nature and the Commission shall comply with every such direction."

Apparently the Commission was not given any discretion regarding inserting this clause, which is inimical to the democratic concept of freedom of speech and press. Tanzanian leaders clearly had learned the importance of the media, not only from its own past experience, but from what's happening in the rest of the world: whoever controls the country's media controls the country's politics."[20]

Togo

In this former French colony, about 45% of those over age fifteen are literate. The principal medium is radio. However, a booming business is the antenna business. If one buys a powerful enough antenna, one can get TV programs from Benin, maybe CNN, and some French stations.[21]

Uganda

This country has been through turbulent times. The current president, Yoweri Museveni, who led the rebellion to end the brutal dictatorships of Idi Amin and Milton Obote, has a more democratic government than in the past. However, he wants to postpone free multiparty elections, and he's found an interesting approach to control of the press. In 1996, Dr. Robert Hilliard was invited to address the Uganda Journalists Safety Committee. They met to discuss new statutes passed following the adoption of a new constitution in 1995. "The new laws," Hilliard reported, "included a requirement that all journalists have university degrees in the field, which would immediately dispossess 90% of the practicing journalists; that all journalists should be licensed by the government, which would guarantee that only journalists who supported the government would be certified; and that the Media Council, which would supervise all the media, would be under the control of the Minister of Information."[22]

It will be difficult to bring about a two-way flow of news and information across the globe when, in some countries, the only way to secure a free flow is to use satellite broadcast from outside one's country—outside the reach of the enemies of free speech.

Zimbabwe

This neighbor to South Africa experienced fifteen years ago the transition to majority indigenous rule that South Africa is experiencing now. Because of that, Zimbabwe offers a case study in the shift to majority rule and the development of a relatively stable, but economically strapped, emerging democracy.

While the racial balance of power has changed, the rich-poor balance is yet to even out. Those with the power to change things find it more in their short-term self-interest to perpetuate the status quo. Those without the economic power find that political power alone can't make the difference. For everyone, changing habits is not easy.

Beryl Neilson, a white owner of an auto parts business, was born in Zimbabwe. She'd be called a "Rhody" (for Rhodesian) by the majority population.

> The biggest change in fifteen years is that the whites have learned to be less racialistic, to get on with the blacks. To you that must sound ludicrous. But to us, it's the way we were brought up. But there's harmony between the races now. Even from them toward us. Only a few people want to stir things up.
>
> We pay here about $25,000 ZM for a satellite dish. That's about $3,000 U.S. I see CNN World Report. We can get SKY as well. The BBC comes onto M-Net, and they do very interesting things on countries all over the world. We pay about $120 ZM per year for satellite TV service. It's not a lot.
>
> On regular TV, the news has changed a lot—but it's the same. When it was a white government, we heard about only the white government. Now, we have a black government, and it's all about the black government and what today's officials are doing. It's the reverse, but it's the same. I think our headlines should be all over the world headlines. If something happens that is a headline, it will be so in England and America. Here we'll only hear what Mugabe is doing tomorrow.[23]

Another perspective on the news in Zimbabwe is offered by Melissa G. Ford, the press attaché with USIA at the U.S. embassy in Harare. She commented on the efforts to make U.S. Public Broadcasting Company documentaries available to the Zimbabwe Broadcasting Corporation (ZBC).

> Worldnet is a USIA channel. We do video-teleconferences, but we don't have enough money to do our own programming, so we acquire many programs from PBS. Because we have the broadcast rights, we offer them to TV stations throughout the world. We've gone over to ZBC and we've offered the programs. There's a program on computer programming, one on how to do business programming, and cultural programs. The man at ZBC says, "Well, this is U.S. propaganda." I say, "No, it's PBS." It's hard to explain that "public" isn't government. They are taking the ones about computers and business. We

get the latest programs off our satellite and take it over to them.
They've gotten some other U.S. programs about people surviving a
bad ghetto drug situation and doing well. One was a story about Ben
and Jerry opening an ice cream parlor in Harlem. So, I'm glad we
can provide some programs to help out.

When President Mugabe was in the United States, we had our
Worldnet cameras there and got a lot of footage of the president with
Secretary of Commerce Ron Brown, things that ZBC didn't get and
couldn't get delivered back here in time. So that night in news they
used a lot of our footage. That was a help because ZBC still doesn't
have the equipment and the money to get footage fast.

There's been a law on the books from the Rhodesia era that essen-
tially gives the government a monopoly on the broadcasting because
they have the transmitters and the dishes and nobody can get a license. The government, however, because of the drought and because
of its huge deficit has decided to make some money by privatizing.
Among other things, they are granting licenses to people who want
to start cable companies. In granting them the license to broadcast
cable they have also thrown in a license for an independent radio
station. So they are almost circumventing the broadcast act and are
preparing for the future. Soon people can have a cable instead of a
dish. There are a lot of things opening up since South Africa opened
up with the end of apartheid. Regional trade is happening. All these
products are available.[24]

Fortunately, the racial barriers are breaking down, and African-owned
media are entering the marketplace. Cosmos Communications is at the
head of the line for a new cable TV license. Chemist Siziba, chairman of
Cosmos Communications, describes his efforts.

We are consulting engineers in telecommunications in particular, electronics in general. Seven of us formed a partnership to assess the
opportunities, not only here, but to work for U.S. programs. Our
company started about eight years ago. We've been working on starting this TV station for five years now. It will be a pay television—
similar to those in America. It will be cable.

The first thing we had to do was to convince the authorities that
it was possible to have private broadcasting stations. That was very
difficult pitch to change their thinking. Broadcasting was considered
a security issue—possibilities of subversion and things like that. Five
years ago they agreed in principle. It took another year to make it
legally possible. Then, the question was how to make it work. Nobody knew how to go about doing it. Nobody had even seen anything
called a broadcast license. We were asked to produce one. We got

English lawyers to write a draft for us. As we were embarking, the national broadcasting entity decided they wanted in. We wanted to be sure they didn't get our license. Although the broadcasting law has a provision providing for a license, it had never been used. When we got our letter, the broadcasting officials wanted to make it their project. We got bogged down in a lot of politics. We were thrown back for a while. Now, just today, we hear that ZBC has objected to our application for a piece of land.

Originally, when we decided to start a station, it was because a close friend wanted to watch the games on a satellite dish. It cost $50,000 or so. You can't pay that kind of money for an aerial. That's all a dish is. So the idea started from there, and developed much larger than that. Originally we thought we'd get CNN, BBC, MTV, and other channels from around the world and make them available to the general public with their ordinary TV sets and UHF aerials. There'd be no cable. As we developed it, it became a station in its own right. We began to see the possibilities of a global station, thinking globally and acting locally. We'd now develop a world-class station to solve African problems. Also we're engineers, and broadcasting is people. If you have five broadcasters, you can span the world and we can do it.

We have signed agreements for live transmission, not as program distributors. We've signed with CNN, MBC, and BBC. We'd like to get in touch with WTN. Our culture is closer to Europe. The actual material we have on our TV is mostly American, although the people who handle it are largely European. The programming will be sport, music, current affairs. We won't do news gathering because it is extremely expensive. We'll buy it from others. We hope to start to broadcast by November 1995. Our aim is to get revenue as we go. We have already placed an order to have a satellite downlink. We put our small antenna and a transmitter at ZBC. We already have an agreement with ZBC to make this happen.

We got a grant at the beginning. We have a five-year development program. We started with very little infrastructure. Most equipment is out there in the weather—antenna, tower, satellite dish. We have temporary structures where we put the actual transmitter. I visited CNN, MTV, BBC in London and I was amazed at the simplicity of the CNN broadcasting infrastructure. It's just rudimentary. So we can do that too. The obstacles are mostly political and bureaucratic. When people know what we're doing, they want to be part of it. They've made certain that at every level where we have to have permission, things are delayed. It's frustrating. Engineers here are being left behind. We have the technical capacity. For a third world country, there is no gap in telecommunications. We could develop the capacity.

Bureaucratic problems mean there's no will to see a project through. We sent engineers to Mauritius because I can broadcast from anywhere in world. We have looked at what MBC is doing. We went to see how things work from Mauritius, in case we can't do it from here.

Our revenue will be mainly from subscriptions and advertising and some connections. In the next three years, we plan to get our own uplink and a transponder. We can then rebroadcast back. This is mostly to assist communities to develop their own programs. For example, a small community with a small transmitter can cover local sports, news, club activities, etcetera. We can use it as a marketing techniques.

Once our service is started, we'll buy back dishes that people have bought across the country and donate them to schools, etcetera. The minister of education can buy space to broadcast to schools, special lessons, etcetera.[25]

Veneliah Mhlanga Thatha is an educational psychologist from Bulawayu, whose opportunity to study in England made it possible for her to have a career beyond the dreams of others from her family neighborhood in a local black township. She summarizes the consumer view of what's developing.

I think we've gone a long way in improving our ways of giving news and information to our people. It's not just news on TV and radio. Lots of people are writing on paper and circulating information about what's happening. It's no longer just the elite, the upper classes. Now a lot of people have access to information. We still have the problem that most of the news is in English, not Ndebele or Shona. For a person out in the bush who wants to read something, that's a problem. But the news on radio and TV is in all three languages. That's good.[26]

Additional information on Zimbabwe can come from the following Internet sites:

<http://www.zimweb.com>

<http://www.harare.iafrica.com>

<http://www.samara.co.zw>

<http://www.icon.co.zw>

<http://wwwl.zimbabwe.net>

CASE STUDIES IN DEMOCRATIZATION

In 1996 there were eighteen multiparty elections in Africa, more than ever before in one year. Sub-Saharan Africa has taken the first major step toward democratization, but it will take a while before the process becomes democratic. In Chad, Niger, and Gambia, former military dictators who had taken power by force managed to become civilian elected leaders, largely by barring their critics from campaigning and by controlling the administration of the elections. In Ghana, on the other hand, Jerry Rawlings, once he had seized power, won his second election in a competitive election widely viewed as fair, and winners and losers appeared to close ranks after the election. Similarly, Benin, Sierra Leone, and Uganda had elections generally considered free in 1996. Madagascar had a democratic election in early 1997. Other multiparty elections occurred in 1997 in Nigeria, Zaire, Kenya, Cameroon, Burkina Faso, and Mali. Fair democratic transitions may be difficult, but at least the concept is being examined. On the other hand, the Congolese want a long transition before elections. And in the Ivory Coast and Zambia, the opposition boycotted elections as unfair.[27]

At other levels, democratization efforts are in process. Below are two case studies.

Media for Rwanda and Burundi Refugees

After completing his master's degree in communication studies in the United States in 1994, Otieno R. J. Ndong'a returned to his native Kenya to a new post of communication director for the Jesuits' East African operation. In this capacity, he's setting up a radio station in Tanzania to provide news and information to thousands of refugees from Rwanda and Burundi. He described the project.

The radio station is a joint project of the Jesuit Refugee Services and the UN High Commission for Refugees. The purpose is to provide information to the refugees who live in that area. There are over 700,000 refugees there.

The station has three main purposes: first, to disseminate information from UNHCR to the refugees; second, to inform them of what is happening in Rwanda and Burundi and the region at large; and third, to inform the refugees about health and educational matters. Three languages will be used. The first is Kirwanda, the language spoken by the bulk of refugees who are from Rwanda. Second, we will broadcast in Kiswahili. The local people in Tanzania speak Kiswahili, and if there are problems with the government in Tanzania, they will be at ease if they can understand it. Third, English broadcasting will provide access to information for the community of aid agencies.

The idea was first proposed in November 1994, when the refugees first went into that region. But at the time there was nobody to put it into place. So this year I was asked if I could take six months to set it up. Now, everything is in place. The equipment was bought by the Jesuits. The salaries are paid by UNHCR. The governments are not involved at all. And we hope to start transmitting on the seventeenth of July 1995.

The audience wants objective information. It's a very delicate situation. For instance, in Rwanda the fighting was encouraged by radio reports. Starting a project like this, one needs to be aware of the problems that might arise. Even an innocent remark can trigger problems. We must be very very careful. That's my main worry. You need to get the refugees involved in programming. You need to identify the refugees who are not going to be biased, who are going to be open-minded, who are able to see both sides. That's not easy. Another problem is getting program material that will satisfy both the Hutu and the Tutsi.

When we were getting the equipment together, we had different kinds of problems from people not understanding the technical equipment to problems of missing parts that needed to be special ordered. Another problem was logistics. Equipment was flown from Rome to Rwanda. From Kigali, Rwanda, to the camps is about 400 kilometers of very bad roads. There are six camps in the Ngara area. In the first three months, we'll concentrate on broadcasting to these six camps. Later we'll have booster stations to Karaga where there are two major camps.

I ask the UNHCR and field officers in the camps to help identify local people for me—residents in the camps. I work with them now for three months. I've worked closely with the community services coordinators in identifying, screening, and training the people to run the station. We are over twenty now.

In terms of programming, we'll have news followed by entertainment—music. We did a survey, and found that the bulk of the refugees are worried about their relatives. We'll get news from the various camps and work with the BBC's program on addressing missing persons.

The most important ingredient to the success of such a project is to work with the community.[28]

The project illustrates how communication of news and information can contribute to stabilization in a volatile situation. The thing is, it's done as a project for charities and relief organizations. It certainly is important that the Jesuits and the United Nations are there to contribute when an apolitical operation is needed.

The question is, why can't independent news and information provided by the private sector in general also meet this need? After all, the market overall is helped when the "we versus they" categorization doesn't occur. Who defined news and information as only that which produces profit because it is by or about affluent people? Who draws this artificial line that relegates news and information by and about poor people to someone aside from the mainstream? Is it possible that there is also profit in the larger social good of including everyone as newsmaker and news recipient? Might the stabilization of the region help the overall economy and ultimately expand the media market more rapidly?

To democratize the news in this situation doesn't mean eliminating the Jesuits and the UN. It simply means that while they handle the details parochial to the situation, the common news and information professionals expand their coverage to incorporate the story of the refugees and their needs as told by the refugees, not as told by someone in London or the United States who has purchased stock footage from an agency. With the equipment available today, surely the refugees can tell their own story and have it exported to the larger world. In addition, those on the scene developing cross-community communication could surely have their jobs made easier with interest and assistance from those who use the best of equipment on a daily basis.

South Africa

In this country of 40 million people, about 5 million whites, 3 million colored, 1 million Indian, and 31 million Africans have only recently sat at the decision-making table together. They've emerged from an era where the whites ruled and everyone else endured economic, political, social, and personal hardships of the most atrocious sort. The new South Africa is an exciting if sometimes difficult place to be in the late 1990s. Everyone is working very hard to make this transition without bloodshed and with a democratic system of justice. The stakes are high. So is the level of creativity and the energy for change. It's what the United States must have been like in 1776 at the time between the Declaration of Independence and the drafting of the Constitution.

The new government policies toward media and the new technologies are arriving at the same time creating all sorts of opportunity. Before the end to apartheid, the National Party government was opposed to the introduction of TV because it would show racial integration in other places. Consequently, South Africa didn't get any TV until 1976, and then it was tightly controlled. Only in the early 1990s did the South African Broadcasting Corporation (SABC) begin to escape this mold. By 1996 SABC had a six-channel satellite subscription service called ASTRASAT. The SABC also had a new board and a new director general inclined to give favorable publicity to the new government and its majority component, the ANC. Former and current national party members say the SABC has just switched parties. That's only partly true. But other things have changed. Now there are many black faces on the air, where formerly there were not. There are some independently operated radio stations, but most are run by the state. There is a liberalization in more people getting access to the airwaves.

Radio is the principal way to reach the rural communities. That's been a problem because of a lack of electricity and an inability to buy batteries. "Freeplay," a radio invented in the mid 1990s by Britain's Trevor Baylis, can solve the problem.[29] It plays without batteries or electricity. It's being tested in Russia, Ukraine, and South Africa. You wind the handle twenty-five seconds for twenty-five minutes of play. If electricity is accessible, the radio can be plugged in. The only problem is that it costs $116 U.S., which will keep it out of the market for a few years.

For those who do have radios, however, William Henry Siemering, creator of the U.S. news and information program *All Things Considered*, is working with South Africa's Independent Broadcasting Authority, which awarded broadcast licenses for radio to nonprofits to provide regional dialect news and information. He's linking new stations with American mentors. The idea is to introduce the U.S. model of independent public radio. The Open Society Foundation for South Africa is financing this effort.

TV may not have reached the really rural areas, but it's easily accessible in the cities and even in the very poor areas of the former black townships like Soweto. "Everyone has a TV. That has a bit impact, especially among those where there's no literacy," says retired educator Franz Auerbach.

I think the state does a good job now using TV as an educational medium. It uses TV and radio for information purposes since we have seven to eight million adult illiterates in South Africa. In fact, in the last year or two, the ANC found that it wanted to discuss policy issues with its mass support base. They discovered it's very difficult to discuss policy with people who can't read. There's a concerted effort to reach the population. The state says there must be language parity among all eleven languages spoken in South Africa.

Regarding the ending of apartheid and the media, scores of foreign journalists came for the Mandela election. They expected a bloodbath and when they found there wasn't a bloodbath, but it was all peaceful, many of them just packed their bags and went somewhere where they'd find the next conflict. So, you see, for South Africa to get the rest of the world to pay attention to our news, it has to be a catastrophe. I bet the news you get now in 1995 in the United States about South Africa is much less than it was five years ago. That's a tragedy, because what's happening here now is much more exciting and much more significant for global questions about how people get along with each other dispite differences of color, gender, whatever. The media should look not only at what we get wrong, but at what we get right. And we're getting quite a lot of things right. For example, we started schooling this year within this province which is most densely populated, with the minister of education saying that no child is to be denied access because they can't pay. Imposing that might be expected to cause huge upheavals, based on the past behavior of white parents when black children wanted to go to school. It caused problems, but minor ones. That in itself is a remarkable story.[30]

Barbara Meyerowitz, a teacher and the president of a small publishing house, comments on the news she gets now and the news she got before apartheid ended.

I have in the last year realized that I have been an absolute victim of propaganda and a closed news media system. Even though I have traveled and read outside magazines and tried to encompass as much as I could, nevertheless, I think a brainwashing system went on affecting many of us in South Africa. I feel furious to think that a government can close the media in such a way and censor things in order to have things all their own way. Of all the people I hate in Nazi Germany, I hate Goebbels the most. I think deceptive information and brainwashing is a most insidious and vile way to twist people's minds. I am of course very aware of how open the media is now, and very relieved.

SABC has made quite vast changes. It has even made changes in accent and the way people say things. Up to now, we've had a kind of Eurocentric way of presenting news. The new director is trying to make it much more Afrocentric. He's caused a lot of comment among white South Africans who have always been used to a particular kind of menu of broadcasting—like their nice plays with people who live in some rural town in England, an Agatha Christie mystery. He doesn't want that any more. He doesn't want some of the famous BBC programs. Even the actual newscasters now speak with a broad South African accent. The director of Radio at SABC, Govan Reddy, says Radio South Africa is for everyone and it should represent the community and not just a tiny minority. It's fascinating to hear him. It's made for very lively interesting new radio.

SABC TV has a marvelous program. It's called *Unbanned*. They are replaying a lot of things which were once banned. Once was not so long ago. The program I saw was stunning. It was the history of the rise of African nationalism in South Africa. It's being put from a perspective of African nationalism—not Afrikaner nationalism. It

starts with the hut tax in 1903, when people were forced to pay a
hut tax. Therefore they were forced to work to get cash. To do this,
the men were forced to go to town and work in the mines. So it's the
history of how whites began to exploit black labor. And they soon
began a process of deteriorating social conditions. The men were
working in the towns. The women were virtually starving in the
homelands (as they were called later on). Family life was really set
asunder. It started there and went through to the infamous land act—
1913, I think. Then it showed the 1930s, when the Nationalist government got into power and on through all the great treason trials.
People here have not seen this. It is part of the history that people do
not know at all. It's not in the history books. Now it's becoming part
of our history. They present it, they say, in a spirit of reconciliation.[31]

Franz Auerbach commented on the news.

There is now a change in news content. There was a time when the
news avoided things like squatter camps, strikes and things that reflected unfavorably on the national party government. Now we get a
bit of the opposite—every strike, every protest gets thrown onto our
TV screens because the new management wants to show that the
sufferings of the people are not hidden from those who watch TV.

We get a limited hostile reaction to these changes. There's a radio
station called Radio Pretoria that's for radical right. Our president
bends over to include whites. Some blacks think he does this too
often. The older people think only of him as a terrorist who was life
imprisoned for terrorist activity. Mandela never was a communist,
but ANC has had an alliance for sixty years with the South African
communist party. The ANC has been challenged to sever this. But
Mandela says that in the 1920s and 1930s almost no whites spoke
against oppression except for the communists and we don't ditch our
friends just because some people don't like them.

One more cautious about the changes in South Africa is Bob Steyn, an
Afrikaner clergyman, lawyer, and later journalist who was awarded a Nieman Fellowship at Harvard. "Democracy has become a buzz word and a
lot of people don't know what it means. I walked up to a demonstrator
and discussed what he was protesting. I said, 'People are about to get together to talk through this problem. Isn't that what democracy's about?'
He said no. He said, 'Democracy is about my right to kill whites.' "[32]

The African National Congress is well aware of the difficulties of developing an informed constituency prepared to take the initiative to keep democracy alive. The newspapers were filled with inserts, comic-book
fashion—lots of pictures and few words, describing what a local govern-

ment did and how it differed from the national government. This was in anticipation of the first local elections held in 1995 following up the national election to end apartheid in 1994. Just one of many task forces working on creating a workable democracy was the Task Group on Open Democracy.[33] Their efforts were designed to ensure that the new government and its constituents work in an environment of maximum government transparency. "The Interim Constitution enshrines an aspiration to a kind of democracy which empowers the people to participate in their governance, and which requires government to account to them for its decisions. If South Africa is to achieve participatory and accountable government, our citizens need to know and understand what government is doing for them and in their name, and how it works. For this reason, one of the central ideals of the Constitution is an aspiration to an open democracy." The purposes of this law are to provide access to information of government bodies, access to proceedings of government bodies, protection of privacy, and protection for officials who disclose lawbreaking, serious maladministration, or corruption and to empower the citizenry by ensuring that they have access to material describing the services of each office of government, how one accesses those services, and how one objects to those services.

The level of creativity and commitment to the new South Africa is inspiring indeed. It will be an important case study to watch in the decade ahead as government, citizenry, and the all-important media work together to realize the dream. For updated information on South Africa see the following:[34]

<http://sabc.co.za> South African Broadcasting Corporation (SABC) home page

<http://www.saix.net/speed/satpress.htm> SABC's satellite TV venture

<http://www.ee.ic.ac.uk/misc/bymap/africa.html> International Email Accessibility

<http://www.mnet.co.za> M-Net satellite communications "front page"

SUMMARY

In the Middle East and North Africa one sometimes hears the argument that global news and information and global TV aren't relevant, but "news from nowhere." Yet, the number of people risking fines and maybe jail by having illegal satellite dishes contradicts that claim. Of course, entertainment TV is a critical reason for having a satellite dish, but access to the news and information channels is nearly always part of the equation.

The other half of the full and fair exchange of news and information, a critical part of the democratization of the media, is the realization of opportunities for local people in a region to have their news be part of what others receive—in Europe, Asia, and the Americas. The growth of regional satellite services in this area is a first step in that direction. Of course, the content cannot be so tightly controlled that it is unbelievable and boring to watch. It may be transmitted, but it won't be watched.

In sub-Saharan Africa, on the other hand, democratization may be occurring at a more rapid pace, albeit a less affluent pace. The problem is that, except for South Africa, the infrastructure isn't in place to encourage intracontinent communication and the accompanying economic growth.

Getting one's story out of Africa has been extremely difficult, because the main global broadcasters are only interested if there is a famine or a bloodbath to report. Such prejudicial coverage doesn't do much for the same broadcasters, who would benefit themselves by expanding the market.

The question is, can Africans be welcomed as partners in the global marketplace? Can they receive the benefits available to the emerging middle classes in other parts of the world? Maybe more important, can they share their story with the rest of the world, where modern technologies have contributed to people forgetting the value of face-to-face communication and cultural traditions? Will it be possible to democratize communication to the extent that the "have–have not" gaps can be bridged, if not closed?

NOTES

1. *The Progress of Nations*, UNICEF, 1995.

2. Nachman Shai, Director General of Israel's Second Television and Radio Authority, 3 Kanfei Nesharim St., Jerusalem. Interview with the author in Jerusalem, January 18, 1994.

3. *Progress of Nations.*

4. Carla B. Johnston, *Winning the Global TV News Game* (Boston and London: Butterworth, Heinemann/Focal Press), 1995, p. 222.

5. I. Girmaw, "The PANAFTEL Project," *Working Documents* (Harare, Zimbabwe: African Telecommunications Development Conference), 6–11 December, 1990.

6. Johnston, *Winning*, p. 218.

7. George Wood, "Communications in Space, Edition 5.5: The Last Dxers Guide to the Galaxy," at <*http://www.funet.fi/pub/culture/tv+film/satellite/misc/galax55.txt*>.

8. Peter Vesey, Vice President, CNNI, One CNN Center, 4th Floor, North Tower, Atlanta, GA 30303. Telephone interview with author, October 25, 1994.

9. Mary Roodkowsky, UNICEF Regional Programme Officer for the Middle East and North Africa. Email telelecture, to Emerson College, Boston, in November 1996.

10. Johan Ramsland, Editor, BBC-WSTV, Television Centre, Wood Lane, London, W12 7RJ, U.K. Interview with the author in London on January 27, 1994.

11. Said Aburish, *The House of Saud* (New York: St. Martin's Press, 1995). Also see "Satellite Dishes Banned in Iran," *San Francisco Chronicle*, May 30, 1995, p. B6.

12. Mordechai Kirshenboim, Director General of Israeli Broadcasting Authority, Khalal Building, Jaffa Street, Jerusalem, Israel. Interview with the author in Jerusalem on January 19, 1994.

13. Radi A. Alkhas, Director General, Jordan Radio and Television, P.O. Box 1041, Amman, Jordan. Interview with the author in Amman on January 10, 1994.

14. Aburish, *House*. Also Rassim Al Jamil, *Communication in the Arab World* (Al Saqi Books, 1995.)

15. Associated Press Wire, "Pirate TV Stations Provide Outlet for Frustrations." *Ketchikan Daily News*, Ketchikan, Alaska, July 3, 1996, p. C6.

16. Francis Naolo Musili, Tawa-Machakos, Kenya. Interview with the author in Kenya on July 2, 1995.

17. Louise M. Bourgault, *Mass Media in Sub-Saharan Africa* (Indianapolis: Indiana University Press, 1995), pp. 134f.

18. *Progress of Nations*.

19. Isaack Mwita, News Editor, CTN-Coastal Television Network, Box 100137, Dar es Salaam, Tanzania. Interview with author in Dar es Salaam on July 5, 1995.

20. Dr. Robert L. Hilliard, former chief of public broadcasting, U.S. Federal Communications Commission, Professor in Mass Communication, Emerson College, Boston. Interview with author in Boston on August 20, 1997.

21. Melewosi Sam Adissem, former reporter from Togo personal interview with Donald Coleman, researcher, Emerson Program in Mass Communication, December 1996.

22. Hilliard, interview.

23. Beryl Neilson, Bulawayu, Zimbabwe. Interview with the author in Bulawayu on June 15, 1995.

24. Melissa G. Ford, Press Attaché, USIS, U.S. Embassy, Harare, Zimbabwe. Interview with the author in Harare on June 20, 1995.

25. Chemist Siziba, Chairman of COSMOS Communications, 88 Robert Mugabe Road, Harare, Zimbabwe. TEL: 724891, FAX: 796630. Interview with the author in Harare on June 20, 1995.

26. Veneliah Mhlanga Thatha, educational psychologist, Bulawayu, Zimbabwe. Interview with the author in Bulawayu on June 16, 1995.

27. Howard W. French, "Despite Setbacks, Democracy Gains in Africa." *New York Times*, January 11, 1997, p. 3.

28. Otieno R. J. Ndong'a, Communication Director for the Society of Jesus, East African Province, Nairobi, Kenya. Interview with author in Nairobi on July 10, 1995.

29. See *Parade* Magazine, April 13, 1997, p. 21.

30. Franz Auerbach, Berea, Johannesburg, South Africa. Interview with the author in Johannesburg on June 1, 1995.

31. Barbara Meyerowitz, Johannesburg, South Africa. Interview with the author on June 6, 1995.

32. Bob Steyn, Cape Town, South Africa. Telephone interview with author in Cape Town on June 10, 1995.

33. See <http:"pc72.law.wits.ac.za/docs/oda4ms.html>. The convenor of the task group was Mojanku Gumbi, Office of the Executive Deputy President T. M. Mbeki, Private Bag 911, Pretoria 0001, South Africa.

34. Donald Coleman, "In Africa's Best Interest: Economic, Cultural and Political Issues in Global Communication," Emerson Graduate Program in Mass Communication, December 12, 1996.

7

Asia, Australia, and New Zealand

OVERVIEW

At the turn of the twenty-first century, two-thirds of the globe's population lives in Asia. The land area is vast—one-third of the globe's surface, from Afghanistan to Japan. Within this region are six of the ten most populated countries in the world: China, India, Indonesia, Japan, Pakistan, and Bangladesh. China and India alone have more people than North America and Europe combined.

By and large, the governments keep a tight control on the media and on freedom of speech, except in Japan, Australia, New Zealand, and India. Growth is rapid and the economic clout of this region may surely rival that of the European Union and the North American Free Trade Organization before the end of the twenty-first century.

DEVELOPMENTS IN COMMUNICATIONS TECHNOLOGY

Fiber Optics, Digital TV, and Cellular Systems

The use of these new technologies varies greatly across the region, depending on where one is. Japan is a model for the globe in employing new communication technologies. Nippon Telegraph and Telephone (NTT), formerly public and now private, spent enormous sums on modernizing in the late 1980s and early 1990s. Integrated service digital network (ISDN) testing in Japan is way ahead of the rest of Asia. On the other hand, North Korea, Afghanistan, and others are decades away from such practices.

South Korea is rapidly moving into a leadership position in the region. Together with the telecommunications authorities of Japan, Hong Kong, China, and AT&T from the United States, they've constructed the first trans-Pacific fiber optic cable system.

The activity in Australia typifies the activity within similar economic markets of the region.[1] Australia sees a major nationwide upgrade of telephone lines as critical to improving international competitiveness economically. The digital service company that provides ISDN, the Internet, and high-speed data transfer for business cannot operate in most places with the current telephone lines. The current government telecom company hasn't invested in modernization and has a price structure no longer appropriate to the technology changes. Hopefully, improvements will come with privatization of one-third of The Australian Telecom, Telstra.

System upgrades and modernization are a slow process in some of the less developed countries in the region. They have not only been hampered by lack of basic infrastructure and lack of resources, they've sometimes encountered management problems. India provides the example that is everyone's nightmare. In the early 1990s a decision was made to rebuild India's phone system. The Telecom Minister awarded 40 million dollars worth of contracts.[2] The project was to have doubled the current number of phone lines by the end of the 1990s, which was to add 10 million new lines. Only recently, in 1997, was it discovered that much of the money was stolen, and little has been done on the project.

Occasionally something really inventive has occurred, making it possible for countries to catch up by leapfrogging whole generations of technology. For example, rural Bangladesh has few, if any, telephone lines. But by 2003, each village will have a cell phone.

Mohammed Yunus, the same man who founded the Grameen Bank in the 1970s to give no-collateral loans in amounts as low as $50 to poor people who wanted to start businesses, has a new idea. It may spread worldwide, as did his microbusiness plan.[3] He started the Grameen Phone Company in Dakar, Bangladesh, planning to put a cell phone in each of Bangladesh's 65,000 villages within six years. For example, Laili Begum, age twenty-seven, borrowed $430 for a cellular phone. People in her village come to her to use it. She repays her loan at a rate of $3.50 week. Calls cost her four taka per minute. She charges five taka. That gives her about $4.50 per day in profit. Yunus's company also sells cell services at commercial rates to businesses. He's signed a joint venture with companies in Norway, Japan, and the United States to install 50–60 signal-relay towers that will insure that the cell phones can transmit over one-third of Bangladesh.

Global TV

Satellite television moved into this region in the early 1990s and is expanding very rapidly. Cable does exist, but it's not nearly as important, primarily because of the time delays required for wiring and the costs of wiring communities.

Fred Brenchley from the *Australian Financial Review*, writes that it is "estimated that by [the year] 2000 some 790 commercial satellites will service the Asia Pacific area with more than 500 transponders suitable for TV. With digital compression, this could add up to 2,000 to 3,000 TV stations. Digital will allow more regional targeting. STAR plans to begin broadcasting Mandarin, Hindi, Bahasa Indonesia, Arabic, and English. They may form separate subsidiaries for China, India, Indonesia, and the Middle East."[4]

Why the rapid growth in satellite TV? Think of the numbers of subscribers one could attract in an area so densely populated. Even if the middle class who can afford satellite TV is only a small percent of the total population, that's millions and millions of people. Besides, English is the first language of global TV, and Asia has 150 million fluent English speakers, more than in Europe, as a legacy of colonialism.

The major global TV news and information broadcasters are all in the region. In the mid 1990s, CNN expanded its distribution in the region by using the new APSTAR II satellite, which reaches two-thirds of the world's population. The satellite footprint provides upgraded service to India and across the entire region. ASIASAT reaches thirty-eight countries with 2.7 billion people—from Israel to Taiwan and Mongolia to the Philippines as well as Australia. STAR TV started in this region in 1991, as is described below. By 1993, it was doing very well even though most of STAR's 45 million potential viewers were concentrated in a few countries—3.3 million in India, 1.98 million in Taiwan, 300,000 in Hong Kong, and according to the Chinese government, 4.8 million households in China received STAR in early 1993. Since 1997, it all belongs to Rupert Murdoch.[5] In 1995, he became the sole owner by purchasing 36.4% to add to the 63.6% bought in 1993. The BBC's WSTV initially relied on STAR to reach Asian audiences. By February 1993, after only fifteen months on the air, 11 million homes across Asia could watch WSTV. But WSTV lost its access to the northern tier footprint when Rupert Murdoch thought it best not to offend the Chinese by providing transponder space for the BBC.

As satellite TV matures beyond its debut years in the early 1990s, more attention is paid to program content and to communicating better with the audiences of the region. For example, CNN began experimenting with Mandarin subtitling for some new distributions over the Pacific, using a technology that enables distribution of subtitling without it having to be seen by those viewers who don't want to see it, that is, without the proper decoding equipment. Rupert Murdoch, on the other hand, has spent some

50 million dollars to attract new writers, producers, and talent.[6] Aside from an effort in the United States to build up Twentieth Century Fox studios as a major TV production house, he has located local companies that are successful and invested in them without tampering with what makes them successful. For example, he purchased half of Bombay-based Zee TV and made it possible for them to increase the number of programs they produce in India.

Nonetheless, in some countries like Malaysia, Singapore, Thailand, and Burma, it is illegal to own satellite dishes. That doesn't mean they aren't there.

The Internet

It certainly is possible to obtain information about countries throughout this region, and it's possible to contact business, government, and academic institutions by the Internet. Yet, in many parts of the region, the Net is a figment of Western imaginations. The highly developed countries like Japan, Australia, and New Zealand are the exception. Open access is expected.

In Hong Kong, access has been relatively easy for the affluent classes of people, but that policy is quite different from the rest of China. Since July 1, 1997, Hong Kong was returned to the Chinese government. In China, ChinaNet was launched in May 1995, and by March 1996 it had about 1,000 subscribers.[7] The Minister of Posts and Telecommunications invested over 10 million dollars into ChinaNet. The minister warned of the need to limit access to prevent "politically dangerous" ideas from entering China. In 1996, there were about 200,000 personal computers in China. Potentially, half of these could use the Internet. On February 1, 1996, the government issued its regulations for the Internet, stating that all access must be through a channel designated by the Ministry of Posts and Telecommunication. There are regulations for application for access and requirements for safety and security control.[8] At the top of the list of regulations is a clause warning that "producing, retrieving, duplicating, or spreading information that may hinder public order is forbidden."

To familiarize the rest of the world with Chinese freedoms, the Chinese government has already begun using the Net to state their case to all those for whom words speak louder than actions. A Web site called "Human Rights in China" is provided by the propaganda department of Xinghua News Agency, China's official news agency. It offers topics like "Citizens Enjoy Economic and Social Rights," "Guarantee of Human Rights in China's Judicial Work," "Guarantee of Rights of Minority Nationalities," and "Active Participation in International Human Rights Activities." They just don't seem to have anything about the individual's right to a role in setting government policy, the right to exercise free speech and free movement, or the right to a fair trial.

Singapore has found its own way to mesh its affluence and technical sophistication with its control of the population. The government of Singapore arranged with Singapore Cable Vision (SCV) to provide all households with interactive multimedia services like Internet access, home banking, and videoconferencing via a project called IT 2000. They hope for 750,000 connections by 1998.[9] These homes will get ABN, CNNI, WSTV, Discovery, ESPN, Prime Sports, MTV Asia, TV5 from France, TV 3 from Malaysia, NHK from Japan, and more in English, Mandarin, and Tamil. There are only two problems. First, only 15% of the population can afford this luxury. Second, the Singapore Broadcasting Act of 1994 restricts what is broadcast on satellite TV, forcing broadcasters to cut pornography and negative messages about the Singapore government. Specifically, "No program should be broadcast which promotes or propagates any religious belief or view or cause of any political party or prejudices relations between the Republic of Singapore and any foreign government."[10] (See Table 7.1 for selected Asian Internet Sites.)

REGIONAL MEDIA GIANTS

The most outstanding of the regional giants was Satellite Television Asia Region, or STAR. It was started in 1990 by Richard Li, the twenty-three-year-old son of a Hong Kong billionaire, Li Ka-ahing. It began as a free service in 1991, delivering five channels including the BBC. He started it because Hutchison Whampoa, a publicly traded conglomerate that his father controlled, owned an interest in ASIASAT I. People were dubious because advertisers would have no way to estimate audience size in a free start-up service. His father helped find initial advertisers. The rate of growth was uncontrollable. In 1993, he sold the majority share to Rupert Murdoch, and its base is no longer really Asian.

The Asian Pacific Broadcasting Union (ABU) was launched in 1989 and was a natural outgrowth of the Asian-Pacific News Network (ANN) started some years earlier and based in Malaysia. ABU launched Asiavision in 1989. Like the EBU and Eurovision, Asiavision is designed to enhance interregional communication. By the mid 1990s, it was particularly proud of its capacity to do "hot-switching" to allow members to directly exchange news with simultaneous downlinking.

In the economic area, the South East Asian Alliance (ASEAN) is more and more assuming the role that the EEC used to play in Europe. This promises better regional collaboration in the early part of the twenty-first century. As the resources of this region begin to reinforce each other, new regional giants will surely emerge.

Table 7.1
Internet Sites in Asia

<http://www.majic.co.jp> Japan Telecommunications

<http://www.tbs.co.jp> Japan Tokyo Broadcasting

<http://www.nmjc/org/jiap/jdc/cyber/japan/html> Deregulation

<http://www.nb-pacifica.com/reg/nocensorship of interne-545.html>

    Internet Censorship Issues

<http://www.gov.sg/sba/policy/satguide.htm> Singapore Satellite Broadcasting

<http:www.gov.sg> Singapore government Web site

<http://cmp.lucr.edu/essays/edward-earlelmillenium/singapore.html> Singapore

<http://www.rcti.co.id> first private TV in Indonesia

<http://www.kompas.com> Indonesian daily newspaper

<http://www.gatra.com> or <http://www.tempo.com> Indonesian weekly news

<http://www.indobiz.com> Indonesian entertainment/TV

<http://www.nationmultimedia.com> Thai multimedia organization running

    newspaper, radio, TV, and online business news

<http://www.bangkokpost.net> First English newspaper in Thailand

<http://www.tvnz.com> New Zealand television updates

<http://www.abc.net.au> Australian Broadcasting Corporation

<http://www.123india.com> Indian based Net browser

Source: Anna Matsuzaka, Vidya Iyer, Karen Karitka, Varin Sachdev, and Aditya Kishore, Emerson researchers.

SELECTED NATIONAL DEVELOPMENTS

Australia

The continent of Australia, in the South Pacific, has been a bit of England for over a century. By 1992, 97% of the households had TV sets. The citizenry relied heavily on the Australia Broadcasting Company (ABC) to bring balanced news and information, just like the BBC. The Special Broadcasting Service (SBS) complemented the ABC by offering multilingual radio services to the aborigines in the out-back and to the few other minorities in the country. The Australian Broadcasting Tribunal (ABT) monitored the entire communications operation as does the FCC in the United States. Only ABT has the power to censor program content. By 1997, things in Australia had changed. The immigrant population has grown very rapidly. Now, 40% of the population was not born in Australia. Australia, more and more, sees itself as part of the Pacific basin region.[11]

Bangladesh

In 1993 in Bangladesh there was one TV set for every 339 people, considerably less than in most countries in the region. Nonetheless, the number of sets is growing, and certainly in the urban areas there's a market. In 1994 state TV negotiated agreements with WSTV and CNN transmitted through the terrestrial system a set number of hours each day. WSTV's rebroadcast reached a potential 6.6 million viewers. Prior to WSTV's arrival, CNN was the only English service rebroadcast in Bangladesh.

Indonesia

Some 87% of Indonesian households had TV in 1993. The government actively encouraged satellite TV as a way to reach its 3,000 islands. Nonetheless, the content of what's communicated is at question. When the International Federation of Journalists says that individual journalists are victimized and receive death threats when they attempt free expression of ideas; democratization does not exist.

Japan

Being prohibited from spending money on a military budget after the end of World War II had the effect of realigning Japanese markets and enabling them to create one of the leading economies in the world. In fact, Japan is the second most prosperous country in the world, after Switzerland. Its 1993 GNP per capita was $31,450.[12] It's not surprising, therefore, to find them at the leading edge of the communications technologies revolution. Not only does everyone have TV, but as of August 1992 there were 6 million households equipped with DBS receivers.

Nippon Hoso Kyokai (NHK), the public broadcasting system in Japan, is one of the world's largest broadcasting organizations. The structure is modeled on the BBC. NHK has two satellite channels, one of which is DBS-1, a channel with 57.3% news and information bulletins from seventeen broadcasters in ten countries and Hong Kong. NHK notes that no other single channel in the world provides the same news from the different perspectives of people in Asia, Europe, and the Americas, presented through their news programs in the original format, with simultaneous translation in Japanese

Of the NHK budget, 96% is financed by 34 million household fees. According to NHK's Etsuzo Yamazaki, NHK executive producer and liaison officer at ABC, "Some people think it is not necessary for NHK to do broadcasts abroad. But, even as a nation, Japan should explain itself more for the foreign countries. TV programs are one of the best ways to explain Japan. So, the Japanese Diet approved NHK's spending some amount of money for international service."[13]

Today's Japan is a general news program in English broadcast six days a week and picked up in the United States, Thailand, Korea, and Singapore. Similarly, *Asia Now* with news on Asian countries is picked up on sixty-four PBS stations in the United States and in Thailand. *Japan Business Today* is broadcast five days a week and seen in the United States on CNBC, in Europe on Superchannel and SKY, and in Singapore. *Asian Business Now* is provided to CC/ABC in the United States daily, in two-minute program segments on market results and trends.

In August 1989, NHK changed its fee structure for TV households. It added its receiving fee for DBS, 930 yen, to its terrestrial fee for a charge of 2,300 yen per month for a household. Social welfare facilities, educational facilities, the handicapped, and the needy receive discounts or full exemptions.

In preparation for the next phase of technological advancement, NHK is preparing to use Integrated Services Digital Broadcasting (ISDB), a system that can realize new services such as HDTV, multimedia, facsimile service, teletext, telesoftware, HDTV stationary images, and data transmission, through a single broadcasting channel that may now have just one analog program. Satellite and terrestrial channels, optical fiber, and other means can all transmit ISDB. NHK is only one of many examples one could cite of the advancements in communications in Japan.

WSTV, a twenty-four-hour news and information channel, began in spring of 1994 as a joint venture with a Japanese partner, Nissho Iwai Corporation. It's translated into Japanese at peak audience times, available in English on a twenty-four-hour basis and in Japanese from 8:00 P.M. to midnight. Translators based in London translate news bulletins live. Other programs such as documentaries, current affairs features, and information programs are translated in advance. Both languages, English and Japanese, are transmitted in stereo so viewers can balance how much of each language they wish to hear.

Cable and Wireless Japan Communications Services Ltd. has its head office in London with a British executive. Established in 1990 a 50–50 joint venture with Tokyo Information Services (TIS), a Sanwa Bank subsidiary operating in Osaka and Tokyo, the two major economic cities in Japan.[14] It provides international connections from Japan to other parts of the world. They are especially active in Hong Kong and Macau. The increases in international communications and in mobile phones mean that business is very good just now.

Digital satellite TV is already becoming a market competitor in Japan. For more information see <*http://economist.iconnect.net/issue/05-10-96/wb8359.html*>. PerfecTV began on October 1996. For $26 per month plus $460 for the setup of the dish, you get fifty-seven TV channels and 103 radio channels. In summer 1997, JSKYB, a joint venture of Rupert Murdoch and Softbank, began to offer a 100-channel digital service. DirecTV launched a 100-channel service in 1997. While Japan's commercial TV stations are in a strong position and still get the advertising dollars, to maintain a competitive edge, they will have to invest in digital. The present plan is that all Japanese TV will be broadcast digitally by 2010, and there's pressure to move the date up to 1999.

Malaysia

By the mid 1990s, well over 90% of households in Malaysia receive at least the basic two TV channels, RTM TV1 and TV2, broadcast through the Ministry of Broadcasting. In July 1995 the government had privatized TV3; allowed another commercial station, Metrovision, to broadcast, and was privatizing certain time slots on other stations. In 1996 Malaysia began to receive satellite TV and twenty channels.

Rahmah Bt. Hashim, Ph.D, a faculty member at Universiti Kebangsaan Malaysia, Department of Communications, comments on what's happening to the Malay industry.

Ownership is still Malaysian. Many of the owners of production houses are still local. But there is a tendency now of joint ownership with foreign partners. I think this is reflected in Malaysia, Inc., where the government and the private sector work as partners. It's a reflection of the globalization era. They know that there is not enough market to concentrate on the local scene. If you make just twelve dramas a year, you cannot make money. It's just basic math. The overhead costs are high.

For example, there is a local company, HVD (Home Video Distributors), with a board that is mostly local, but they have ventured out into the Asian market and signed an MOU with STAR TV. Initially, it was initially a video outlet. The owner had connections in the Ministry. Consequently, they had opportunity to produce local dramas with the help of some Hong Kong directors.

Focusing on news, there is a tendency to focus on economic news. We have an increasing number of programs on business trends, on money matters, on shares. This is new. When I was younger we didn't have these things that ordinary laymen don't understand. I think we're in a period of transition where there is some confusion—even on the part of the stations. I think the bottom line is money.

Also, there's a lot of accommodation. As a nation, we've put considerable emphasis on use of the Malay language as a way to bring together our heterogeneous population. The media privatization has meant more programs that are not in Malay. It's more pocket oriented.

I think society cannot stop the invasion of satellite communications, but I think the individual strength and individual resilience can surpass whatever invasion is coming from the sky. For the individual to be strong, we are talking about the children—future generations and whether they can be resilient. It's up to adults and parents. And as far as the broadcasters are concerned, in the final analysis, the views and aspirations of the different peoples in the international community need to be respected, not just the voice of the powerful and the vocal, but also the deafening sounds of the silent majority.[15]

New Zealand

The small South Pacific country of New Zealand remains another nation built in the image of England. Over time the European population and the Maori natives have generally made peace, although economic differences still remain. In early 1990s, Television New Zealand found itself challenged by the arrival of commercial stations, similar to the events in Australia. In 1994, TCI, the U.S. cable giant, launched a partnership with TV New Zealand.

North Korea

As is the case in China, public loudspeakers mounted on utility poles blast out radio broadcasts in North Korea to the entire population at designated intervals. The Korean Central Broadcasting Committee decides what's transmitted on these radio substitutes. When people have real radios, the dials are fixed to prevent reception of external broadcasting. It's not clear how many people have TV, but the government broadcasting system fills about half of program time with broadcasts about the government leader. However, beginning in 1995, North Koreans able to construct a satellite dish found themselves able to receive programs from the new South Korean satellite—in Korean.

South Korea

Of the households in South Korea, 99.4% have TV sets. Since the Korean War in the 1950s, prosperity has come quickly to the republic on the southern half of the Korean peninsula. Cable TV was implemented in 1993, and DBS satellite TV in 1995. This well-controlled "democracy" has a tradition of valuing regulation and has devoted considerable time to discussion of how one regulates these new technologies. While responsible entities are designated, accomplishing such regulation may be another matter. Within the state-run TV networks, the government has exercised its assumed parental role. For example, in December 1996, they banned teenage singers from TV so that they could refocus on their studies.

Cultural differences across the globe do alter views of what is or isn't appropriate on TV. For example, Kyeong B. Kwon, a Korean student in the United States, doesn't understand the constant display of guns on U.S. TV. "Violence, to me, is more like when a TV show uses guns. That's because it is prohibited in Korea for a citizen to own a gun." He goes on to say martial arts is not real violence. It's a kind of sport.[16]

Regarding the Internet, South Korea recently warned that a person's putting information on the Internet might be interpreted as compromising their security from North Korean danger.

Singapore

Vitually every household has access to TV. There are two public channels owned by the government and two cable stations—one government owned and one partially owned by the government. This second station carries MTV, STAR, Fox, UPN, BBC, and HBO. However, the government controls the content of what these global broadcasters rebroadcast on Singapore's stations. If it is violent or otherwise offensive, the broadcasters lose their license.

While Singapore is an economic hub for the region and many corporations have offices here, it doesn't mean much for local residents. For example, CNN's Asia Business News (ABN) is broadcast from Singapore, but in the mid 1990s Singaporeans did not receive ABN.

At this point, the plan to provide Internet access to all households is in its early stages, and only 20% of people have access to the Internet. That rate is still far higher than in most Asian countries.

The Singapore government promised that it wouldn't overregulate the Internet, but it wants to protect its citizens and the country. One way to do this is to punish those who use the Internet for pornography or for materials on the wrong political or religious views. Internet providers register with the government and pay a license fee to allow the Singapore Broadcast Authority to investigate any violation of the law. This procedure went into effect September 15, 1996. What's interesting is that people who live in Singapore, knowing no alternative, have no problem with the censorship.[17]

CASE STUDIES IN DEMOCRATIZATION

India

Only 27% of India's households had TV in 1994. The absence of TV gives some indication of the country's economic conditions. The wealth-poverty contrasts are incredible. India is, however, not one of the globe's ten poorest countries. All of them are in Africa.

Of the country's 600 million people, 350 million live below the official poverty line. Some 48% of the population is illiterate. One hundred million city dwellers live in slums called "jhuggis," where those who are fortunate find metal and timber scrap to erect shacks. Some 70% of Indians have no access to toilets, and 30% lack a safe water supply. The 1993 GNP per capita was $290, which gives a perspective on both the poverty and the concentration of wealth. In contrast, while the jeweled maharajahs of the past are fading away, a new overclass of business, political, and mafia leaders parade the new wealth. A middle class exists, significant in numbers—200 million—if not in its percentage of the whole population. The issue in India is not this new concentration of wealth, but the failure to create more wealth.[18]

One of the most remarkable things about India is that despite the fact that half of its 600 million people are illiterate, the country has been able to keep a democracy alive for fifty years. The ability to maintain this open system continues to be challenged by the 18-million-person-a-year growth in population. By 2025, India may have 1.3 billion people and exceed China in population.

It is argued that the poverty is not as bad as fifty years ago. People note that fifty years ago, if you grew up low-caste and poor, you wouldn't have proper clothes, and you'd be emaciated. Some say that most people today have some clothes and a meal or two a day. Then life expectancy was thirty; now it is more like sixty. The country has fed a population three times the size of the 1947 population. To some extent things have improved, in some circles. However, the lower-caste people living on the streets by the sea in

Bombay certainly don't have clothes or, for that matter, scraps of wood or metal.

Even in the mid 1980s, people in villages were gathering at centers to watch TV or videos. In the early 1990s, Doordarshan, the state TV, was considered so bad that local stores rented videotapes of news that had been sent in from other countries. Soon thereafter, the STAR TV satellite footprint was over India. People joined together in home-rigged neighborhood cable hookups and found ways to make their own satellite dishes. Much to Doordarshan's amazement, this thirst for television was unquenchable. The market took off.

Because India has the world's second largest single market, the global broadcasters were there to assist in any way possible. By the year 2000, it's estimated that the middle class will be 400–500 million strong. That's a spending power of about 1 trillion rupees per year. A lot of money. These people are impatient for progress. They compare India with Indonesia, South Korea, and Malaysia, which were as poor as India in 1947. They point out that these countries have leaped ahead with a per capita income now ten to twenty times that of India. They point out that those countries have 90% literacy rates. Even those aspiring to be middle class are impatient. Mohammed Rafiq, twenty-eight, a Muslim who makes his living selling vegetables, comments, "When we sit in our homes at night, we see pictures on our television sets of the rich man's life, with cars, refrigerators, air-conditioners, everything we don't have. So naturally we think: why is it that God caused us to be born here? Is it our fate to live always as we do?"[19]

Those in the media industry hustling to meet this growing market demand finally got a government acknowledgment that the country needed to be freed from the grip of the very boring Doordarshan state TV. Doordarshan was encouraged to sign an agreement with CNNI to lease space on INSAT IIB, the Indian government's satellite. CNNI would broadcast a twenty-four-hour channel into India. R. Basu, director general of Doordarshan, noted that this was the first step toward Doordarshan offering channels to other broadcasters on INSAT IIC when it went into orbit in 1996.[20]

By the mid 1990s, Indian markets were producing $6 billion annually on video games, $16 billion to rent home videos, $80 billion in the phone service sector, and $80 billion in sales through home catalogues. This is happening in the context of the Asia-Pacific market, which is twice the size of the European and American markets. The Asia-Pacific market has had growth at a rate of $3 billion a week. That's $3 trillion a year. If cable TV reaches 50% penetration into the top 5% of Asian households, and each pays $100 per year for the service, that's $15 billion a year in revenue.[21]

At the head of the television privatization line is Zee TV. Ashok Vaishnavi, general manager and one member of the leadership team at Zee, explains.

> We're three years old. We started in 1992. We're dynamic, energetic, young and we're full of fun. Within the country we reach about 25% of all cable and satellite homes. We'd like to reach 50–75% within two years. We have about 15 million cable and satellite homes. It's about one-quarter of the total TV homes. This industry is amazing. In the beginning the growth of satellite television was about 100% every 3–6 months.
>
> The problem in India is the Telegraph Act. It's responsible for the fact that there's been no Indian broadcast industry. The British came up with this act in 1895 in order to protect the British rule in India. The fact is that you can have international broadcasters come to our country, compile programming, beam it out, and then beam it back down to us. On the other hand an Indian broadcaster cannot beam directly to our audiences in the country or to audiences outside the country. This is not a level playing field. The satellite uplink and downlink has needed to happen outside the country for anyone other than Doordarshan.
>
> But that's only part of the story. India is the only reliable democracy between Europe and Australia. Nobody can dispute this. We are the strongest liberal democratic influence in the region. Anyone can tell you that. We are equidistant from Japan, Europe, Africa, and Australia. We're right there in the center. We intend to be the center of communications in the region. We have an internal economy which is driven by this huge population. Logistics-wise, I don't see why we shouldn't be number one. The world's liberal democracies must see to it that India's liberal and democratic roots are strengthened because we're going to be the kind of influence in this area that the United States has been in North and South America.
>
> We're not talking about hegemony, not expansionism. We're talking greater invention, greater independence, about improving the standard of living. We're not talking control or expansionism. We're talking about a smile on the face of every human being in this global village. I don't think there's another country in the region positioned to do this yet. You see we're not just a national channel. We're seen in sixty countries. They're selling our programs to Indonesia. We're seen in half-dozen southeast Asian countries. We have an Arabic band on our transponder until midnight. We don't want to tell our audiences only what's happening in India. We want to give the news of the third world the way it should be told. Western media has never projected the Indian or the Asian point of view the way it should be.

It's nice to know that this is the first Asian channel seen on Asian terms. We've done no marketing yet. With the right effort, the data that says we're seen in 1% of satellite and cable homes in the region could easily shoot up to 10–15% in a couple years time.

At home in India, we have tremendous trouble. One-third of our population is below the poverty level. I don't see why we shouldn't work for a better tomorrow. Liberalization of the economy cannot come without liberalization of the telecom and the broadcasting at the same time. You see what's key in today's economy is the rapidity of the response and that depends on how good, how reliable, how responsive your communications network is. So I look on the telecom and broadcast picture as a part of the totality—all of it together generating wealth. Commercial television is directly driven by advertising. Advertising is linked to creation of wealth—selling products and creating jobs.

In the next five years, we'll provide greater and more audiovisual services besides television programming—multimedia, interactive, databases, educational, home shopping. You name it, we intend to do it. We've already started home shopping. We've also started data education. One of the ambitions of the chairman is that we should have a twenty-four-hour state-of-the-art television channel covering India and the region. We have that education at the moment—teaching computer sciences, computer management, etcetera. I think as these technologies become available we should have a twenty-four-hour TV education channel—distance education, yes. There'll be immense backup. Something like BBC, open university. I'm fully convinced that as this sector grows, we'll be an important part of it.

In the future, one of our strong commodities will be software. Even now, in 1995, computer software is one of our largest commodities. It will be about a billion dollars a year in a couple years. We have the world's third largest pool of scientists and engineers. We have the world's second largest pool of computer software specialists. Now tie that to the world's largest film industry and the convergence of video, audio and computer. Talk about the information superhighway. We have everything to be a key player.[22]

No doubt India will be a key player, and its role as a leading democracy can help set a tone for the region, unless the uncontrollable population growth exacerbates the poverty problem. People may not be literate, but television already exposes them to the lifestyles available to other people. At what point do these enormous numbers of people become impatient? Might another Gandhi emerge to lead them toward demanding a change in the status quo? How destabilizing would that be for the emerging markets in the region? Will those in control of the economy realize that it's in their self-interest to find ways to upgrade the quality of life for India's poor and to find ways to curb the rate of population growth?

China

In 1994, there was one TV set in China for every forty-four people, and the number of households with sets was growing very rapidly, especially in urban areas. Zhaow Wanli, a young engineer, said that in 1996 in most big cities people have access to more than twenty TV stations and pay TV exists for the first time.[23] This is a change from a few years earlier, when there were only a handful of stations. China Central Television (CCTV), the government system, has been supplemented with cable. Zhaow indicates that they don't encourage satellite TV because cable "is better in image quality."

While not encouraged and sometimes illegal, satellite is creeping in. The first satellite dishes began to appear in shops in late spring 1992. By spring 1993 they were everywhere in Beijing. As in other countries all over the world, the national television, CCTV, was more the spectator than the instigator. Dozens of shops sold satellite dishes despite the 1990 Chinese law banning the use of satellite dishes to receive foreign TV signals—unless there was permission from the police. The law didn't ban the sale of dishes or their installation as long as they are used to watch CCTV. If the police come, people tell them they only watch CCTV. The dishes sold are about five feet in diameter and cost about $500 including the receiver. That's not much more than a VCR.

Peter Vesey, former vice president of CNNI, commented in 1994 about global TV in China.

> We've had a signal strength problem there [in China], but yes, CNN has been seen in China on a semiofficial or official basis since 1987. It has taken a huge dish to pick up our signal, but we've been seen at CCTV. Our signal has been distributed through their facility to diplomatic and foreign communities and compounds in the Beijing area and to hotels which have receivers that can pick up the signal in China itself recently. In fact, the end of September 1994, we went on a new satellite which is partially owned by the Chinese—APSTAR I, which was specifically designed to carry Chinese programming for Chinese-speaking Asia. We've got a good clear strong signal on that satellite, which should make us available to a number of the many many dishes that exist either semi-officially or illegally in China. We have no idea what the viewership is. But it certainly has addressed our signal strength problem there, and we're now much more readily

receivable there in China. You have to be a diplomat as well as a businessperson in this part of the world. Ted Turner has always put a premium on that aspect of the business. Hopefully, over time, not tomorrow or the next day, but over the next several years, we would hope to achieve a legal circulation in China to a wider audience than just those who live there who are non-Chinese or who are government officials, to be legally distributed and to be legally paid for that distribution I would hasten to add.

I think we have always been honest and straightforward in our dealings with the various Chinese authorities. They have always known what we were doing, and I think they have come, over many years, to respect our service and our intentions, such things as Tiananmen Square coverage notwithstanding. I think that puts us in a pretty good position there overall. And we hope to enhance that position. Obviously, for the long term, China represents an amazing opportunity. But, realistically, both on the short to intermediate term, the English language service, going into a country with a tiny percent of its population fluent enough to understand it, I don't think we represent either a tremendous opportunity or a tremendous threat politically.[24]

Rupert Murdoch's STAR TV, after the incident of removing the BBC from his program lineup in order to appease the Chinese, eventually signed a $20 million deal to build four TV studios in Tianjin, China, and he shows STAR in hotels.[25]

China's Ministry of Radio, Film and Television announced in November 1996 that it approved digital television expansion in China working with the Hundai Electronics America TV/COM unit. The system will use satellite transmission coverage of ASIASAT II.[26]

Technology aside, the real question for the twenty-first century is, how will the media be used? Will its uses foster democratization? Will it exacerbate the control government has over its citizens? Will it increase the gap between the haves and the have-nots, thereby contributing to social and political unrest and market instability? The People's Republic of China has spent several generations instilling clear directives issued by government regarding the role of the media. The purpose of the media and of journalism, as Party Chairman Hu Yaobang puts it, is to serve as the "mouthpiece of the party." To get the South China Morning Post Internet Section, try <http://www.scmp.com/news>.

The concept of individual rights being subservient to government has become a norm for the population. A prominent journalism professor at Shanghai Institute of International Studies, when asked in 1992 about individuals making or receiving news on the Internet, replied, "I've never heard of foreigners wanting to send a specific story. Foreigners wanting news will call or write a station. The feedback is mostly by mail. It's not urgent enough to use a computer."

Zhaow Wanli, the young engineer, held the same view about paternalistic government when he commented about the Internet. "TV is for the common people and the Internet is something sophisticated and thus for young people or scientific experts in China. When I went to my ISP, I had to tell them how I was going to use the Internet. There is no legislation for Internet use in China yet."

That's a mindset that can certainly affect democratization. It's quite different from the mindset that assumes that people have rights unless prohibited. It champions the idea that people have no rights unless stipulated.

The other threat to democratization of the media globally comes as major communications corporations compromise their standards in order to make money in Chinese markets. For example, in November 1996 the Walt Disney Company received a message from China's Minister of Radio, Film and Television warning that China was concerned about the new film about the Dalaí Lama, *Kundun*. The film, coproduced by Disney and Touchstone, covers the years of the Dalaí Lama's story from 1950, when the Chinese invaded Tibet, to his exile in 1959.[27] Disney has considerable business interest in China including radio programming, merchandising through its "Mickey's Corner" stores, theatrical releases, filmed animation, a news bureau, comic-book publishing, and plans for a theme park. The minister just wanted Disney to know that he thinks the Dalaí Lama film will affect Disney's potentially profitable Chinese market. The choice: capitulate to Chinese political attitudes and tolerate censorship in order to make money. Fortunately they seemed to have gotten out of the problem by not owning the international distribution rights. Disney distributes in the United States and in the U.K., but the rights to distribute in the rest of the world were sold to a French company, UGC. However, two other studios, Universal and Warner Brothers, did turn their heads on championing free speech. They each rejected the idea of producing this film before it even went to Disney because they wanted to avoid a political problem.

Murdoch's decision to remove the BBC from the satellite distribution to China is another example of economic interests mattering more than democratic standards for freedom of expression.

Hong Kong

This former British colony and economic mecca for Asia was returned to the government of the People's Republic of China on July 1, 1997, and is just beginning to understand the rules for life as a part of the PRC. It's been a very prosperous place. There's one TV set for every three people, and it's where STAR TV started in 1991. In 1994 a Hong Kong reporter was sentenced to twelve years in prison for revealing state secrets with an article on an alleged planned increase in interest rates in China. He published it in a paper in Hong Kong that wasn't even circulated in China. The action had a chilling effect on Hong Kong reporters. As early as 1995, Hong Kong journalists engaged in self-censorship out of fear of Chinese retribution.[28]

SUMMARY

The Asia-Pacific region is moving rapidly into a major economic market force in the twenty-first century. The potentials are enormous. However, the jury is out on whether all this opportunity will result in improved quality of life and market prosperity or whether it will lead to conflict.

Global media and the new communication technologies are a double-edged sword in many parts of this region. On the one hand, millions of people are exposed to new ideas, to new information, education, and to entertainment. Expectations rise and maybe standards of living rise. On the other hand, those wanting to control are fearful of new ideas and work over time to seek ways to constrain people from access to the new media. They try to prohibit freedom of information and censor free speech. How much constraint will people tolerate, especially when they know that they are being controlled?

In addition to the question of how the population will react to exposure to or denial of new technologies, another question arises. For this region to work collaboratively, it will need to transcend the diversity of cultures and religions and political philosophies. The village borders have indeed expanded, and it is no longer possible to be sheltered from people who are different. Will Asia find ways to build pluralism?

Perhaps the ultimate question falls in the laps of the global communication giants—especially the TV and film producers. As their market expands to include the Pacific region, how will they modify their product to reach this market? Will they compromise democratic values and resort to censorship because they are driven by greed? Will they be so delighted to be victors that the viewers will end up victims?

NOTES

1. For more information, see <www.scv.edu.au> and <www.dca.gov.au>.

2. "An independent India looks back on 50 years of progress and pain." *New York Times*, August 14, 1997, p. 1f.

3. Associated Press, "Cellular system to link villages." *Boston Globe*, April 3, 1997, p. A7.

4. Fred Brenchley, "Revealed: Murdoch's Star War's Strategy," *Australian Financial Review*, April 20, 1994, pp. 1, 15–16.

5. "Murdoch buys out remaining Star TV shares from Li family." *The Straits Times*, Kuala Lumpur, July 19, 1995, p. 2.

6. Diane Mermigas, "The Murdoch Map: Exclusive Q&A with News Corp. leader." *Electronic Media*, 41 (1996):26. Also see Diane Mermigas, "What's Murdoch Want Now? Programming." *Electronic Media*, 41: 8, 45. See News Corp. *<http://www.newscorp.com/report/letter.htm>*.

7. "Invasion from Cyberspace." *World Press Review*, March, 1996, p. 40.

8. Seth Faison, "Chinese Tiptoe into Internet." *New York Times*, February 5, 1996, p. A3.

9. Anna Matsuzaka, Unpublished papers, Emerson Program in Mass Communications, February 17, 1997, and March 24, 1997. Also see *<http://www.iipl.com.sg/whatsnew/text/cable.html>*. "Development of Cable TV in Singapore."

10. *<http://.gov.sg/sba/policy/satguide.htm>*, April 1996.

11. For more information see web sites: *<www.abc.net.au>* and *<www.scv.edu.au>*.

12. *Progress of Nations*, UNICEF, 1995.

13. Etsuzo Yamazaki, executive producer, NHK, Japan Broadcasting Corp., 1177 Avenue of the Americas, New York. Interview with the author in New York on May 19, 1994.

14. Matsuzaka, "Development of Cable TV."

15. Rahmah Hashim, Ph.D., faculty, Universiti Kebangsaan Malaysia, Department of Communications, Faculty of Social Sciences and Humanities, U.K.M., 43600 Bangi, Selangor Darul Ehsan, Malaysia. Fax: (6) 03–8256484. Interview with the author in Kuala Lumpur on July 20, 1995. Also see her article "Media Development" in *Journal for the World Association for Christian Communications*, 41(April 1994).

16. Kyeong B. Kwon, Emerson Program in Mass Communications, Spring 1997.

17. See *<http://cmp.lucr.edu/essays/edward-earlelmillenium/singapore.html.>*.

18. "An Independent India Looks Back on 50 Years of Progress and Pain." *New York Times*, August 14, 1997, p. 1f.

19. *Ibid.*

20. Reuters, "India Will Allow CNN Broadcasts." *International Herald Tribune*, July 1–2, 1995, p. 9.

21. Ashok Vaishnavi, General Manager, ZEE Telefilms Ltd., Bombay. Unpublished paper, written December 7, 1993.

22. Ashok Vaishnavi, General Manager, ZEE Telefilms Ltd., Continental Bldg. 135, Dr. Annie Besant Road, Worli, Bombay, 400018, India. FAX: 91–022–4931938. Interview with the author in Bombay on July 1995.

23. Wanli Zhaow, a young engineer in Beijing. Telelecture from China to International Communications class, Emerson College, Boston, November 15, 1996.

24. Peter Vesey, Vice President CNNI, One CNN Center, 4th Floor, North Tower, Atlanta, GA 30303. Telephone interview with the author, October 25, 1994.

25. Jonathan Karp, "Buttering Up Beijing." *World Press Review*, September 1995, p. 32.

26. See *<http://www.mediacentral.com>*.

27. Willie Brent, "Disney Tangled in Lama Drama." *Variety*, 365, no. 5, December, 1996, p. 11.

28. Charles A. Radin, "Hong Kong Press Feels Beijing Pressure: Self-censorship Cited as China Takeover Nears." *Boston Globe*, April 2, 1995.

8

Conclusions

Nothing is neutral. Those who decide the content of the media have benefits; those excluded from having their viewpoints represented in the media have problems competing for economic opportunity in the marketplace. Those who decide news priorities, hence society's priorities, make value judgments that benefit their own self-interest; those whose priorities are decided for them make their own value judgments regarding how to retaliate against institutions they deem unhelpful. Those who begin as victors, by winning a battle, sometimes lose a war and become victims themselves. Those who begin as victims sometimes end as victors.

This is the complex dynamic of human society over which a thin veil of dazzling new communications technologies have been placed. The globe spins faster for those caught up in the technological developments. How will convergence work? Imagine a global network of satellites that enables you to phone from somewhere to nowhere and vice versa! What if it's possible to send the same picture to the little box in every home across the world at the same time? So far, it's all been about seductive technology and money. Make lots of money. Get to new markets first.

Get there with what? Will the news and information that create the reality on which society bases its development have a positive or a negative impact on the quality of life in the decades ahead? Is anyone thinking about that? What's happening to the viewers? Will there be victims of this era? Who? Are there any victors? Is it possible to merge industry and consumer self-interest so that there are many victors?

THE VIEWERS

In the cyclical pattern of society, it's nearly time for the pendulum to swing away from the decade or two of deference to corporate profits. There comes a turning point when public opinion says "enough," that profit has gone beyond the acceptable level and has become greed. The pendulum then shifts into a pro-consumer period. This happened in the 1930s and again in the 1960s and 1970s. How will it play out when it happens now at the end of the 1990s? The world is a smaller place now. As life expectancy is longer, those who learned their skills in the 1960s are simply more skilled, and definitely still working. The technologies make communication much easier now so more people can play a role in whatever direction this pro-consumer shift takes. Hopefully, the shift won't be in the direction of fascism. Hopefully it will be in the direction of democratization. With democratization, the consequences for the majority of people are far healthier.

The media does set priorities and therefore has an enormous role to play in which the pro-consumer approach is chosen. The media creates the myths by which we live. As George Gerbner said, "Those who tell the stories hold the power in society. Today television tells most of the stories to most of the people, most of the time."[1] At this time of transition, what stories are the media telling the viewers?

It's more complex than at the time of past societal readjustments. "Viewers" have much more choice. The affluent can get far more news and information than they want because of the enormous choice on the Internet and on television. They can get either more than they want or such narrowcast information that they may have less than is needed to see the forest in which the trees are placed. The poor can get news and information they never knew existed until television came into their lives. This can be information from other cultures, with implications that they do not understand because there's no one to "translate." Or they can simply view, absorb, and become increasingly impatient for their share of what they see that other people have.

Equally important to what viewers get is what viewers don't get. This matters because it is at the heart of whether or not viewers become informed enough and empowered enough to be an effective anchor to hold steady political freedoms, economic growth, and social opportunity throughout the storms of change that sweep through the airwaves. Studies of democracy show that the public functions as this anchor, preserving the values of fairness, survival, and strength.[2]

Journalists may leap to cover only soap-opera-type scandal and call it news. It's easy to report. It doesn't require investigative reporting. It brings easy rating points. But at the end of the day, what do the viewers know about the important decisions made that affect their livelihoods? Can't important stories also be told so they bring high ratings?

Media owners may choose to capitulate to dictatorial governments in order to make profits. Look at Murdoch's dumping the BBC news in order to curry the favor that brings more business from China. Look at the contortions Disney went through when China pressed them not to tell the Dalai Lama story, lest they lose the ability to make money in China's giant market. In the short run, the media owners will make more money by capitulating. What will they lose in the long run besides control of their companies? Their integrity? Does that have a value any more?

What the media chooses to let the masses know determines whether or not there will be victims or victors in society's next period of pro-consumerism.

THE VICTIMS

How can there be victims? Those who like TV and the Internet will happily play with their "remote" or their "mouse." Those who don't like it or can't access it will just do other things. That's true, except there are moments when everyone is part of a community, a society. In that context, everyone either benefits or is hurt.

This holds true even for those who isolate themselves. Where does the food come from—and that which is needed to grow it and store it and buy it or sell it? Where does the housing come from—and that which is necessary to build it and insulate it and supply it with light and water? Where does the health care come from—and that which is necessary to make it available and to pay for it and to have transport to it? How does one avoid being harmed by warfare, toxic spills, or severe climate when it surrounds one? How does one dream dreams, pursue interests, see the world, encourage the children to be all that they want to be, if one lives in a place where speech is limited, movement is limited, and career opportunity is dictated?

How do people know how to create opportunities that enhance the quality of their lives? The stories told on the media become the models. It's such a waste of time, and it can result in serious mistakes, to simply say, "just change," to people who have no idea how to create viable market economies, transparent governments, and democratic societies. Why reinvent the wheel when there are countless models in what could be the news and information provided as a daily exchange? Whose news is it anyway?

Those who do nothing to create the opportunities of life become the victims controlled by others. It's easy to see how this can hold true for the viewers. Might it also hold true for the industry whose leaders either do nothing to change to meet the interests of a new market in a new era or who do nothing to take a stand for integrity? Might they end up like the frogs in the pan of water, accommodating to ever hotter water until they are cooked?

THE VICTORS

What are the criteria for deciding who's a victor? The prevailing thinking at the end of the twentieth century is that there are two criteria—in reality they become one. First, make the most money. Second, beat out the competition by getting to the new market first, so you can make the most money.

Once upon a time, a business plan included a description of a product or service provided to a market—central to the criteria for being a victor. When the pendulum swung into the corporate profit decades of the 1980s and 1990s, as it did before in the 1940s and 1950s and before that in the 1890s and 1910s, the market changed. So did the product and service. In these very narcissistic times, the market became the stockholders of the company itself. The product became money the company delivered to itself. For those at the top of this power-prestige-greed game, it was easy never to see a "public." They were invisible—just statistics, if that. They certainly weren't priorities in any way. They didn't need to be. They were always there, always subservient, and enough of them bought whatever one sold.

In the pro-consumer decades, the criteria for defining the victors are different. The popularity of the product or service is weighted most highly, because from that one wins in the market competition and the result is making the most money. That money will, of course, fill the pockets of the stockholders, but it will be deemed important to not put it all in those pockets. Expanding the market to win more popularity for one's product or service is deemed equally important because it is the way to make more money. So, profits go into philanthropic efforts, into investing in smaller businesses, into public projects, into job creation. Because the gap between rich and poor decreases, the market can expand. The pro-consumer corporate efforts build good will. Public ideal merges with self-interest. The self-interest of the company is served. Everyone can be a victor. The self-interest of the consumer is served.

So, what kind of news and information will the media offer at this time of social readjustment? How will this thin veil of dazzling new communications technologies affect society?

Will the stories told in the news create myths that perpetuate the early 1980s corporate profit ideal described by former New York governor Mario Cuomo as making "the denial of compassion acceptable?" Will the media enable people to understand government transparency—to let the sun shine on those decisions that will result in strengthening either fascism or democracy? Will anyone apply the lessons learned from the models describing Bangladesh, South Africa, Bulgaria, Bolivia, and Boston?

It's time to think. Not about the technology—we're consumed in that. It's time to think about how we *use* the technology. It's a moment of enormous opportunity to merge self-interest and ideal, to make victors of the many and not the few. Unless we hear Einstein's reminder that "everything has changed except the way we think," it's the victims, not the victors, who may multiply, to the detriment of haves and have-nots alike.

NOTES

1. George Gerbner, "Society's Storyteller: How Television Creates the Myths by Which We Live." *Media and Values*, No. 59–60 (Fall 1992), Los Angeles.

2. Everett Carl Ladd, "Public Opinion: Questions at the Quinquennial." *Public Opinion*, April/May 1983. Alexis de Tocqueville, *Democracy in America*. Also see Carla B. Johnston, *Reversing the Nuclear Arms Race* (Boston: Shenkman Books, 1986), p. 31f.

Further Reading

The author strongly recommends that readers interested in this topic monitor periodicals, newspapers, and the Internet for new developments. The topic is current, and consequently there are not a lot of books addressing the impact of the new communication technologies.

Akwule, Raymond. *Global Telecommunications*. Boston and London: Butterworth Heinemann/Focal, 1992.

Barnouw, Erik, et al. *Conglomerates and the Media*. New York: The New Press, 1997.

Bourgault, Louise M. *Mass Media in Sub-Sahara Africa*. Indianapolis: Indiana University Press, 1995.

Frederick, Howard. *Global Communication and International Relations*. Belmont, CA: Wadsworth, 1993.

Hilliard, Robert L., and Michael C. Keith. *Global Broadcasting Systems*. Boston and London: Butterworth Heinemann/Focal, 1996.

Johnston, Carla B. *International Television Co-Production*. Boston and London: Butterworth Heinemann/Focal, 1992.

Johnston, Carla Brooks. *Winning the Global TV News Game*. Boston and London: Butterworth Heinemann/Focal, 1995.

Negraponte, Nicholas. *Being Digital*. New York: Random House, 1996.

Parker, Richard. *Mixed Signals: The Prospects for Global Television News*. New York: Twentieth Century Fund Press, 1995.

Smith, Anthony. *The Age of the Behemoths: Globalization of Mass Media Firms*. New York: Twentieth Century Fund, 1992.

Styles, Thomas A., and Leonard Styles, eds. *The 1000 Hour War: Communication in the Gulf*. Westport, CT: Greenwood, 1994.

The World Satellite Directory. Potomac, MD: Phillips, annually.

UNESCO Communication and Society Series, Communication Policy Series, Reports and Papers on Communications. For recent publications contact UNESCO at the United Nations.

U.S. Department of Commerce, *Globalization of Mass Media*, Washington, DC: Government Printing Office, 1993.

World Radio-TV Handbook. New York: Billboard, annually.

Web sites of interest in addition to those listed within this book:

Browsers and Search Engines

Browsers:
   <webmaster@apic.net>
   or *<http://www.w3.org>*
   or e-mail to *<webmaster@w3.org>*
Key search engines:
   <http://www.yahoo.com>
   <http://lycos.cs.cmu.edu>
   <http://altavista.com>

Communications organizations

<http://cavern.uark.edu/comminfo/www/ACA.html> American Communication Association Web Site

<comserv@vm.its.vpi.edu> International Association of Mass Communication Research. Your message is "join iamcrnet my name" (without quotes). It's free.

<telnet igc.org> Then access iamcrnet for newsletter and other research information.

<Listproc@hawaii.edu> Academy for Global Communication and Education (ACE). Then your message is "SUBSCRIBE ACE-L your name" (without quotes).

Global information

<http://www.odci.gov/cia/publications/95fact/index.html> U.S. CIA Fact Book—a profile of every country in the world

<http://www.igc.apc.org/interact/PeaceNet.html> Global Communications, a nonprofit foundation venture

<http://nearnet.gnn.com/gnn/gnn.html> Global network navigator

Communications, media, and journalism sites around the world

   <http://www.jou.ufl.edu/commres/jouwww.htm>
   <http://www.clearinghouse.net>
   <http://www.analysys.co.uk/commslib.htm> Virtual Library—communications and journalism sections

Newspapers

<http:www.clarinet.com> Wires
<http://www.newslink.org/> Newspapers, broadcasts
<http://wwww.aãuburn.edu/~vestmon/news.html> Newsroom (from Reuters,
    USA Today, networks, etc.)
<http://www.iht.com> International Herald Tribune
<http://www.nyt.com> New York Times
<http://www.wsj.com> Wall Street Journal
<http://www.csmonitor.com> Christian Science Monitor
<http://www.enews.com/> Electronic Newsstand
<http://www.dowjones.com.pj.html> Personal journal—your own news

Broadcasters

<http://www.informatik.uni-aldenburg.de/~thkoch/> especially shortwave
<http://www.teleport.com/~celinec/tv__usent.htm>
<http://www.rtvf.nwu.edu/links/broadcasting.html> Radio and TV
<http://www.service.com/stv/home.html> Science TV
<gopher:gopher.voa.gov/voa news> Voice of America
<http://www.bbc.com>

Government initiatives and infrastructure

*<http://www.rpi.edu/Internet/Guides/decemj/icmc/applications-government-
    initiatives.html>*
<http://www.ntia.doc.gov> U.S. National Telecommunication and Informa-
    tion Administration
<http://www.cto.int> Commonwealth (British) Telecommunication Organi-
    zations
<http://www.fundesco.es> Spain
<webmaster@echo.lu> European Community
<http://www.sds.no> Internet use in Europe
*<http://www.rpi.edu/internet/guides/decemj/icmc/applications-government-
    initiatives.html>*
<gopher://gopher.undp.org> United Nations
<http://www.worldbank.org> World Bank

Influence of computers, telecommunications, satellites, and information technology

<http://www.webcom.com/pcj/it-nf/itn-open.html>
<http://www.mit.edu> Check Media Lab at MIT.
<hkb@nic.funet.fi> information on European satellites
<http:///www.intelsat.int:8080/> Intelsat

Regulation

<http://alnilam.ucs.indiana.edu:1027/sources/com.html>
    - Check International Telecom Union
    - Check Asian Mass Comm Research and Info Center

- Check GLOCOM-Global Communication, International University of Japan
- Also a route to MIT Media Lab

<http://town.hall.org/radio/index.html> computers, freedom, and privacy
<http://www.igc.apc.org/fair> Fairness and Accuracy in Reporting
<http://zippy.sonoma.edu/ProjectCensored>

North America
<http://www.atv.ca> Canadian TV on ATV
<http://www.mediacentral.com>
<http://www.nbc.com> and similar format for other networks

Latin America
<http://www.zonalatina.com>
<http://www.hispanstar.com>
<http://latin-america.com>

Europe
<gopher://gopher.nato.int> NATO
<germnews@vm.gmd.de> Germany, subscribe eMail
<gopher://utsainfo.jpl.utsa.edu/axtualites dans la Presse Francaise/Le Journal de RFI> Radio France
<gopher://smile.srce.hr/english/subject/news/> Europe—from U.S. embassy daily Bulletin Board
<FSUMedia@sovam.com> Media about former Soviet Union eMail. Free to subscribe as follows: <listproc@sovam.com> with message "SUBSCRIBE FSUMEDIA your   name   here" (without quotes).
<http://red.path.net/internews> Updates on press freedom violations, subscription by email <ifex@web.apa.org>
<gopher://poniecki.berkeley.edu> E. Europe and Russia
<http://www.yahoo.com/news/international/name country> Any country

Middle East and Africa
<http://www.afrika.com/>
<http://www.africaonline.co.ke/AfricaOnline/eastafrican.html> East   Africa news
<gopher://israel-info.gov.il> Israel
<http://gwis2.circ.gwu.edu/~chip42/africa.html>
<http://sbweb.2.med.iacnet.com/infotrac/session/592> South African dailies

Africa, the Caribbean, and the Americas
<http://majorca.npr.org/programs/afropop/>

Asia and Oceana
<http://www.cuhk.hk/rthk> Hong Kong Radio and TV
<http://www.asiaonline.net>

<http://www.iipl.com.sg/whats new/text/cable.html.> Cable TV in Singapore
<http://cmp.lucr.edu/essays edward-earlelmillenium/singapore.html.> Singapore cracks down on Net.
<http://www.tbs.co.jp/tbsannual/television.html> Tokyo Broadcasting System
<http://www.abc.net.au> Australia Broadcasting System

Index

About the Author

CARLA BROOKS JOHNSTON is founder and president of New Century Policies, a consulting firm that focuses on creating and sustaining democratic public policy innovation. She is the recipient of a Loeb Fellowship at Harvard and a Bunting Fellowship at Radcliffe, and she lectures worldwide on global communications and the importance of media access to effective development. She is the author of five books, including *International Co-Production of Television Programs* (1992) and *Winning the Global TV News Game* (1995).